Perfect
PIES

Perfect PIES

BETH ALLEN

PHOTOGRAPHS BY
BETH GALTON

Reader's Digest

THE READER'S DIGEST ASSOCIATION, INC.

PLEASANTVILLE, NEW YORK • MONTREAL

ACKNOWLEDGMENTS

As the author and co-producer of PERFECT PIES, *I was extremely fortunate to be able to work with a superb team of professionals who helped me turn my manuscript and recipe creations into a beautiful, delicious reality.*

A Great Big Pie goes to —

THE EDITORIAL TEAM

Food Editor *Judith Sutton, for her unlimited baking knowledge and keen editing skills*

Researcher *Judith Blahnik, for her astonishing ability to find countless pie facts, pie bakers, and pastry chefs*

CANADIAN LIVING *Food Director Elizabeth Baird, for her in-depth knowledge of traditional Canadian pies from British Columbia to Newfoundland*

Recipe Testers *Michelle Gurdon and Lorna Charles, for their professional testing and retesting of endless pies*

Nutritionists *Annette B. Natow, Ph.D., R.D., and Jo-Ann Heslin, M.A., C.H.E., R.D., for their accurate analyses and nutritional consulting*

Indexer *Catherine Dorsey, for her accurate cataloguing that works*

Camilla Yost, for sharing her community cookbooks and for locating some great pie bakers

THE PHOTOGRAPHY TEAM

Award-winning Photographer Beth Galton and her expert studio team, including Kathryn Shertzer and Rochelle Jensen, for the sensational photographs

Master Food Stylist Delores Custer and her professional team — Elizabeth Duffy, Sally-Jo O'Brien, Mina Cho, and Marie Haycox — for their appetizing recreations of the pies

Prop Stylist Francine Matalon-Degni, for the artistic assembly of photography props — including over one hundred pie plates

THE DESIGN TEAM

Art Director and Co-Producer Lynn Yost, for her creative ideas and enthusiasm, book design, and how-to illustrations — plus her husband, Christopher Kent, for his support

Illustrator Bob Steimle, for his decorative color art

Hand Model Beth Connelly, for her help developing the step-by-step illustrations

THE READER'S DIGEST TEAM

Executive Editor, Trade Books, Joseph Gonzalez, for his enthusiastic support — from the first presentation and tasting session

Senior Editor, Trade Books, Carolyn Chubet, for her expert editing and continuous support

Senior Design Director, Trade Books, Henrietta Stern, for her artistic vision and guidance

Production Editor, Trade Books, Lisa DiConsiglio, for her creative support

THE SUPPORT TEAM

Husband John Frederick Allen, for being my best friend, believer, supporter, and enthusiastic taster (even after sampling the five-hundredth piece of pie)

Family, friends, neighbors, and colleagues who always found an appetite to "taste another pie"

And last, but certainly not least, all the pie bakers, chefs, and food professionals cited on page 144 and throughout the book

— *Beth Allen*

A Reader's Digest Book

Created and Produced by
BETH ALLEN ASSOCIATES, INC.
EDITORIAL DESIGN PRODUCTIONS

Copyright © 1998 Beth Allen Associates, Inc.
Photographs copyright © 1998 Beth Galton, Inc.
Illustrations copyright © 1998 Lynn Yost

Library of Congress Cataloging-in-Publication Data

Allen, Beth
    Perfect Pies: by Beth Allen.
        p.   cm.
    Includes index.
    ISBN 0-7621-0080-X
    1. Pies.   I. Title.
TX773.A35724   1998
641.8`852—dc21   97-32726

A Pie Book with a Difference

You can make perfect pies whether you're an experienced baker or not, thanks to this book. PERFECT PIES takes all the guesswork out of baking pies, whether you choose a pie that comes out party-perfect or homemade, with love.

Not only are there the hows and whys of making and baking pies, but also there are over 180 kitchen-tested recipes. They'll help you serve delicious pies morning, noon, and night, any season of the year, for any reason.

Want to make a quick pie? A traditional pie? The perfect pie for a special occasion, or just a comfort pie for a winter's eve? Here's all you need to know — whether you use our recipes or experiment on your own, following our charts. You'll find recipes from famous people, celebrity chefs, food professionals, and just plain good cooks.

Browse through this book and pick your favorites — from pancake puffs to start your day to hearty supper pies for a savory ending. You'll find tiny snackin' pies, fabulous fruit orchard pies, very very chocolate pies, creamy custard pies, and country kitchen pies.

Step by step, this new world of heavenly homemade pies is ready for you to explore. Whatever your "pie IQ," this book is for you.

CONTENTS

PIE SMARTS

♥

Behind every good pie is a pie-smart baker, one who chooses the freshest ingredients, selects the perfect savory or sweet filling for the perfect shell, and knows what makes crusts tender and flaky.

To become pie-smart, begin with the basics in this chapter. There are tips for choosing the right pans, a guide to the baker's tools that help simplify tasks, and techniques for rolling and shaping the crust neither too thin nor too thick. You'll find ideas for topping off the pie with a mile-high meringue, lacing it up with a lattice crust, or finishing it off with a fancy flute or swirls of sweetened whipped cream.

Start by learning more about making and baking pies — you'll find many tips, techniques, hand-me-down hints, and a trouble-shooting guide. You'll quickly discover the wonders that the sensational world of pies holds for you.

✦ *Grandma Phyllis's Fresh Raspberry Pie (see recipe, page 131)*

THE PIE BAKER'S TOOLS

Check your kitchen for these baking tools and kitchen equipment. Some are essential, while others are just nice to have.

MEASURING

■ **DRY MEASURES** For measuring flour, sugar, shortening, shredded cheese, cream cheese, nuts, coconut. For the most accurate measuring, choose cups with straight sides and without rolled edges. Spoon in the ingredient (don't pack it, unless the recipe specifies, such as packed brown sugar). Run a spatula straight across the top to level it off.

■ **LIQUID MEASURES** Choose durable heatproof glass cups (instead of plastic) with pour spouts. Use for measuring milk, water, cream, sour cream, other liquids.

■ **MEASURING SPOONS** Metal spoons hold their shape and measure more accurately longer than plastic.

■ **KITCHEN SCALE** Takes the guesswork out of measuring fruits or other ingredients by weight — digital scales are the most accurate.

MIXING

■ **HEAVY-DUTY MIXER** Stands alone, so you can do other things while it mixes. To reduce spattering, look for one equipped with a deep bowl with a splatter cover. Use the wire whip for aerating creams and meringues; the paddle for general mixing. A portable mixer works fine too, but it takes longer to do the same job. A cordless mixer goes anywhere.

Pastry blender *Food processor* *Whisks* *Digital scale* *Heavy-duty mixer* *Sifter*

✦ HANDY INGREDIENTS ✦

The Drys *Flours: All-purpose, unbleached all-purpose, cake, whole-wheat, pastry — Sugars: Granulated, superfine, confectioners', light & dark brown — Cookie & cracker crumbs: Graham, chocolate, vanilla, macaroon — Nuts: almonds, hazelnuts, pecans, walnuts, peanuts, coconut*

The Fats *Butter, shortening, sour cream, egg yolks, cream cheese, specialty cheeses, chocolate*

The Liquids *Ice water, milk, cream, eggs, fruit juices, vinegar, liquid flavorings*

Sweet Spices *Allspice, cinnamon, nutmeg, ginger, mace, cloves*

Savory Spices *Curry, cumin, pepper, paprika, saffron*

Herbs *Basil, thyme, marjoram, oregano, sage, rosemary, dill, tarragon*

Flavorings *Vanilla, orange, lemon, or almond extract — Orange, lemon, & lime zest — Fruit liqueurs — Coffee*

■ **FOOD PROCESSOR** Mixes pastry in minutes, grinds nuts for crusts and toppings, chops vegetables for main-dish pies, and crumbles crumbs for crusts.

■ **SIFTERS** A 5-cup sifter is best for flour that must be presifted; a 3-cup sifter with a triple screen is handy for dusting flour over your work surface. A heavy-duty stainless steel sifter with a steel spring action in the handle is best, since it takes less energy to do the job. A duster-shaker is great for stenciling cocoa or confectioners' sugar on top of pies.

■ **WIRE WHISKS** The long French sauce whisk with its contoured shape is best for batters. The flat whisk removes lumps from custards easily. A wide balloon whisk, with its many thin flexible wires, is great for fluffing up egg whites and whipping cream. The horizontal whisk with curly, thicker wires is a "must" for reaching into the edges of a saucepan when cooking custard fillings. A piano whisk with many thin wires whisks eggs and liquids together quickly.

■ **PASTRY BLENDER** Use to cut fat into dry ingredients quickly and evenly.

■ **COPPER MIXING BOWL** A nice extra. When egg whites are beaten in the bowl, the copper acts as a catalyst to give a more stable foam (and a higher meringue).

ROLLING

■ **WOODEN PASTRY BOARD** Buy one just for pastry; never use it for cutting onions or meats. Look for one about 18 x 22 inches, that is marked with inches around the edges and circular cutting guides in the center.

■ **MARBLE SURFACE** Maintains a colder temperature than a wood surface. This means it keeps dough chilled longer, reducing the possibilities of sticking.

■ **PASTRY CLOTH** with circular roll-out guide lines (usually 8-, 9-, and 10-inch circles). Comes in plastic or cloth. I prefer a woven cloth one, since it's porous enough to work in flour (this helps prevent the dough from sticking during rolling).

■ **ROLLING PIN SLEEVE** A stretchable cloth sleeve that slips over a rolling pin. Rubbing flour into the cloth helps prevent the dough from sticking.

■ **SOLID ROLLING PINS** A solid wooden one with tapered ends enables you to work the dough easily into a circle. A simple wooden cylinder without handles gives you the best control and even rolling. The more common one is cylindrical with ball-bearing handles, in wood or stainless steel, or with a nonstick surface.

■ **HOLLOW GLASS ROLLING PIN** Designed to be filled with ice water. Keeps the dough colder when rolling, helping prevent sticking. Perfect for rolling puff pastry and other soft rich doughs.

■ **DOUGH SCRAPERS** A metal one is great for scraping dough off the work surface. The ones with a built-in ruler double as a guide for cutting pastry. Some have a nonstick coating. Plastic scrapers are flexible and great for cutting dough, scooping up dough from the work surface, and getting that last bit of batter out of the bowl.

SHAPING

■ **PASTRY WHEELS** Come with either a straight or a scalloped edge. Use the straight-edged wheel for cutting out rounds of pastry for pie shells and the fluted one to make decorative zigzag edges.

■ **PASTRY BRUSHES** Come with either plastic or natural bristles (I prefer the natural ones, as they are more gentle to the pastry). The flat brushes (usually 2 to 3 inches wide) with extra-soft bristles are best for applying glazes on delicate pastry. The round brushes are sturdier and best for basting top crusts with melted butter or cream.

■ **PASTRY CRIMPERS** Small serrated tweezers give pastry a professional-looking crimped edge and come in many sizes.

■ **PASTRY BAGS & TIPS** The best are heavy cotton pastry bags with polyurethane plastic coating and reinforced tips. Invest in a set of fluted and plain tips for piping creams and icings onto sweet pies and for topping savory pies with mashed potatoes.

■ **VOL-AU-VENT CIRCLES** A set of concentric metal disks in graduated sizes. Ideal for cutting out different sizes of dough circles, perfectly every time.

■ **PASTRY CUTTERS** (see page 63) Smaller than cookie cutters, these are handy for cutting out decorative pastry shapes, such as fruits, hearts, and leaves for topping pies.

BAKING

■ **GLASS & POTTERY PIE PLATES** Essential for old-fashioned rolled pastry and crumb crusts. Come in sizes from 8 to 11 inches in diameter. Some come in clear or tinted heat-resistant glass. Others come in thicker, ovenproof ceramic pottery that goes from the freezer to oven, which distributes heat evenly, resulting in crisp pastry. All pie plates have slightly sloping sides. Standard pie plates are about 1½ inches deep, with

a narrow flat edge. Deep-dish pie dishes are 2 inches deep, often with a fluted edge; these are ideal for baking juicy fruit pies.

■ **METAL PIE PLATES** The best come in aluminum with a nonstick coating or in heavier stainless steel. Some metal plates come with a perforated double bottom that bakes the shell extra crispy and brown.

■ **TART PANS** The best have a removable bottom so you can easily remove the tart from the pan. Check that the bottom fits tightly. If either piece gets bent, replace the pan. It's best to have at least a few sizes: a 9-inch, a 10- or 11- inch, and a 12-inch. Traditional pans are tin-coated steel; others are heavy aluminum with a nonstick coating. To clean, wipe with a damp cloth. Never scrub or place tin pans in the dishwasher.

■ **QUICHE DISHES** The classic quiche dish is made from glazed white pottery with straight fluted sides. Available in sizes from an individual 3-inch dish to party-size, usually from 12 to 14 inches in diameter.

■ **TINY TART & TARTLET PANS** For individual tarts, use 4½- to 5-inch tart pans with straight (not slanted) fluted sides, about 1 inch high. Pans with removable bottoms are worth the extra cost, since the tarts are then easier to remove. For tiny round tartlets, in 2- or 3-bite size, look for pans about 3 inches across the top and only about ½ to 1 inch deep, with sloping fluted sides.

■ **BARQUETTE & FANCY TARTLET MOLDS** Barquette molds are boat-shaped, about 3 inches long and 1¾ inches wide, with sloping sides. Other tiny tartlet molds come as diamonds, ovals, rectangles, triangles, and hearts. Pastry shells can be a little more difficult to remove from fluted molds than from straight-sided ones.

■ **READY-MADE SHELL IN A FOIL PIE PLATE** Buy a deep-dish shell and follow the package instructions carefully. If you are

baking the filling in the unbaked shell, reduce the oven temperature 25 degrees and add 5 to 10 minutes more baking time as needed. Be sure not to fill the shell too full, as these shells often hold less than homemade ones.

■ **SKILLETS** For morning pies, supper pies, cobblers. Choose cast iron or porcelain enamel on steel with an ovenproof handle, 10 to 12 inches in diameter, with 2-inch sides.

■ **BAKING DISHES** For poultry and meat pies, fruit cobblers, pandowdies, and slumps. Choose a glass or glazed ceramic dish, 13 × 9 inches with 2-inch sides.

■ **PIE WEIGHTS** Metal pellets, about the size of peas, used for weighting down an unfilled pie shell during blind-baking.

■ **PIE BIRD** A decorative, ovenproof ceramic bird that's placed in the center of a fruit pie or a meat pot pie before going into the oven. The hole in its beak acts as a steam vent, helping to bake the filling, not steam it.

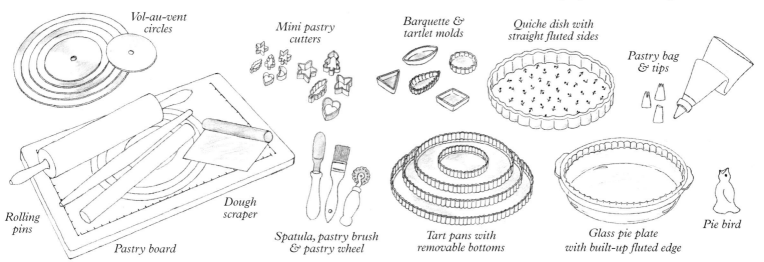

Vol-au-vent circles

Mini pastry cutters

Barquette & tartlet molds

Quiche dish with straight fluted sides

Pastry bag & tips

Rolling pins

Dough scraper

Pastry board

Spatula, pastry brush & pastry wheel

Tart pans with removable bottoms

Glass pie plate with built-up fluted edge

Pie bird

PIE PASTRY BASICS

*Most pies start with a pastry crust, whether it's on the bottom, on the top, or both. But some pies have no crust at all —
just sweet streusel crumbs, a sprinkling of nuts, or a piping of mashed potatoes on top. Here are the basics for pastry crusts.*

PERFECT PIE PASTRY

Follow these tips and you'll be sure to bake tender, flaky, tasty pastry, pie after pie.

■ **Check the correct temperature and size of fat ingredients**. Use shortening that is room temperature and butter that is firm, cold, and cut into ½-inch dice, no smaller. Cut the fat into the flour just until the mixture resembles coarse crumbs about the size of peas. Fat particles this size stay solid in the oven just long enough to produce many flaky layers. Smaller fat particles melt too fast, making fewer flaky layers.

■ **Use the recommended mixing method** to give a dough that rolls out consistently.

■ **Mix just until the mixture comes together into a dough — no more.** Over-mixing creates tough pastry. Then shape the dough into 6-inch disks, about 1 inch thick.

■ **Chill the disks of dough** before rolling. Most pie pastry recipes suggest 30 minutes to an hour of chilling (if you chill it longer, let it stand at room temperature for about 15 to 30 minutes before rolling). The crust will shrink less in the oven and the edging will keep its shape better.

■ **Roll the dough to the exact thickness** called for in the recipe — don't guess, use a ruler. Pastry that's rolled too thin can tear easily and brown before the filling is cooked. Pastry rolled too thick is tough, not tender and flaky.

■ **Freeze the shaped crust in its pie plate** for 15 minutes before baking to help it hold its shape in the oven even better.

■ **Bake the crust at the exact temperature and for at least the time specified** in the recipe or until it turns the color suggested.

ROLLING & SHAPING PASTRY

Mix and chill the pastry as the recipe suggests. Lightly flour a large work surface and your rolling pin. Work quickly, so the pastry stays chilled while you're working.

Beginning at the center of the pastry disk, roll the dough from the center out into a large circle, ⅛ inch thick. Work in a circle, turning the dough as you go. Using a pastry wheel or the tip of a knife, trim the dough to a circle 5 inches larger than the diameter of your pie plate (6 inches for a deep-dish). Vol-au-vent metal guides make it easy, or cut free-hand.

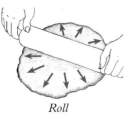

Roll

Transfer the pastry to the pie plate by rolling it up loosely around the rolling pin. Unroll the pastry, starting from one edge, shaping and easing the pastry gently into the plate as you go. To prevent shrinkage during baking, do not stretch the dough. Trim away any excess, leaving a 1½-inch overhang, and finish the crust with a fancy flute or flat edging.

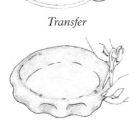

Transfer

Shape and trim

BASIC PASTRY CHEMISTRY

The ingredients and techniques for making a crust tender are the direct opposite of those that make it flaky. The secret? A delicate balance.

THE DRYS — Mainly flour, which contains a strong, elastic protein called gluten. Bread flour contains the most gluten; cake flour the least. All-purpose flour, a blend of the two, contains the right amount of gluten to produce a flaky yet tender crust. The gluten in the flour starts developing as soon as liquid is added. To prevent it from developing too much, coat the flour with fat *before* adding liquid. Other dry ingredients, mixed with flour before fats and liquids are added, are sweeteners, flavorings, and rising agents such as baking powder.

THE FATS — Butter, shortening, cream cheese, egg yolks, sour cream — the more fat, the more tender and flakier the crust. Room-temperature fats, such as shortening, coat flour particles quickly and easily, making a crust tender. Cold fats, such as butter, hold the flour layers apart, making a crust flaky. In a hot oven, they remain solid just long enough for the dough surrounding them to cook. As they melt, they release steam, pushing the dough apart into many flaky layers. The more fat globules, the more layers and the flakier the pastry.

THE LIQUIDS — Ice water, milk, cream, eggs, fruit juices, and flavorings such as vanilla bind the flour and fat together into a dough, making it possible to roll it out. Liquids also turn into steam in the oven and activate any baking powder, making the pastry flakier. Ice water moistens evenly and quickly. Milk adds protein and is likely to produce a tougher pastry, so I stick with water. I often add a little acid, such as lemon juice, a sprinkle of vinegar, or sour cream, which breaks apart any long gluten strands, making the crust even more tender.

BLIND-BAKING

Blind-baking a crust means to prebake it partially or completely before filling.

1 **Prick small holes all over the bottom and up the sides of the shell,** using the prongs of a fork. This allows steam to escape during baking, letting the shell bake evenly without puffing up.

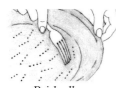

Prick all over

2 **To insure that the crust holds its shape in the oven,** line the crust with parchment paper or buttered

aluminum foil, extending it 1 inch above the rim. Fill with pie weights or uncooked rice or beans.

3 **To partially prebake,** bake in a hot oven (400° to 425°F) for 10 to 12 minutes; transfer to a rack. Lift out the lining and pie weights.

Use pie weights

4 **To completely prebake,** return the unlined crust to the oven for 5 to 8 minutes more or until golden and crisp. Transfer to a cooling rack.

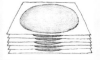

FANCY FLUTES & EASY EDGINGS

Fancy flutes and edgings add your personal touch. They also increase the amount of filling the crust will hold, helping prevent bubble-overs during baking. Choose a pie crust recipe that's sturdy enough to hold an edge, but not so rich in butter that the design melts away in the oven (see Pick-a-Crust Pie Wheel, page 14). Fancy flutes work fine in either a standard pie plate or a deep-dish one; flat edgings work best in a standard plate with a flat edge. Roll and shape the pastry without stretching and freeze the shaped crust before baking (see opposite).

To shape a 1-inch stand-up pastry edge Gently ease and fit the pastry into a pie plate (flat or fluted edge), leaving a 1½-inch overhang. Fold the pastry under, making a 1-inch stand-up edge. Finish with a flute or a design that starts with a stand-up edge. Freeze 15 minutes before baking.

PINCH-PUSH FLUTE (see photo, page 129) Begin with a 1-inch stand-up pastry edge (see left). Holding the thumb and index finger of one hand ½ inch apart on the outside of rim, pinch a V-shape of pastry. At the same time, push the dough into the pinch from the inside with the index finger of your other hand. Continue making flutes at ¼-inch intervals around the pie.

ZIGZAG FLUTE (see photo, page 133) Begin with a 1-inch stand-up pastry edge (see left). Hold the pointed edge of a small diamond- or star-shaped cookie cutter against the inside of the pastry edge. Pinch the pastry from the outside of the edge with the thumb and index finger of your other hand, making a sharp zigzag flute. Continue fluting at ¼-inch intervals around the pie.

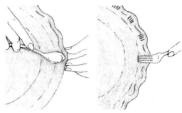

FEATHERED PETAL FLUTE Begin with a 1-inch stand-up pastry edge (see left). Holding the thumb and index finger of one hand 1 inch apart on the outside of the edge, pinch a V-shape of pastry. Push the dough into the pinch from the inside with the tip of a small spoon, pressing down to make petals. Lightly feather the center of each petal with the tines of a fork.

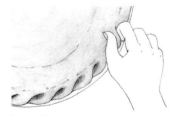

ROPE EDGE (see photos, pages 8, 117 and 127) Begin with a 1-inch stand-up pastry edge (see above at left). Make a fist and gently grasp the pastry on the diagonal, pushing forward with the knuckle of your index finger and pulling back with your thumb. Continue by placing your thumb in the groove left by your index finger.

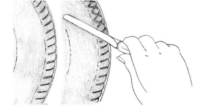

CROSSHATCH Begin with a 1-inch stand-up pastry edge (see above at left). Using the blunt edge of a kitchen knife, make diagonal indentations every ½ inch around the pastry edge two times around the pie — first in one direction, then in the opposite direction.

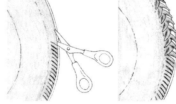

SHEAVES OF WHEAT Begin with a 1-inch stand-up pastry edge (see above at left). Using scissors, cut the dough on a slant at ½-inch intervals around the edge of the pie. Turn one point toward the center of the pie. Shape the next point in the opposite direction, then continue around the pie.

POINTED SCALLOP (see photo, page 96). Shape the pie shell with a flat pastry edge ¼ inch thick. Using a bottle opener, cut out triangular points of pastry at ½-inch intervals around the edge of the pie. Use enough pressure to cut the pastry with a sharp clean edge.

BRAIDED EDGE Start with enough pastry for a 2-crust pie. Shape the bottom crust with a flat pastry edge. Roll out extra dough ⅛ inch thick. Using a ruler and a knife, cut out 9 strips, 14 x ½ inch. Starting at the center, braid 3 strips out to each end. Make two more braids, and connect all 3 by moistening with water and pinching together. Moisten pastry edge of pie with water and gently press on the braid.

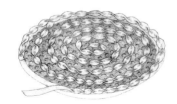

PINWHEEL Start with enough pastry for a 2-crust pie. Shape the bottom crust with a flat pastry edge. Roll out extra dough ⅛ inch thick. Cut into 10 strips, 16 x 1 inch. Make a pinwheel of pastry strips, starting at the center of the pie and twisting the strips as you go. Connect the ends of strips by moistening them with water and pinching together. Finish the edge with a tightly twisted strip of pastry.

WREATH (see pages 102-103 and 123) Start with enough pastry for a 2-crust pie. Shape the bottom crust with a flat edge. Roll out extra dough ¼ inch thick. Cut out 24 leaves or hearts with a cookie cutter (about 1½ inches long) and brush one side of each cutout with slightly beaten egg white. Place the cutouts on an angle around the rim, brushed-side down, draping and curving them. Gently press in place.

RUSTIC PLEAT (see photos, pages 69 and 75) Start with enough pastry for a 2-crust pie. Roll out the pastry into a large circle, ⅛ inch thick, and trim into a large enough circle to give a 4-inch overhang (you'll need a 20-inch circle for a 9-inch deep-dish pie plate). Spoon in the filling. Fold the edges of the dough over the filling, pleating them as you go, and letting the filling in the center show. Great for fruit pies.

PICK-A-CRUST

PICK-A-CRUST PIE WHEEL

Each pie in this book that uses a crust gives at least one suggested crust recipe, sometimes two or three. But don't stop there. You can create your own variation by using our Pick-a-Crust Pie Wheel. Locate the type of pie you'd like to make on the inner circle of the wheel. Every crust in each pie slice mixes and matches with that type of pie. Most of the crust recipes are in this chapter.

For instance, for Custard & Cream Pies, choose from ten different crusts, such as an old-fashioned Buttery Crust or the very easy Whipped Pastry. You'll find many other crusts on this wheel too — easy Pat-in-the-Pan tart shells, cookie and nut crumb crusts, on up to the professional French pastries, such as Pâte Brisée, Pâte Sucrée, and Pâte Sablée. There are even specialty crusts such as Rapid-Rise Yeast Dough and Beth's Snickerdoodle Cookie Crust.

All crusts are not created equal when it comes to baking them out perfectly. For spectacular results, choose a crust that matches up with the type of pie you're making. Some crusts are just right for shaping a fancy flute, while others are too rich to stand up during baking. Recipes marked with a star (★) hold fancy edges the best.

The pie bird in the center of the wheel can be used for baking deep-dish fruit pies and savory pot pies (see The Pie Baker's Tools, page 11).

All pie recipes come to you kitchen-tested by professional experts. When baking a pie, choose only the crust suggested in the recipe or this chart — for perfect results, pie after pie after pie.

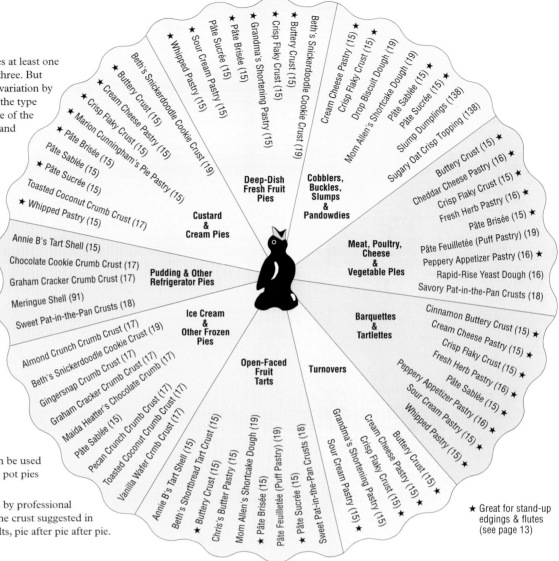

★ Great for stand-up edgings & flutes (see page 13)

LATTICE-TOP CRUST

Create an old-fashioned lattice by weaving strips of pastry together. Pick a pastry that is easy to roll using the Pick-a-Crust Pie Wheel above, making enough for a double-crust pie. Roll out two circles of dough, ⅛ inch thick.

Shape the bottom crust into the pie plate, leaving a 1½-inch overhang. From the other circle, cut out 10 to 12 strips, 1 inch wide (try a fluted pastry wheel). Now start weaving. Finish with a fluted edge.

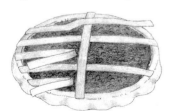

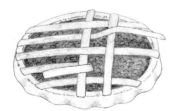

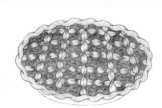

1 Lay half of the strips evenly across the top of the pie in one direction, then fold back every other strip halfway. Place one of the remaining strips across the center of the pie. Replace the folded strips.

2 Fold back the alternate strips, place a second strip crosswise, about ¾ inch from the first one, and replace the folded ones.

3 Repeat the weaving, using the remaining strips, until a lattice crisscrosses the top of the pie. Flute the rim with a fancy flute or a rope edge (see page 13), then glaze the crust and bake as the recipe directs.

NO-WEAVE LATTICE Twist pastry strips as you place them at right angles on the pie.

VERSATILE ROLL-OUT PASTRY CRUSTS

PICK-A-PASTRY	THE DRYS	THE FATS	THE LIQUIDS	CHILL/ FREEZE	PREBAKE PARTIAL / COMPLETE
Annie B's Tart Shell ▲ MIXER *2 tart shells (9-, 10-, or 11-inch)*	3½ cups cake flour ⅔ cup granulated sugar	10 tablespoons (1¼ sticks) unsalted butter, at room temperature 10 tablespoons (1¼ sticks) margarine, room temperature	1 large egg, slightly beaten ½ teaspoon vanilla extract	Chill 1 hr	350°F 12 to 15 min *(completely blind-bake)*
Beth's Shortbread Tart Crust ● HAND or ■ PROCESSOR *1 shell (9-, 10-, or 11-inch)* **TIP**: Fold edge double to reinforce sides.	1 cup all-purpose flour ⅓ cup cake flour ⅔ cup granulated sugar 3 tablespoons ground almonds ¾ teaspoon salt ½ teaspoon baking powder	½ cup (1 stick) cold unsalted butter, cut into small pieces	1 large egg 2 tablespoons Cointreau or ice water	Chill 1 hr or freeze 30 min	400°F 12 to 14 min *(completely blind-bake)*
Buttery Crust & Cinnamon Buttery Crust ● HAND or ■ PROCESSOR *2 shells or 1 double crust (8-, 9-, or 10-inch)*	3 cups all-purpose flour 3 tablespoons granulated sugar ½ teaspoon baking powder ½ teaspoon salt ½ teaspoon cinnamon (optional)	¾ cup (1½ sticks) cold unsalted butter	⅓ cup ice water 1 large egg yolk, slightly beaten 2 tablespoons fresh lemon juice	Chill 30 min / Shape, then freeze 15 min	400°F 8 to 10 min / 15 to 18 min
Chris's Butter Pastry ■ PROCESSOR *1 tart shell (8-, 9-, or 10-inch)*	1 cup all-purpose flour 2 tablespoons granulated sugar	½ cup (1 stick) cold unsalted butter	1 tablespoon ice water ¼ teaspoon vanilla extract	Shape, then freeze 15 min	375°F 15 min *(completely blind-bake)*
Cream Cheese Pastry ● HAND ONLY *2 shells or 1 double crust (8-, 9-, or 10-inch)*	2½ cups all-purpose flour 1 teaspoon baking powder ½ teaspoon salt	½ cup (1 stick) cold unsalted butter 2 3-ounce packages cold cream cheese	5 tablespoons ice water 1 large egg yolk, slightly beaten 2 teaspoons fresh lemon juice	Chill 30 min / Shape, then freeze 15 min	400°F 10 min / 15 min
Crisp Flaky Crust ● HAND or ■ PROCESSOR *2 shells or 1 double crust (8-, 9-, or 10-inch)*	2½ cups all-purpose flour 2 tablespoons granulated sugar ½ teaspoon baking powder ½ teaspoon salt	½ cup (1 stick) cold unsalted butter ⅓ cup cold shortening	6 tablespoons ice water 1 tablespoon fresh lemon juice	Chill 30 min / Shape, then freeze 15 min	400°F 10 to 12 min / 15 to 18 min
Marion Cunningham's Pie Pastry ● HAND ONLY *1 shell (9- or 10-inch)*	1½ cups all-purpose flour ¼ teaspoon salt	½ cup shortening	3 to 4 tablespoons ice water	Chill 1 hr	425°F 15 min *(completely blind-bake)*
Grandma's Shortening Pastry ● HAND ONLY *2 shells or 1 double crust (8-, 9-, or 10-inch)*	2½ cups all-purpose flour 1 teaspoon salt	1 cup + 1 tablespoon shortening, at room temperature	1 large egg yolk, beaten, plus enough ice water to make ½ cup	Chill 15 min	400°F 10 to 12 min / 15 to 18 min
Pâte Brisée ● HAND ONLY *2 shells or 1 double crust (8-, 9-, or 10-inch)*	2½ cups all-purpose flour 2 tablespoons granulated sugar ½ teaspoon baking powder ½ teaspoon salt	¾ cup (1½ sticks) cold unsalted butter	⅓ cup ice water 1 tablespoon fresh lemon juice	Chill 30 min / Shape, then freeze 15 min	400°F 10 to 12 min / 15 to 18 min
Pâte Sablée ● HAND or ■ PROCESSOR *2 shells or 1 double crust (8-, 9-, or 10-inch)*	1½ cups all-purpose flour 1 cup cake flour ¼ cup confectioners' sugar 1 teaspoon baking powder ½ teaspoon salt	¾ cup (1½ sticks) cold unsalted butter	1 large egg, slightly beaten, plus additional beaten egg if necessary to make a dough	Chill 1 hr	400°F 10 to 12 min / 15 to 18 min
Pâte Sucrée ● HAND or ■ PROCESSOR *2 shells or 1 double crust (8-, 9-, or 10-inch)*	2¼ cups all-purpose flour ⅓ cup confectioners' sugar ½ teaspoon baking powder ½ teaspoon salt	¾ cup (1½ sticks) cold unsalted butter	4 to 6 tablespoons ice water 2 large egg yolks, slightly beaten	Chill 30 min / Shape, then freeze 15 min	400°F 10 min / 14 to 15 min
Sour Cream Pastry ● HAND or ■ PROCESSOR *2 shells or 1 double crust (8-, 9-, or 10-inch)*	2½ cups all-purpose flour ⅓ cup confectioners' sugar ½ teaspoon baking soda ½ teaspoon salt	¾ cup (1½ sticks) cold unsalted butter	1 cup sour cream	Chill 30 min / Shape, then freeze 15 min	400ªF 10 to 12 min / 15 to 18 min
Whipped Pastry ▲ MIXER *2 shells or 1 double crust (8-, 9-, or 10-inch)*	3 cups all-purpose flour 1 tablespoon granulated sugar 1 teaspoon salt	½ cup (1 stick) unsalted butter, softened ½ cup shortening, at room temperature	½ cup boiling water 1 tablespoon fresh lemon juice	Chill 1 hr / Shape, then freeze 15 min	400°F 10 to 12 min / 15 to 18 min

● BY-HAND METHOD
1-In a large bowl, mix **The Drys** together.
2-Cut in **The Fats** with a pastry blender, your fingers, or 2 knives until coarse crumbs form.
3-Stir in **The Liquids** just until a dough forms.

■ FOOD PROCESSOR METHOD
1-Process **The Drys** in the processor bowl for 2 seconds to mix.
2-Add **The Fats** and pulse until coarse crumbs form.
3-With the motor running, pour **The Liquids** through the feed tube. Process for 30 seconds more or just until a dough forms.

▲ ELECTRIC MIXER METHOD
1-In a large bowl, with mixer on HIGH, whip **The Fats** with the sugar (a **Dry**).
2-Blend in **The Liquids** (room temperature or hot first, then cold). Reduce the speed to LOW.
3-Add the remaining **Drys** and beat just until a dough forms.

SAVORY ROLL-OUT PASTRY CRUSTS

PICK-A-PASTRY	THE DRYS	THE FATS	THE LIQUIDS	CHILL	PREBAKE PARTIAL / COMPLETE
Cheddar Cheese Pastry ● HAND ONLY *2 shells or 1 double crust (8-, 9-, or 10-inch)*	2½ cups all-purpose flour ½ teaspoon baking powder ¼ teaspoon salt ¼ teaspoon cayenne pepper	1 cup (4 ounces) coarsely shredded Cheddar cheese 6 tablespoons (¾ stick) cold unsalted butter	½ to ⅔ cup ice water (depending upon the moistness of the cheese)	30 min	400°F 8 to 10 min / 15 to 18 min
Fresh Herb Pastry ● HAND or ■ PROCESSOR *2 shells or 1 double crust (8-, 9-, or 10-inch)*	2½ cups all-purpose flour ½ teaspoon baking powder ½ teaspoon salt 1 tablespoon snipped fresh herbs (see list below)	½ cup (1 stick) cold unsalted butter ⅓ cup shortening, at room temperature	7 to 8 tablespoons ice water	30 min	400°F 8 to 10 min / 15 to 18 min
Peppery Appetizer Pastry ● HAND or ■ PROCESSOR *2 shells or 1 double crust (8-, 9-, or 10-inch)*	2½ cups all-purpose flour ½ teaspoon baking powder ½ teaspoon salt ½ teaspoon freshly ground black pepper	½ cup (1 stick) cold unsalted butter ¼ cup shortening, chilled 1 large egg yolk	5 tablespoons ice water	30 min	400°F 8 min / 13 min 5-inch tartlet 10 min / 15 min 8-, 9-, or 10-inch shell
Spicy Mustard *Variation*	***Substitute*** for the black pepper: 1 teaspoon dry mustard		***Add***: 1 teaspoon Worcestershire sauce		
Tex-Mex *Variation*	***Substitute*** for the black pepper: ½ teaspoon chili powder ½ teaspoon ground cumin		***Add***: ⅛ teaspoon hot pepper sauce, or to taste		

● BY-HAND METHOD
1-In a large bowl, mix ***The Drys*** together.
2-Cut in ***The Fats*** with a pastry blender, your fingers, or 2 knives until coarse crumbs form.
3-Stir in ***The Liquids*** just until a dough forms.

■ FOOD PROCESSOR METHOD
1-Process ***The Drys*** in the processor bowl for 2 seconds to mix.
2-Add ***The Fats*** and pulse until coarse crumbs form.
3-With the motor running, pour ***The Liquids*** through the feed tube. Process 30 seconds more or until a dough just forms.

TIP: You can also experiment with **Buttery Crust, Cream Cheese Pastry, Crisp Flaky Crust, Pâte Brisée, Sour Cream Pastry,** and **Whipped Pastry** (see page 15) by adding your favorite herbs and spices.

RAPID-RISE YEAST DOUGH

Here's another great savory dough that's perfect for hearty pies such as pizzas, calzones, or meat supper pies. Thanks to rapid-rising yeast, this dough is ready to shape in 20 minutes. The addition of oil makes it easier to shape.

MAKES ONE 14-INCH PIZZA PIE OR 12 MINI PIZZAS

- 3 **cups all-purpose flour**
- 1 **packet (¼ ounce) rapid-rising active yeast**
- 1 **teaspoon sugar**
- 1 **cup warm water (120° to 130°F)**
- ¼ **cup extra virgin olive oil**
- 1 **teaspoon minced fresh rosemary**
- 2 **teaspoons salt**
- 1 **teaspoon freshly ground black pepper**
- **Yellow cornmeal**

1 In a food processor or a large bowl, process or mix 1 cup of the flour, the yeast, and sugar. Pulse or stir in the warm water until the mixture is smooth and blended. Add 1 cup of the remaining flour, the oil, rosemary, salt, and pepper. Pulse or stir just until the mixture pulls together into a smooth dough.

2 Sprinkle the remaining 1 cup of flour on a work surface (a marble one is great). Gradually knead the flour into the dough by pressing it down and away from you with the heels of both hands.

Knead

Pull up dough from the back, fold it over itself, and rotate a quarter turn. Repeat only until the dough is smooth, elastic, and no longer sticky. The dough will spring back when pressed. Let the dough rest for 5 minutes.

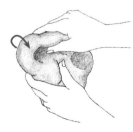

Fold

3 Shape the dough, add toppings, and bake as the recipe suggests. Or shape into a 14-inch circle in a pizza pan or on a large baking pan with 1-inch sides. Sprinkle with your favorite pizza toppings (pepperoni, salami, sautéed vegetables, cheese) and bake for about 20 minutes or until golden.

YOUR CHOICE OF HERBS Try substituting other herbs in the yeast dough for the fresh rosemary — basil, marjoram, oregano, thyme.

✦ FRESH HERB PASTRY ✦

1 teaspoon crumbled dry herbs may be substituted for each tablespoon of fresh

Basil for vegetable pies
Chives for egg and cheese pies
Dill for fish pies
Marjoram for pork or lamb pies
Oregano for tomato pies
Rosemary for chicken pies
Sage for turkey pies
Savory for poultry pies
Tarragon for fish or seafood pies
Thyme for beef pies

COOKIE CRUMB & NUT CRUSTS

PICK-A-CRUST	THE DRYS	BUTTER & LIQUID	DIRECTIONS	FREEZE	BAKE
Almond Crunch Crumb *1 shell (8-, 9-, or 10-inch)* *(No-bake crust)*	¾ cup finely chopped blanched almonds 1 cup vanilla wafer crumbs (25 to 30 wafers) 3 tablespoons granulated sugar	½ cup (1 stick) unsalted butter, melted	1-Toast almonds at 375°F for 5 to 7 minutes. Cool. 2-Toss all ingredients. 3-Press into a buttered pie plate.	Freeze crust for 15 min before filling	No
Chocolate Cookie Crumb *1 shell (8-, 9-, or 10-inch)*	1½ cups chocolate cookie crumbs (40 to 45 cookies) ¼ cup granulated sugar	6 to 7 tablespoons unsalted butter, melted	1-Toss all ingredients. 2-Press into a buttered pie plate.	Freeze crust 15 min before baking	350°F 7 to 10 min
Gingersnap Crumb *1 shell (8-, 9-, or 10-inch)*	1½ cups gingersnap crumbs (35 to 40 gingersnaps) ⅓ cup packed light brown sugar 1½ teaspoons grated lemon zest	6 to 7 tablespoons unsalted butter, melted	1-Toss all ingredients. 2-Press into a buttered pie plate.	Freeze crust 15 min before baking	350°F 8 to 10 min
Graham Cracker Crumb *1 shell (8-, 9-, or 10-inch)*	1½ cups graham cracker crumbs (10 large crackers) ⅓ cup granulated sugar ½ teaspoon ground cinnamon (optional)	6 to 7 tablespoons unsalted butter, melted	1-Toss all ingredients. 2-Press into a buttered pie plate.	Freeze crust 15 min before baking	350°F 8 to 10 min
Maida Heatter's Chocolate Wafer Crumb *1 shell (8-, 9-, or 10-inch)*	1½ cups chocolate cookie crumbs (40 to 45 cookies)	¾ cup (1½ sticks) unsalted butter, melted	1-Line pie plate with foil, with 1-inch overhang. 2-Toss all ingredients. 3-Press into a foil-lined pie plate. Bake, then freeze.	Freeze crust after baking until hard. Lift crust out; peel off foil. Return crust to pie plate. Fill.	300°F 7 to 10 min
Pecan Crunch Crumb *1 shell (8-, 9-, or 10-inch)* *(No-bake crust)*	1 cup finely chopped pecans 1 cup vanilla wafer crumbs (25 to 30 wafers) 3 tablespoons granulated sugar	½ cup (1 stick) unsalted butter, melted	1-Toast pecans at 375°F for 5 to 7 minutes. Cool. 2-Toss all ingredients. 3-Press into a buttered pie plate.	Freeze crust for 15 min before filling	No
Toasted Coconut Crumb *1 shell (8-, 9-, or 10-inch)* *(No-bake crust)*	1½ cups flaked coconut 1 cup vanilla wafer crumbs (25 to 30 wafers)	½ cup (1 stick) unsalted butter, melted	1-Toast coconut at 350°F for 10-15 minutes. Cool. 2-Toss all ingredients. 3-Press into a buttered pie plate.	Freeze for 15 min before filling	No
Vanilla Wafer Crumb *1 shell (8-, 9-, or 10-inch)*	1½ cups vanilla wafer crumbs (40 to 45 wafers) ¼ cup granulated sugar	6 tablespoons (¾ stick) unsalted butter, melted 2 teaspoons vanilla extract	1-Toss all ingredients. 2-Press into a buttered pie plate.	Freeze crust for 15 min before baking	350°F 8 to 10 min

MAKING CRUMB CRUSTS

Crumb crusts are among the easiest to make — some are not even baked, just pressed into the pan and chilled. If you are in a hurry, you can use a ready-made crumb crust from the supermarket. However, they usually do not hold all of the filling in our recipes. Plus, don't expect them to have that great homemade taste.

1 TO MAKE CRUMBS
By hand Place cookies or crackers in a large heavy plastic bag. Close partially, leaving a small space for air to escape. Roll with a rolling pin until finely and evenly crushed.
In a food processor Pulse until crumbs form, being careful not to grind the cookies too fine (they should not look powdery).

2 TO SHAPE THE CRUST
Coat the pie plate well with softened, not melted, butter (keeps the pie from sticking to the pie plate, making serving easier).
Pat the crumbs firmly and evenly over the bottom and up the sides of the pie plate.
For a perfect shape, place another pie plate (same size) in the crust and press down gently.

3 TO FINISH THE EDGE
Press the crumbs firmly to make a stand-up rim about ½-inch high.
Shape the edge by pressing the rim of crumbs from the inside of the edge with the thumb and fingertips of the other hand from the outside — pinching, pressing, and fluting as you go. To set the crust, freeze for 15 minutes before baking.

BETH'S PAT-IN-THE-PAN TART CRUST

Here's my simple, never-fail tart crust — just mix, pat in the pan, and bake.

MAKES ONE 12-INCH TART SHELL
PREP TIME 15 MIN ✦ BAKE TIME 15 MIN

★ EASY

- 2 **cups all-purpose flour**
- 1 **teaspoon baking powder**
- ½ **teaspoon salt**
- 1 **cup (2 sticks) unsalted butter, at room temperature**
- ¾ **cup sifted confectioners' sugar**
- 2 **teaspoons vanilla extract**
- 2 **tablespoons milk**

1 Butter a 12-inch tart pan with a removable bottom. In a small bowl, stir the flour, baking powder, and salt.

2 In a large bowl, with an electric mixer on HIGH, beat the butter and sugar until light yellow and creamy. Beat in the vanilla. Using a spoon, stir in the flour mixture, then the milk, just until a dough forms.

3 Turn the dough into the tart pan. Flour your hands well and pat the dough evenly with your fingertips over the bottom and up the sides. The crust will be about ⅜ inch thick.

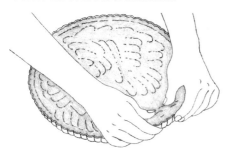

4 Using a fork, prick the bottom and sides of the crust all over. Run a long sharp chef's knife, slicer, or rolling pin along the top edge, evenly cutting off the excess dough.

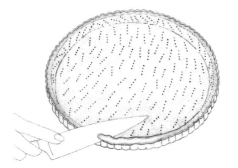

5 If your recipe calls for an unbaked crust, fill and bake the tart. Or, before filling, prebake crust at 350°F for 10 minutes for a partially baked shell or 15 minutes for a completely baked shell (see Blind-Baking, page 12).

6 Cool the tart as your recipe directs. To remove the cooled tart from the pan, loosen the sides of the crust with a small kitchen knife. Holding the bottom of the tart, push the ring away, letting it fall onto your arm. Set the crust on a serving plate (no need to remove the bottom of the pan, unless you wish).

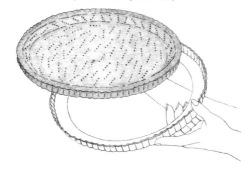

✦ BAKER'S TIPS ✦

No tart pan? *Use a 12-inch quiche or flan dish with straight sides instead (not a pie plate with slanted sides). Slice and serve the tart straight from the dish (do not try to remove the whole tart).*

Dough too sticky to pat in the pan? *It's just too warm. Refrigerate in the pan for 30 minutes and try again.*

Pat-in-the-pan tart shells freeze well *after they are baked, right inside the pan they were baked in. Wrap tightly in freezer paper and use within 1 month.*

To thaw a frozen baked shell, *unwrap and let stand at room temperature for 1 hour before filling. Avoid freezing this pastry unbaked, as the baking powder will lose its rising properties.*

DELICIOUS PAT-IN-THE-PAN OPTIONS

Begin with Beth's Tart Crust recipe (above), vary a few ingredients, and create many different crusts — savory as well as sweet. Pat into a regular tart pan with a removable bottom or a flan dish. A fluted pan or dish gives the fanciest finish.

SWEET

TOASTED ALMOND CRUST Add ½ cup finely chopped toasted almonds (see page 21) to the flour mixture. Add ½ teaspoon almond extract with the vanilla. Perfect for apricot, peach, plum, and blueberry tarts.

PECAN PRALINE CRUST Add ½ cup finely chopped toasted pecans (see page 21) to the flour mixture. Substitute ¾ cup packed light brown sugar for the confectioners' sugar. Ideal for ice cream pies and creamy custard fillings.

ORANGE MARNIER CRUST Add ½ cup finely chopped toasted almonds (see page 21) to the flour mixture. Omit the vanilla and add 2 tablespoons Grand Marnier liqueur. Great for fancy tarts with creamy custard fillings.

ZESTY LEMON CRUST Decrease the vanilla extract to 1 teaspoon and add 2 teaspoons grated lemon zest (Step 2). A perfect match for fresh berry and whipped cream fillings.

SUGAR 'N' SPICE CRUST Substitute ¾ cup granulated sugar for the confectioners' sugar. Add 1 teaspoon pumpkin pie spice to the flour mixture. Great for sweet custard fillings.

SAVORY

SAVORY SCALLION CRUST Decrease the sugar to 1 tablespoon and omit the vanilla extract. Increase the flour to 2¼ cups and add ⅓ cup minced scallions, both white and green parts. Great for cheese and seafood quiches; complements meat and vegetable fillings too.

CRACKED PEPPER CRUST Omit the sugar and the vanilla extract. Increase the flour to 2¼ cups and add ¾ teaspoon cracked black pepper and ½ teaspoon paprika. Use for spicy chicken, beef, and pizza fillings.

FRESH BASIL CRUST Decrease the sugar to 1 tablespoon and omit the vanilla extract. Increase the flour to 2¼ cups and add ¼ cup minced fresh basil. The perfect complement to vegetable and beef fillings.

MEXICANA CRUST Omit the sugar and the vanilla extract. Increase the flour to 2¼ cups and add ¾ cup (3 ounces) grated Monterey Jack cheese with jalapeño peppers. Use for chili, cheese, and beef fillings.

BACON CRUST Omit the sugar and the vanilla extract. Increase the flour to 2¼ cups and add ½ cup crumbled cooked bacon. Great for cheese quiches and potato tarts.

PÂTE FEUILLETÉE (PUFF PASTRY)

A rich buttery dough that bakes into hundreds of light, crispy layers of pastry that melt in your mouth. It's golden, puffy, and perfect for fruit tart shells, galettes, and for topping pot pies.

PASTRY FOR TWO 12-INCH TARTS OR TWELVE 5-INCH TARTLETS (FREE-FORM OR TART PAN)

- 1 **pound (4 sticks) chilled unsalted butter, cut into ½-inch dice**
- 3 **cups all-purpose flour, plus a little more for sprinkling**
- 1 **cup cake flour**
- 1 **teaspoon salt**
- 1 **cup ice water (about)**

1 Be sure the butter is well chilled. In a large bowl, toss the butter, both flours, and salt together. Using an electric mixer fitted with a flat paddle, mix the dough rapidly on LOW until the butter is well coated with the flour. If the butter begins to soften, place the mixture in the refrigerator until the butter hardens.

2 Mix in ¾ cup of the iced water, then add as much of the remaining ¼ cup of iced water as needed to form a dough. Transfer the dough to a lightly floured surface.

3 Quickly push, pat, and roll the dough into a rectangle about 18 × 12 inches. Work fast and handle the dough gently.

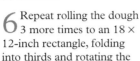
Roll into a rectangle

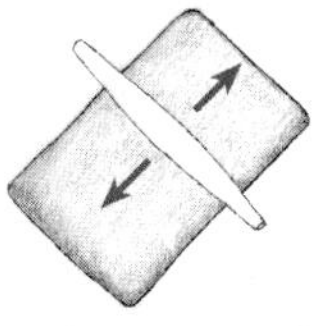

4 Fold the dough into thirds: first fold one narrow end over the middle, then fold the other end on top, forming a rectangle, 6 × 12 inches.

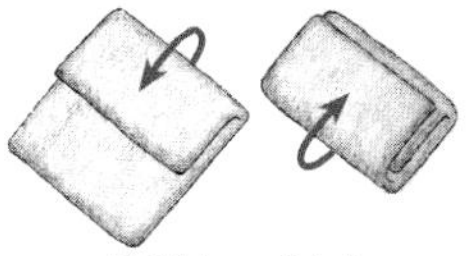

5 Rotate the dough a quarter of a turn. If the dough loses its chill, wrap in plastic wrap and chill for 30 minutes.

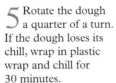
Fold into thirds

6 Repeat rolling the dough 3 more times to an 18 × 12-inch rectangle, folding into thirds and rotating the dough a quarter of a turn each time. Wrap the pastry in plastic wrap and chill for 45 minutes. Repeat the rolling and folding the dough 2 more times, then use immediately or refrigerate for up to 3 days. Or wrap in freezer paper, seal, and freeze for up to 3 months. Thaw in the refrigerator for about 3 hours or until pliable.

Rotate & roll again

BAKED TART SHELL Divide pastry in half, then roll into a round ⅛ inch thick and 3 inches larger than tart pan. Fit into the pan and trim pastry even with the top. Completely prebake at 400°F for 15 minutes or until golden and puffed (see Blind-Baking, page 12). Cool.

BAKED TARTLET SHELLS (5 inch) Divide pastry into 12 even pieces; roll as for tart shells, but only 2 inches larger than tartlet pans. Bake at 400°F for 12 minutes.

BETH'S SNICKERDOODLE COOKIE CRUST

Snickerdoodles are a popular New England butter cookie generously showered with cinnamon and sugar. Here, those ingredients are mixed into a rich cookie crust.

PASTRY FOR 2 SINGLE SHELLS OR 1 DOUBLE-CRUST PIE (8-, 9-, OR 10-INCH)

★ **EASY**

- 2¼ **cups all-purpose flour**
- ½ **cup granulated sugar**
- ¼ **cup finely chopped pecans**
- ½ **teaspoon baking powder**
- ½ **teaspoon ground cinnamon**
- ½ **teaspoon salt**
- ¼ **teaspoon ground nutmeg**
- ½ **cup (1 stick) cold unsalted butter**
- 2 **large egg yolks**
- 6 **tablespoons ice water**
- 1 **teaspoon vanilla extract**

1 In the bowl of a food processor, place the flour, sugar, pecans, baking powder, cinnamon, salt, and nutmeg. Process for 1 second to mix thoroughly. Add the butter and pulse for 30 seconds, or just until the mixture resembles coarse crumbs.

2 Add the egg yolks, water, and vanilla. Process 30 seconds more or until a dough forms. Divide the dough in half and shape each into a 6-inch disk. Wrap in plastic wrap and chill for 30 minutes.

3 Use as your recipe directs, or prebake at 375°F for 10 minutes for a partially baked shell or for 15 minutes for a completely baked shell (see Blind-Baking, page 12).

DROP BISCUIT DOUGH

A quick and heavenly biscuit dough that tops fruit cobblers, slumps, buckles, and pandowies.

DOUGH FOR ONE 13 × 9-INCH PAN

★ **EASY**

- 1 **cup milk**
- 1 **large egg**
- ¼ **cup unsalted butter, melted**
- 1½ **cups all-purpose flour**
- ⅓ **cup packed light brown sugar**
- 1 **tablespoon baking powder**
- ½ **teaspoon salt**

1 Butter a 13 × 9 × 2-inch baking pan. Fill with the fruit mixture as the recipe directs. Or fill with 8 cups of your favorite ripe fruit, tossed with 1 cup sugar, 3 tablespoons all-purpose flour, and 2 tablespoons instant tapioca.

2 In a liquid measure, whisk the milk, egg, and butter. In a medium-size bowl, mix the flour, sugar, baking powder, and salt. Make a well in the center and pour in the milk mixture. Stir until well mixed. Drop by spoonfuls on top of the filling. Bake as recipe directs or at 400°F for 25 minutes or until the filling is bubbly.

MOM ALLEN'S SHORTCAKE DOUGH

A rich biscuit dough that pats out easily and turns fresh fruits into fabulous shortcake pies.

DOUGH FOR ONE 14-INCH ROUND OR ONE 15½ × 10½-INCH PAN

★ **EASY**

- 3 **cups all-purpose flour**
- ⅓ **cup sugar, plus 2 tablespoons for sprinkling**
- 1½ **tablespoons baking powder**
- 1 **tablespoon grated lemon zest**
- 1½ **teaspoons salt**
- ¾ **cup (1½ sticks) cold unsalted butter (not margarine)**
- ¾ **to 1 cup cold heavy (whipping) cream**
- 2 **large eggs**

1 Butter a 14-inch deep-dish pizza pan or a 15½ × 10½ × 1-inch baking pan. In a large bowl, mix the flour, the ⅓ cup of sugar, the baking powder, lemon zest, and salt. Cut in the butter with your fingers or a pastry blender until coarse crumbs form. In a cup, whisk the ¾ cup heavy cream and the eggs until frothy. Add to flour mixture and work it in until a dough forms, adding the additional ¼ cup of cream if needed.

2 Flour your fingers. Pat the dough into the pan and flute the edges. Sprinkle with the remaining sugar and chill 15 minutes. Top and bake as recipe directs; or bake dough at 425°F for 10 to13 minutes or until golden and set (don't overbake). Top with your favorite fresh fruits, plus whipped cream, if you wish.

TOPPINGS, TIPS & TECHNIQUES

MIX & MATCH PIE TOPPINGS

Here are some of my favorite pie toppings for finishing off a pie in a delectable way. Pick your favorites and look for others scattered in recipes throughout this book (see Index for more pie toppings). Be as creative as you wish.

TOPPER	PIE	INGREDIENTS	DIRECTIONS	YIELD
Beth's Mile-High Meringue ▲ MIXER	• Chocolate pies • Cream pies • Custard pies • Key lime pies • Lemon pies	5 egg whites (large, extra-large, or jumbo) 2 teaspoons fresh lemon juice or ½ teaspoon cream of tartar ⅛ teaspoon salt ⅔ cup granulated sugar	1-In a medium-size bowl with an electric mixer on HIGH, beat the egg whites, lemon juice, and salt until fluffy. Beat in the sugar, 2 tablespoons at a time, and continue beating until the meringue stands in glossy soft peaks. 2-Score hot filling with the tines of a fork. Spoon on meringue, making high peaks and sealing edges well. 3-Bake at 350°F for 12 to 15 minutes or until golden.	Meringue for one pie (9- or 10-inch)
Chocolate Curls ★ EASY	• Chocolate Silk Pie • Chocolate cream pies • Ice cream pies • Whipped-cream-topped pies	A 3-ounce bar of bittersweet (dark) chocolate, warmed in microwave on MEDIUM for 15 to 20 seconds (or under a desk lamp for 5 minutes)	1-Using a vegetable peeler, scrape the chocolate bar from top to bottom in one long motion, making long curls of chocolate. 2-Spread on a plate in a single layer and chill until ready to use.	Curls to decorate two 9-inch pies
Crème Fraîche *(Spoonable)* ★ EASY	• Dip for savory empanadas • Fresh fruit dumplings • Pudding pies • Warm fruit crisps	1 cup heavy (whipping) cream 1 tablespoon buttermilk or sour cream	1-In a small bowl, whisk the cream and buttermilk. 2-Cover with plastic wrap and let stand at room temperature for at least 4 hours or overnight until thickened. Refrigerate and use within 10 days.	1 cup spoonable crème fraîche
Crème Fraîche *(Whipped)* ▲ MIXER ★ EASY	• Fresh berry pies • Fresh fruit cobblers • Pudding pies • Pumpkin pies • Slumps & Pandowies	1 cup cold heavy (whipping) cream 2 tablespoons sifted confectioners' sugar ⅓ cup sour cream	1-In a medium-size bowl with an electric mixer on HIGH, beat the cream until frothy. 2-Add the sugar and beat until thickened. 3-Fold in the sour cream. Cover and refrigerate. Best when served immediately.	2 cups whipped crème fraîche
Decorator's Secret Whipped Cream ▲ MIXER	• Chocolate pies • Custard pies • Fancy fruit tarts • Fresh fruit cobblers • Fresh fruit turnovers • Fruit galettes • Ice cream pies • Pecan pies • Slumps & Pandowdies	1 teaspoon unflavored dry gelatin 4 teaspoons cold water 1 cup heavy (whipping) cream ⅓ cup sifted confectioners' sugar 2 teaspoons vanilla extract	1-In a small bowl, mix the gelatin with water and let stand until thick. Completely dissolve gelatin over hot water or heat in the microwave on HIGH for 1 minute. (Be sure mixture is clear, not grainy.) Cool to lukewarm. 2-In a small bowl with an electric mixer on HIGH, beat the cream just until it starts to thicken. Beat in the gelatin all at once, then the sugar and vanilla. Continue beating until soft peaks form (do not overbeat). Spread or pipe the cream right away. Refrigerate until serving time.	2 cups whipped cream
Fancy Pastry Cutouts Use Crisp Flaky Crust recipe (page 15)	• Apple pies (apples) • Cherry pies (hearts) • Fruit dumplings (leaves) • Meat pot pies • Pumpkin pies (leaves or turkey) • Tiny turnovers	½ recipe pastry for 2-crust pie ½ cup granulated sugar ½ teaspoon ground cinnamon ¼ cup heavy (whipping) cream 1-inch cookie cutters for cutouts for pie edge and 2-inch cutters for top of pie	1-On a lightly floured surface, roll out the dough ⅛ inch thick. Cut out desired shapes. 2-Toss the sugar and cinnamon. Brush the cutouts with cream and sprinkle with the cinnamon-sugar. 3-Attach small cutouts with a little water on edge of unbaked pie (see page 63). Bake as recipe directs. 4-Bake larger cutouts at 350°F for 10 minutes.	About 24 small cutouts plus about 6 large cutouts for a 9-inch pie top
Praline Nut Crunch ♦ SAUCEPAN ★ EASY	• Apple pies • Custard pies • Fresh fruit cobblers • Peach pies • Pudding pies • Pumpkin pies	6 tablespoons (¾ stick) unsalted butter 1 cup packed light brown sugar ½ teaspoon ground cinnamon 1½ cups chopped pecans 1 tablespoon dark corn syrup	1-In a small saucepan, melt the butter over low heat. Stir in the sugar and cinnamon and cook until smooth and bubbly. Remove from the heat. 2- Add the pecans and syrup, and toss until well coated. 3-Transfer to a piece of waxed paper to cool. Break up. Sprinkle on pie during last 5 minutes of baking.	Topping for two 9-inch pies Any extras can be frozen
Rum Crème Anglaise *(Rum-flavored custard sauce)* ♦ SAUCEPAN ▲ MIXER ★ EASY	• Chocolate ice cream pies • Chocolate pudding pie • Fresh fruit dumplings • Fresh peach pie • Hot apple pie • Mincemeat pie • Warm berry crisps	2 cups heavy (whipping) cream 3 large egg yolks ½ cup granulated sugar Dash salt 2 to 3 teaspoons light rum	1-In a medium-size heavy saucepan, bring the cream to a simmer over medium heat. 2-In a small bowl with an electric mixer on HIGH, beat egg yolks, sugar, and salt until thick ribbons form. 3-Stir in some of the hot cream, then return to the saucepan. Cook for 2 minutes or just until thickened. Stir in rum. Place pan in a bowl of ice water to chill.	2 cups custard sauce
Tart Glaze ♦ SAUCEPAN ★ EASY	• Custard pies • Fresh fruit dumplings • Fresh fruit tarts/tartlets • Ice cream pies	1½ cups red currant jelly, strawberry jelly, or apricot preserves 1 tablespoon fresh lemon juice	1-In a small saucepan, stir the jelly or preserves over medium heat until melted. Remove from the heat. 2-Stir in the lemon juice. Strain if using preserves. 3-Drizzle over tart and chill until set.	Glaze for one 12-inch tart or eight 5-inch tartlets
Vanilla Icing *(for drizzling)* ★ EASY	• Fried fruit pies • Fruit turnovers • Streusel-topped pies	2 cups sifted confectioners' sugar 5 to 6 teaspoons milk 1 teaspoon vanilla extract	1-In a small bowl, stir all the ingredients until smooth (the icing should be thin). 2-Drizzle on top of cooled baked pie.	1 cup icing

FINISHING TOUCHES

GRATING CHOCOLATE This works best when the chocolate is at room temperature. To prevent the chocolate from melting from the heat of your hands, hold the bar of chocolate in a piece of plastic wrap. Grate the chocolate against the coarse side of a hand grater. Or use a food processor fitted with the fine or coarse grating blade. Spread the grated chocolate in a shallow pan and refrigerate until firm.

MELTING CHOCOLATE Microwave chocolate in its paper wrapper on HIGH for 1 to 2 minutes until it's glossy and almost melted. Then scrape into a bowl and stir until it is completely melted. Or heat chocolate in a double boiler over simmering water, stirring until melted. If chocolate gets too hot, or just a drop of water gets into the pan, chocolate can clump up into a grainy mess, called "seizing." Rescue it by stirring in a teaspoon of butter.

TOASTING NUTS A great topping for ice cream pies. If the recipe calls for chopped nuts, chop them first before toasting them. Spread the nuts in a single layer on a shallow baking pan with ½-inch sides. Toast in a 350°F oven for 5 to 7 minutes, tossing the nuts often with a metal spatula. Watch closely; nuts can burn quickly. To make *salted* toasted nuts, see page 92.

TOASTING COCONUT To toast fresh or packaged coconut, spread it out in a shallow baking pan with ½-inch sides. Toast at 350°F for 10 to 12 minutes, tossing the coconut often with a metal spatula. (Fresh coconut takes a few minutes longer to toast than packaged coconut.)

LEMON, LIME, OR ORANGE ZEST The colored part of the rind, called zest, is the part to use. (The white layer underneath is the bitter pith). Here's an easy tip: Fit a piece of parchment paper or plastic wrap over the fine-hole side of a metal grater. Grate a few strokes, removing just the colored part. When you see the white pith, turn the fruit to a new spot. The zest collects on the paper, so you don't have to scrape it off the grater.

Candied Lemon or Orange Zest A lovely, tasty garnish for fresh fruit tarts. Using a vegetable peeler or a small sharp knife, remove long colored strips from the fruits. Cut away any white pith that might remain on the back. Cut strips ¼ inch wide. Bring 2 cups of sugar and 1 cup of water to a boil. Drop the strips into the boiling syrup and cook for about 5 minutes or until glossy and transparent. Using a slotted spoon, remove the strips to a rack to drain. When lukewarm, toss with granulated sugar.

See Index for more Tips & Techniques.

TROUBLESHOOTING TIPS

PROBLEM	CAUSE — THE RESCUE
Crust browns before fruit is cooked or before filling is set	• **Oven is too hot** — Always use an oven thermometer and check the temperature of the oven before putting in the pie. • **Foil liner or shiny baking sheet lining the oven is reflecting heat onto the pie, causing it to cook too fast** — Use foil shiny-side down or a dark (not shiny) baking sheet. • **Foil pie plate is used for baking pie** — Reduce the oven temperature 25 degrees. Give the pie the doneness test specified in the recipe (it may need a few more minutes of baking).
Crust dough crumbly, hard to roll out	• **Too much fat** — Try a recipe with a little less fat. • **Too little liquid** — Try adding a little more of the liquid, 1 teaspoon at a time.
Crust dough too wet and sticks to pastry board	• **Too much liquid** — Try using a little less liquid or sift a little extra flour on the board. • **Dough too warm** — Freeze pastry dough for 5 to 10 minutes to chill the fat. • **Wrong mixing method** — If you're using the food processor and the recipe does not suggest this, cut back the liquid a little.
Crust not flaky	• **Wrong type of fat** — A combination of room-temperature shortening and very cold butter gives the flakiest pie crust. • **Fat was cut too small** — Cut the fat into the flour only until it forms crumbs the size of peas, no smaller.
Crust shrinks	• **Overmixing dough** — Mix just until the pastry dough comes together. • **Stretching dough when fitting** — When shaping the dough into a shell, ease it gently into the pie plate. Pat, don't pull it. • **Shell did not rest before baking** — Shape the crust, then freeze it for 15 minutes before filling and baking, or blind-baking.
Crust soggy	• **Custard filling soaks into crust during baking** — Brush the bottom crust with an egg white (slightly beaten with 1 tablespoon of water) before blind-baking the shell or before pouring in the filling and baking the pie. • **Juicy fresh fruit can result in soggy crusts** — Sprinkle bottom crust with about 1 tablespoon flour before adding filling.
Crust tough	• **Too much handling of dough** — Mix the pastry dough just until it pulls together, no more; pat, don't knead it, when rolling. • **Too little fat** — Try a recipe with more fat, preferably one with both shortening and butter. • **Too much gluten was developed in the pastry by overmixing** — Substitute 1 tablespoon of the liquid in the recipe with lemon juice or vinegar (both are acids which break down the gluten strands in the dough). Mix just until the flour disappears.
Custard pie filling doesn't thicken	• **Undercooking or overcooking of custard** thickened with cornstarch — Bring custard to a full boil, cook only 2 minutes. • **Recipe is thickened only with cornstarch** — Try a recipe that's thickened with both cornstarch and flour. • **Pie is too warm to cut** — Place the pie in the refrigerator until the custard completely sets before cutting.
Custard tart filling topped with fruit softens and breaks in refrigerator	• **Acid in some fruits break down custard's gel** — Avoid using fresh strawberries or fresh pineapple to top custard tarts. • **Undercooking or overcooking of custard thickened with cornstarch** — Bring custard to a full boil, then cook and stir for 2 minutes, no more.
Fresh fruit pie doesn't thicken or too runny to cut	• **Pie hasn't thickened properly** — Use a recipe that's thickened with both cornstarch and quick-cooking tapioca. • **Pie wasn't baked enough** — Be sure to follow baking temperature and time given in the recipe exactly. • **Pie is too warm to cut** — Let pie stand for at least 3 hours at room temperature before cutting.
Meringue not high	• **Sugar was added too soon** — Beat egg whites into a foam with the acid *before* adding the sugar. • **Sugar was added too fast** — Add sugar, 2 tablespoons at a time, beating in plenty of air between additions. • **Fat on bowl and/or beaters** — Be sure the bowl, beaters, and any utensil touching the meringue are clean. • **Underbeating or overbeating of whites** — Beat the meringue until it stands up in soft glossy peaks when beaters are lifted.
Meringue weeps	• **Wrong kind of sugar used** — Use granulated sugar, not superfine or confectioners' sugar. • **Acid added at the wrong time** — Add acid (cream of tartar or lemon juice) to egg whites at the start *before* adding sugar. • **Meringue was placed on a cold filling** — Spoon the meringue on top of the filling while it is still hot. The heat sets the bottom of the meringue quickly, preventing a pool of uncooked "weeping" meringue on the filling.

MORNING PIES

Morning wake-up pies start with a few simple ingredients, such as eggs, milk, and, often, cheese. Some are whipped into puff pies, filled with fresh fruit, and served right from the skillet. Others take a slice from history and turn into plantation pies, pain perdu pies, farmhouse skillet pies, and stratas from the kaffeeklatsches of the 1950s. Frittatas and quiches are filled with garden vegetables, seafood, or meat, making them hearty enough to show up occasionally at the supper table, too. Choose your favorites, invite some friends, and welcome them warmly with freshly baked pie.

✦ *Farmhouse Cheddar Skillet Pie (see recipe, page 24)*

BRIE STRATA WITH TROPICAL FRUIT SALSA

This is a layered cheese pie that's best when assembled the day before, refrigerated, and then baked right before guests arrive.

MAKES ONE 12-INCH STRATA
PREP TIME 30 MIN ✦ BAKE TIME 35 MIN
CHILL TIME 1 HR

BRIE STRATA

- 1 **1-pound wheel Brie, rind removed**
- 1½ **pound loaf unsliced French or Italian bread**
- 1 **cup milk**
- 2 **large eggs**
- 2 **large egg whites**
- ¼ **teaspoon salt**
- ¼ **cup packed light brown sugar, divided**
- 2 **tablespoons unsalted butter (not margarine), melted**

TROPICAL FRUIT SALSA

- 1 **large mango, peeled, pitted, sliced**
- 1 **large papaya, peeled, seeded, and sliced**
- 1 **cup dried cranberries**
- ¼ **cup honey**
- 2 **tablespoons fresh lime juice**
- 6 **whole cloves**

1 Butter a 12-inch fluted quiche dish with 2-inch sides. Place the Brie in the freezer for 15 minutes. Meanwhile, using a serrated knife, cut bread into 1-inch-thick slices. Remove the crusts and cut into 1-inch cubes (you need 8 cups). In a food processor or blender, process the milk, eggs, egg whites, and salt until frothy. Using a sharp knife, thinly slice the cheese, about ¼ inch thick, dipping the knife in warm water frequently.

2 Arrange half of the bread cubes in the quiche dish. Layer with half of the Brie slices, sprinkle with half of the brown sugar, and pour over half of the milk mixture. Repeat with the remaining bread, Brie, sugar, and milk. Cover with plastic wrap and refrigerate the strata for 1 hour, or preferably overnight.

3 In a medium-size bowl, toss all of the ingredients for the Tropical Fruit Salsa. Cover with plastic wrap and let the salsa stand at room temperature for 1 hour or in the refrigerator overnight. Remove the cloves before serving.

4 About 1 hour before serving, remove the strata from the refrigerator. Preheat the oven to 350°F. Uncover the strata, drizzle with the butter, and bake for 35 minutes or until golden-brown and puffed. A kitchen knife inserted in the center should come out almost clean. Cut the strata into wedges and serve immediately with the fruit salsa.

1/10 strata = 500 calories, 19 g fat (11 g saturated), 98 mg cholesterol, 63 g carbohydrates, 19 g protein, 752 mg sodium, 3 g fiber

FARMHOUSE CHEDDAR SKILLET PIE

Down on the farm, breakfasts are hearty. Folks make egg and cheese pies by whipping egg yolks, then folding in beaten whites and sharp Cheddar. The puffy egg pies cook partially in a skillet, then finish puffing up high in the oven (photo, pages 22–23).

MAKES ONE 10-INCH SKILLET PIE
PREP TIME 20 MIN ✦ COOK TIME 17 MIN

- 6 **large eggs, separated**
- ½ **cup light cream or milk**
- ¼ **cup finely chopped green onions (white and green parts)**
- 2 **cups (8 ounces) shredded sharp Cheddar cheese, divided**
- ½ **teaspoon freshly ground black pepper**
- ½ **teaspoon salt**
- ¼ **teaspoon cream of tartar**
- 2 **tablespoons unsalted butter (not margarine)**

1 Preheat the oven to 375°F and set out a deep 10-inch ovenproof skillet (a cast-iron one is best).

2 In a large bowl, with an electric mixer on HIGH, beat the egg yolks with the cream until light yellow and thick. Stir in the onions, 1¾ cups of the cheese, and the pepper. Set aside.

3 In a clean medium-size bowl, with the mixer on HIGH, beat the egg whites, salt, and cream of tartar with clean beaters until glossy stiff peaks form. Fold the whites into the yolk mixture (don't worry if some whites are still visible).

4 In the skillet, melt the butter over medium heat, then swirl the butter up the sides of the pan. Gently spoon in the batter and cook for 7 to 8 minutes or until set on the bottom. As the egg mixture cooks, lift up the edge, tilt the skillet, and let the uncooked batter run underneath (see right, top).

5 Transfer the skillet to the oven and bake for 10 minutes or until set and puffed. Sprinkle with the remaining ¼ cup of cheese and serve immediately right from the skillet (see right, bottom).

1/8 skillet pie = 226 calories, 19 g fat (11 g saturated), 207 mg cholesterol, 2 g carbohydrates, 12 g protein, 370 mg sodium, .3 g fiber

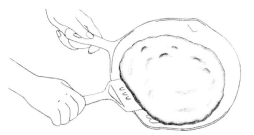

Lift up the edge of the cooked puff, letting the uncooked batter run underneath

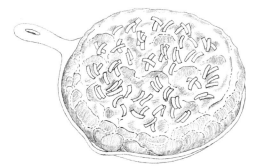

Finish cooking the puff in the oven until it puffs up high and golden

◆ *Brie Strata with Tropical Fruit Salsa*

PAIN PERDU PIE

In French, pain perdu *means "lost bread." It's the name given to French toast, since it is a great way to revive day-old bread. This recipe soaks the bread slices, flavors them with fresh orange and rum, then bakes them into a pie until soft and custardy on the inside, golden on the outside. No need to fry individual pieces of toast — just slice a piece of the pie for each guest.*

MAKES ONE 12-INCH PIE
PREP TIME 20 MIN ✦ BAKE TIME 30 MIN
CHILL TIME 1 HR

- ⅓ cup sugar
- 1½ teaspoons cinnamon
- 4 large eggs
- 2 large egg whites
- 1¼ cups milk
- 1 tablespoon grated orange zest (page 21)
- ½ cup fresh orange juice
- 2 tablespoons light rum or ½ teaspoon rum extract
- 1 teaspoon vanilla extract
- ½ teaspoon salt
- 12 slices French bread, cut 1 inch thick (about 12 ounces)
- 2 tablespoons unsalted butter (not margarine), melted
- ¾ cup fresh orange sections
- ¾ cup fresh ruby red grapefruit sections

1 Preheat the oven to 350°F and butter a fluted 12-inch quiche dish with 2-inch sides or a deep cast-iron skillet. In a cup, toss the sugar with the cinnamon.

2 In a food processor or blender, process the eggs, egg whites, milk, orange zest, orange juice, ¼ cup of the sugar-cinnamon mixture, the rum, vanilla, and salt until light and frothy. Pour into a shallow medium-size bowl.

3 Dip the bread slices into the egg mixture and arrange, overlapping, in the quiche dish or skillet. Pour the remaining egg mixture over the top. Cover with plastic wrap and refrigerate for 1 hour or preferably overnight, turning the slices of bread once. Uncover, drizzle with the butter, and sprinkle the pie and the fruit with the remaining sugar-cinnamon mixture.

4 Bake for 30 to 40 minutes or until the pie is puffed and golden brown. Serve immediately with bowls of orange and grapefruit sections. Or arrange the fruit in a pinwheel design on top of the pie (see below). Serve hot.

⅙ pain perdu pie = 358 calories, 11 g fat (5 g saturated), 159 mg cholesterol, 49 g carbohydrates, 13 g protein, 576 mg sodium, 2 g fiber

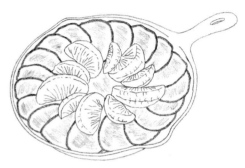

For a special topping, arrange the orange and grapefruit slices in a pinwheel on the baked pie

PLANTATION PUFF PIE

These plantation skillet cakes, as they were originally called, first appeared around the late 18th century in South Carolina. But they're not really cakes at all, but a cross between a popover, a puff pancake, and a skillet pie. They were often accompanied by applesauce and brown sugar. However, I like to top them with fresh blueberries and confectioners' sugar for an extra touch.

MAKES ONE 12-INCH SKILLET PUFF PIE
PREP TIME 15 MIN ✦ BAKE TIME 15 MIN

- 3 tablespoons unsalted butter (not margarine)
- 1 cup fresh blueberries
- 5 tablespoons granulated sugar, divided
- 3 large eggs
- 1 large egg white
- ⅔ cup milk
- ⅔ cup all-purpose flour
- 1½ teaspoons grated lemon zest (page 21)
- 2 tablespoons fresh lemon juice
- ¼ teaspoon ground nutmeg

  Sifted confectioners' sugar

1 Place one of the oven racks in the middle of the oven and preheat the oven to 425°F. Put the butter in a deep 12-inch ovenproof skillet (a cast-iron one is best). Set aside. In a small bowl, toss the berries with 3 tablespoons of the granulated sugar and set aside.

2 In a large bowl, with an electric mixer on HIGH, beat the eggs, egg white, and milk for about 2 minutes or until the mixture is light yellow and frothy. Reduce the speed to LOW and beat in the flour, the remaining 2 tablespoons of granulated sugar, the lemon zest, lemon juice, and nutmeg.

3 Place the skillet on the middle rack in the oven to heat for 1 minute or until the butter is frothy. Remove the skillet from the oven and carefully swirl the butter over the bottom and up the sides. Pour in the egg batter and return the skillet to the oven.

4 Bake the skillet cake for 15 minutes or until golden and puffed. Toss on the blueberries, sprinkle with the confectioners' sugar, and serve the pie immediately, while still puffed and hot.

⅛ puff pie = 160 calories, 7 g fat (4 g saturated), 95 mg cholesterol, 20 g carbohydrates, 5 g protein, 42 mg sodium, 1 g fiber

ORANGE PLANTATION PIE

Substitute 1½ teaspoons grated orange zest for the lemon zest and 2 tablespoons fresh orange juice for the lemon juice (Step 2). Substitute 1 cup of fresh raspberries for the blueberries (Step 2).

✦ *Pain Perdu Pie, served with bowls of orange and grapefruit sections*

VEGETABLE-HAM FRITTATA

Frittatas are open-faced Italian omelets, in the round. Typically, vegetables and meats are mixed and cooked with the eggs, then often finished under the broiler. This frittata resembles a pizza — with eggs holding it together instead of a crust.

MAKES ONE 12-INCH FRITTATA
PREP TIME 20 MIN ✦ COOK TIME 25 MIN

- ½ **pound unpeeled small red potatoes, thinly sliced**
- 6 **large eggs**
- 2 **large egg whites**
- 1½ **cups (6 ounces) shredded provolone cheese, divided**
- ½ **teaspoon salt**
- ¼ **to ½ teaspoon crushed red pepper flakes**
- 2 **tablespoons olive oil**
- 1 **large green bell pepper, cut into thin strips**
- 1 **cup red onion slivers**
- 1 **teaspoon minced garlic**
- 1 **cup (6 ounces) baked ham strips**
- 4 **large plum tomatoes, thinly sliced**
- ¼ **cup slivered fresh basil leaves**

1 Half-fill a large saucepan with water and bring to a boil over high heat. Add the potatoes and cook for 10 minutes or until barely tender. Drain and keep hot.

2 Meanwhile, in a medium-size bowl, whisk the eggs and egg whites until frothy. Fold in 1 cup of the cheese, the salt, and red pepper flakes. Set aside.

3 In a deep 12-inch broilerproof skillet, heat the oil over medium-high heat. Add the bell pepper, onions, and garlic and sauté for 5 minutes or until soft. Stir in the ham and potatoes and sauté 3 minutes more.

4 Pour the egg mixture over the vegetables in the skillet. Reduce the heat to medium-low and cook, uncovered, for 6 minutes or just until the egg mixture is set around the edges. Meanwhile, preheat the broiler.

5 Arrange the tomatoes on top of the frittata and sprinkle with the remaining ½ cup of cheese. Slide the skillet under the broiler for 1 to 2 minutes or until the frittata is bubbling and set in the center. Sprinkle with the basil. Slice and serve immediately, right from the skillet.

1/8 frittata = 249 calories, 15 g fat (6 g saturated), 185 mg cholesterol, 13 g carbohydrates, 17 g protein, 652 mg sodium, 1 g fiber

SPINACH & BACON PIE

Fresh spinach, from the garden or the market, tosses with onion, Swiss cheese, and crisp bacon to make this puffy morning pie.

MAKES ONE 9-INCH DEEP-DISH PIE
PREP TIME 30 MIN ✦ BAKE TIME 50 MIN
STANDING TIME 5 MIN

- ½ **recipe CRISP FLAKY CRUST (page 15)**

  SPINACH-SWISS FILLING
- 1 **10-ounce package fresh spinach, trimmed and rinsed**
- 1 **cup chopped onions**
- 6 **thick slices lean bacon**
- 1 **cup (4 ounces) shredded Swiss cheese**
- 2 **tablespoons all-purpose flour**
- 4 **large eggs**
- 1 **large egg white**
- 1½ **teaspoons salt**
- ½ **teaspoon freshly ground black pepper**
- ¼ **teaspoon ground nutmeg**
- 1⅓ **cups milk**

1 Preheat the oven to 400°F and butter a 9-inch deep-dish pie plate. Roll, shape, and flute the pie shell. Prick the shell all over with a fork. Partially prebake the shell for 10 minutes or just until set (see Blind-Baking, page 12). Cool the shell on a wire rack. Reduce the oven temperature to 350°F.

2 Place the spinach in a large saucepan. Add 1 cup of water, cover, and steam over medium-high heat for 3 minutes or just until it turns bright green. Drain and transfer to a large bowl.

3 In a medium-size nonstick skillet, sauté the onions and bacon over medium-high heat for 7 minutes or until the bacon is crisp. Using a slotted spoon, transfer this onion-bacon mixture to the bowl with the spinach and toss. Spread this mixture over the bottom of the partially baked shell. Toss the cheese with the flour and sprinkle over the spinach.

4 In the same bowl, whisk the eggs, egg white, salt, pepper, and nutmeg. Whisk in the milk and pour over the cheese mixture in the shell. Bake for 40 minutes or until puffed and golden-brown and a kitchen knife inserted in the center comes out clean. Let the pie stand on a rack for 5 minutes before serving.

1/9 pie = 294 calories, 18 g fat (9 g saturated), 128 mg cholesterol, 21 g carbohydrates, 12 g protein, 594 mg sodium, 1 g fiber

✦ *Vegetable-Ham Frittata, sprinkled with slivers of fresh basil*

✦ *Manchego Cheese & Two-Pepper Quiche in a Pâte Brissée tart shell*

Manchego Cheese & Two-Pepper Quiche

One of Spain's most famous cheeses, Manchego is made from the milk of Manchego sheep that graze in the famous plains of La Mancha. It's golden, semifirm, and rich-flavored, and it melts beautifully in this roasted pepper tart.

MAKES ONE 11-INCH QUICHE
PREP TIME 45 MIN ✦ BAKE TIME 40 MIN
COOL / STANDING TIME 20 MIN

½ recipe **CRISP FLAKY CRUST**
(page 15)

MANCHEGO CHEESE FILLING
1 **large green bell pepper**
1 **large red bell pepper**
1 **tablespoon olive oil**
¾ **cup finely chopped onion**
6 **canned plum tomatoes, drained
and coarsely chopped**
1 **teaspoon chopped fresh rosemary
leaves or ¼ teaspoon dried**
¼ **cup thinly sliced pimiento-stuffed
Spanish olives**
¼ **cup minced fresh parsley**
2 **cups (8 ounces) shredded
Manchego cheese or Swiss cheese**
5 **large eggs**
1 **large egg white**
⅓ **cup milk**
¼ **teaspoon freshly ground black
pepper**

1 Preheat the oven to 400°F and butter an 11-inch fluted tart pan with a removable bottom. Roll, shape, and trim the tart shell. Prick the shell all over with a fork. Partially prebake the shell for 10 minutes or just until set (see Blind-Baking, page 12). Cool the shell on a wire rack, while you make the filling. Turn off the oven and preheat the broiler.

2 Place the bell peppers on the broiler pan. Broil about 6 inches from the heat, turning occasionally, for 10 minutes or until the skins are black. Turn off the broiler. Using tongs, transfer the peppers to a clean paper bag, close the bag tightly, and let stand for 10 minutes or until the peppers are cool enough to handle. Cut each pepper vertically into quarters, then core, seed, and cut into long ¼-inch-wide strips. Set aside. Set the oven temperature to 375°F.

3 Meanwhile, in a large skillet, heat the oil over medium-high heat. Add the onion and sauté for 5 minutes or until tender. Add the tomatoes and rosemary and cook 3 minutes more. Remove from the heat and stir in the olives and parsley. Let the onion mixture cool for 15 minutes, then spread over the bottom of the partially baked shell. Sprinkle the cheese over the onion mixture.

4 In a medium-size bowl, whisk the eggs, egg white, milk, and black pepper until frothy. Pour over the cheese in the shell. Arrange the peppers in a pinwheel design on top of the tart, alternating the colors.

5 Bake the quiche for 30 to 40 minutes or until puffed and golden-brown. Let the quiche stand on a wire rack for 5 minutes before serving.

1/10 quiche = 306 calories, 19 g fat (9 g saturated), 140 mg cholesterol, 20 g carbohydrates, 13 g protein, 354 mg sodium, 2 g fiber

Quiche Lorraine

The word quiche *comes from the German dialect* kuche, *meaning "cake," yet the dish itself is from France. The authentic Lorraine version is a simple egg custard pie, flavored only with bacon. It made its debut into North America in the 1970s as a brunch dish. I especially like this variation, with Gruyère cheese, which bakes into a puffy custard.*

MAKES ONE 9-INCH DEEP-DISH QUICHE
PREP TIME 30 MIN ✦ BAKE TIME 40 MIN
COOL / STANDING TIME 20 MIN

½ recipe **PÂTE BRISÉE (page 15)**

QUICHE FILLING
6 **thick strips bacon, chopped**
½ **cup chopped onion**
2 **cups (8 ounces) shredded Gruyère
cheese**
2 **tablespoons all-purpose flour**
3 **large eggs**
1 **large egg white**
1¼ **cups milk**
½ **teaspoon salt**
¼ **teaspoon ground nutmeg**

1 Preheat the oven to 400°F and butter a 9-inch deep-dish pie plate. Roll, shape, and flute the pie shell. Prick the shell all over with a fork. Partially prebake the shell for 10 minutes or just until set (see Blind-Baking, page 12). Cool the shell on a wire rack.

2 In a large skillet, cook the bacon and onion over medium-high heat until the bacon is crisp. With a slotted spoon, transfer to a medium-size bowl. Let the bacon-onion mixture cool for

15 minutes, then toss with the cheese and flour. Spread over the bottom of the partially baked shell.

3 In a large bowl, whisk the eggs, egg white, milk, salt, and nutmeg until frothy. Pour over the cheese in the pie shell. Bake the quiche for 30 minutes or until puffed and golden-brown. Let stand on a rack for 5 minutes before serving.

1/9 quiche = 308calories, 20 g fat (11 g saturated), 124 mg cholesterol, 16 g carbohydrates, 14 g protein, 384 mg sodium, 1 g fiber

DELORES'S APPLE PUFF PANCAKE PIE

Master Food Stylist Delores Custer created this recipe for a family reunion at her beach cottage one summer. Delores suggests using tart crisp apples such as Granny Smiths. For baking the puff pancakes, she prefers a heavy cast-iron skillet.

MAKES ONE 10-INCH PIE
PREP TIME 20 MIN ✦ BAKE TIME 25 MIN

- ¼ **cup granulated sugar**
- ½ **teaspoon ground cinnamon**
- 3 **large eggs**
- ½ **cup milk**
- 1 **teaspoon grated lemon zest (page 21)**
- ½ **cup all-purpose flour**
- ½ **cup (1 stick) unsalted butter (not margarine), divided**
- 2 **tart apples (such as Granny Smiths), peeled, quartered, and sliced ¼ inch thick**

  Sifted confectioners' sugar

1 Preheat the oven to 450°F and set out a deep 10-inch ovenproof skillet (a cast-iron one is best). In a small bowl, mix the granulated sugar with the cinnamon and set aside.

2 In a medium-size bowl, lightly whisk the eggs, milk, and lemon zest. Blend in the flour just until mixed (the batter will be slightly lumpy).

3 In the skillet, melt ¼ cup of the butter over medium heat. Add the apples and sauté for 5 minutes or until tender. Pour the egg batter over the apples and transfer the skillet to the oven. Bake for

20 minutes or until the apples are tender and the pie puffs up high.

4 Meanwhile, melt the remaining ¼ cup of butter. Remove the skillet from the oven, drizzle the puff pie with the butter, and sprinkle with the cinnamon-sugar mixture. Return the pie to the oven for 5 minutes or until the sugar mixture is bubbly. Sprinkle with a little confectioners' sugar and serve immediately, right from the skillet.

1/4 puff pie = 418 calories, 28 g fat (16 g saturated), 226 mg cholesterol, 36 g carbohydrates, 8 g protein, 66 mg sodium, 2 g fiber

FRESH PLUM PUFF PIE

This pie bakes up high into a golden-brown puff pie with plums peeking through the top. Look for the ripest, juiciest, sweetest plums you can find. The large reddish-purple Ace plums with reddish flesh or the purple-black Friar plums are best.

MAKES ONE 10-INCH PUFF PIE
PREP TIME 20 MIN ✦ BAKE TIME 15 MIN

- ⅔ **cup all-purpose flour**
- ⅓ **cup granulated sugar**
- ½ **teaspoon baking powder**
- ½ **teaspoon salt**
- 4 **large ripe, juicy reddish- or dark-purple plums, pitted and thinly sliced**
- ¼ **teaspoon ground cinnamon**
- 3 **tablespoons unsalted butter (not margarine), melted, divided**
- 4 **large eggs**
- ⅔ **cup milk**
- 1 **teaspoon vanilla extract**

  Sifted confectioners' sugar

1 Preheat the oven to 400°F and set out a deep 10-inch ovenproof skillet (a cast-iron one is best). Onto a piece of waxed paper, sift the flour, granulated sugar, baking powder, and salt. In a medium-size bowl, toss the plums with the cinnamon.

2 In the skillet, heat 1 tablespoon of the butter over medium-high heat. Add the plums and sauté for 3 minutes or just until tender. Using a slotted spoon, transfer the plums to a bowl and set aside. Reserve the juices in the skillet.

3 In a medium-size bowl, with an electric mixer on HIGH, beat the eggs

until thick and light yellow. Beat in the milk and vanilla. Blend in the flour mixture (the batter will be slightly lumpy). Pour the batter into the skillet containing the reserved plum juices and top with the plums. Drizzle with the remaining 2 tablespoons of butter.

4 Transfer the skillet to the oven and bake for 15 minutes or until the pie is golden and puffy. Sprinkle the pie with confectioners' sugar and serve immediately, right from the skillet.

1/4 puff pie = 356 calories, 16 g fat (8 g saturated), 243 mg cholesterol, 44 g carbohydrates, 10 g protein, 392 mg sodium, 2 g fiber

✦ *Delores's Apple Puff Pancake Pie, puffed up high with a sprinkling of confectioners' sugar*

SUPPER PIES

♥

Supper pies are hearty pies. Most are substantial enough for the evening meal. Others are small and light enough to serve for lunch. They are savory, not sweet; satisfying, not frivolous; plain eating, not fancy. Often supper pies have an international heritage — meat pies from England, pizza pies from Italy, potato gratin pies from France. Others, such as chicken 'n' dumplings pie, come from generations of hand-me-down recipes. Good-for-you foods are tucked inside many supper pies — fresh-from-the-garden vegetables, just-caught seafood, lean poultry. And best of all, supper pies are stand-alone pies, usually needing only a salad or bread to round out the meal. Discover the delights of savory supper pies.

♦ *Pot Pies (from left to right) —*
Chicken 'n' Dumplings Skillet Pot Pie and
Individual Beef Pot Pies (see recipes, page 36)

CHICKEN 'N' DUMPLINGS POT PIE

When mixing up these old-fashioned rolled dumplings, stir with a wooden spoon just until the dough comes together; overmixing makes tough dumplings. To prevent dumplings from falling apart as they cook, simmer, never boil them.

MAKES ONE 12-INCH PIE
PREP TIME 45 MIN ✦ COOK TIME 1½ HR

- 1 **5- to 6-pound roaster chicken, cut up, giblets removed**
- 6 **cups chicken stock or broth**
- 3 **cups chopped celery, divided**
- 3 **cups chopped onions, divided**
- 1 **tablespoon seasoning salt**
- 1 to 2 **teaspoons ground white pepper**
- 2 **cups peeled carrot circles (¼ inch thick)**
- 1 **cup green peas (fresh or frozen)**
- 3 **tablespoons fresh thyme leaves or 1 tablespoon dried**
- 1 **tablespoon chopped fresh sage or 1 teaspoon rubbed sage**
- 1 **tablespoon sugar**
- ¼ **teaspoon powdered saffron Paprika for sprinkling**
- ¼ **cup chopped fresh parsley**

ROLLED DUMPLINGS

- ¾ **cup (1½ sticks) unsalted butter (not margarine), at room temperature, cut into small pieces**
- 1⅔ **cups very hot water**
- 2 **large eggs, slightly beaten**

- 1½ **teaspoons salt**
- 5¼ **cups all-purpose flour, divided**

1 In a 6-quart Dutch oven or soup pot, place the chicken, stock, 1 cup each of the celery and onions, the seasoning salt, and pepper. Bring to a boil over high heat. Reduce the heat to medium-low and simmer, uncovered, for 45 minutes or until the chicken is tender. Using tongs, transfer the chicken to a bowl; remove and discard the skin if you wish. Cover the chicken and keep it warm.

2 To the broth in the pot, add the remaining 2 cups each of celery and onions, the carrots, peas, thyme, sage, sugar, and saffron. Bring to a full boil. Reduce the heat to medium-low. Cook, uncovered, 15 minutes or until the vegetables are tender. Using a slotted spoon, transfer the vegetables to the bowl with the chicken. Keep broth simmering.

3 Meanwhile, prepare the dumplings: Stir the butter and hot water in a large bowl until the butter melts. Stir in

the eggs and salt. Gradually add 5 cups of the flour, mixing just until the flour is incorporated and the mixture is sticky.

4 On a work surface, sprinkle the remaining ¼ cup of flour and knead the dough for 2 minutes. Roll the dough into a 24-inch square, ⅛ inch thick (a thicker dough can mean tough dumplings). Cut the dumplings into 3-inch squares. One by one, slide the dumplings into the simmering broth in the pot. Cover and cook for 20 minutes or until a toothpick inserted in the center of the dumplings comes out clean.

5 Preheat the broiler. Using a slotted spoon, remove half of the dumplings to a platter. Return the chicken-vegetable mixture to the pot, placing it on top of the remaining dumplings. Layer the rest of the dumplings on top. Sprinkle with the paprika. Broil for 2 to 3 minutes or until bubbly. Sprinkle with the parsley.

⅛ pie = 737 calories, 24 g fat (13 saturated), 202 mg cholesterol, 81 g carbohydrates, 44 g protein, 1,444 mg sodium, 5 g fiber

INDIVIDUAL BEEF POT PIES

Here's a favorite pot pie, topped with flaky homemade puff pastry leaves. For a quick version, use frozen pastry dough.

MAKES SIX 5-INCH INDIVIDUAL PIES
PREP TIME 1 HR ✦ BAKE TIME 20 MIN

- ½ **recipe PÂTE FEUILLETÉE (page 17), or ½ of a 17½-ounce package (1 sheet) frozen puff pastry, thawed**

BEEF PIE FILLING

- 2 **tablespoons vegetable oil**
- 2 **pounds boneless beef chuck, cut into bite-size pieces**
- 8 **ounces fresh mushrooms, washed and sliced vertically (3 cups)**
- 2 **cups chopped yellow onions**
- 1 **tablespoon fresh thyme leaves or ¾ teaspoon dried**
- 2 **teaspoons salt**
- ½ **teaspoon freshly ground black pepper, or to taste**

- ½ **cup all-purpose flour**
- 4 **cups beef stock or broth, heated**
- 1 **pound small red potatoes, cut into 1-inch chunks**
- 2 **cups sliced celery (¼ inch thick)**
- 2 **cups diced carrots (¼-inch dice)**
- 1 **cup green peas (fresh or frozen)**
- 3 **tablespoons light cream**

1 Set out six 2-cup ovenproof ramekins. Prepare or thaw the pastry and refrigerate. In a 5-quart Dutch oven or soup pot, heat the oil over medium-high heat. Add the beef, mushrooms, onions, thyme, salt, and pepper and sauté for 5 minutes or until the beef is brown. Sprinkle on the flour. Gradually stir in the stock, cooking until it thickens. Add the potatoes, celery, carrots, and peas and

bring to a boil. Reduce the heat to medium-low. Cover and simmer for 30 minutes or until the vegetables are tender. Divide among the 6 ramekins.

2 Preheat the oven to 400°F. On a lightly floured surface, roll out the pastry ¼ inch thick. Cut out 6 rounds to match the diameter of your dishes; cover each pie with a pastry round. Then, using a 1½-inch leaf cutter, cut out about 30 leaves, re-rolling the scraps as you go. Attach the leaves with cream, then brush tops of pies with the remaining cream. Bake for 20 minutes or until golden.

1 pie = 654 calories, 29 g fat (13 saturated), 136 mg cholesterol, 56 g carbohydrates, 42 g protein, 1,017 mg sodium, 5 g fiber

SHRIMP POT PIE

Some of the earliest pot pies were made in big iron kettles. The kettle would be lined with a rich pastry, then topped with a partially cooked filling and crowned with a top crust with a large hole in the the center. During cooking, broth was poured into the hole as needed. This double-crust pot pie is filled with shrimp, peppers, and potatoes, then spiced with curry, if you wish.

MAKES ONE 9-INCH DEEP-DISH PIE
PREP TIME 45 MIN ✦ BAKE TIME 30 MIN

1 recipe **FRESH HERB PASTRY made with thyme (page 16)**

SHRIMP FILLING
- 1 **cup red pepper strips**
- 1 **cup green pepper strips**
- 2½ **cups peeled, diced all-purpose potatoes**
- 2 **pounds medium shrimp, thawed if frozen, peeled, deveined, and split down the back**
- 2 **tablespoons unsalted butter**
- 1 **teaspoon curry powder (optional)**
- 2 **cups onion strips**
- 1 **tablespoon minced garlic**
- ¼ **cup all-purpose flour**
- 1½ **teaspoons salt**
- 1 **cup canned coconut cream, plus 1 tablespoon for brushing**

1 Butter a 9-inch deep-dish pie plate. On a lightly floured surface, roll out half of the chilled pastry into a large round, ⅛ inch thick. Trim into a 15-inch circle and fit into the pie plate, leaving a 1½-inch overhang (do not prick). Chill the pie shell while you make the filling.

2 Half-fill a large saucepan with water and bring to a boil over high heat. Blanch the pepper strips and potatoes for 5 minutes. With a slotted spoon, transfer the vegetables to a plate. Add the shrimp to the boiling water and cook for 3 minutes or just until opaque. Drain.

3 In a large skillet, melt the butter over moderately high heat. Stir in the curry, if using, and cook for 1 minute. Add the onions and garlic and sauté for

5 minutes or until soft. Stir in the flour and salt and cook until bubbly, then stir in the 1 cup of coconut cream. Cook and stir for 3 minutes or until thickened, then stir in the cooked vegetables and shrimp. Spoon into the pie shell.

4 Preheat the oven to 400°F. Roll the rest of the pastry into a 12-inch circle and place on top of the filling. Seal and flute the edges. Cut out a small circle in the center for the steam to escape. Brush the top crust with the remaining tablespoon of coconut cream. Bake the pie for 30 minutes or until golden and bubbly. Serve hot. Store any leftover pie in the refrigerator.

1/8 pie = 625 calories, 36 g fat (21 saturated), 213 mg cholesterol, 52 g carbohydrates, 26 g protein, 762 mg sodium, 3 g fiber

VEGETABLE POT PIE UNDER A CHEDDAR LATTICE

When you want a light supper, here's the answer: a potpourri of fresh vegetables tossed with a light basil cream and baked under a lattice Cheddar crust. Slice and serve with a fresh mesclun salad, drizzled with a white wine vinaigrette.

MAKES ONE 9-INCH DEEP-DISH PIE
PREP TIME 45 MIN ✦ BAKE TIME 30 MIN
COOL TIME 5 MIN

1 recipe **CHEDDAR CHEESE PASTRY (page 16)**

GARDEN VEGETABLE FILLING
- 1½ **pounds red potatoes, sliced ¼ inch thick**
- 1 **cup peeled carrot circles (¼ inch thick)**
- 1 **cup red pepper strips**
- 1½ **cups small broccoli florets**
- 1 **cup light cream plus 1 tablespoon for glazing**
- 1 **cup milk**
- 1 **vegetable bouillon cube**
- 2 **tablespoons unsalted butter**
- 1 **large red onion, slivered (1½ cups)**
- 2 **teaspoons minced garlic**
- ⅓ **cup all-purpose flour**
- ¼ **teaspoon freshly ground black pepper**
- ½ **cup slivered fresh basil**
- 1 **large egg yolk**

1 Butter a 9-inch deep-dish pie plate. On a lightly floured surface, roll out half of the chilled pastry into a large round, ⅛ inch thick. Trim it to a 15-inch circle and fit into the pie plate, leaving a 1½-inch overhang (do not prick). Chill the pie shell while you make the filling.

2 Half-fill a large saucepan with water and bring to a boil over high heat. Cook the potatoes and carrots for 20 minutes or until tender, adding the red pepper strips for the last 3 minutes of cooking. Drain the vegetables well; toss with the uncooked broccoli florets.

3 In a small saucepan, heat the 1 cup of cream, the milk, and bouillon cube over medium heat until the mixture simmers and the bouillon cube dissolves; remove from the heat. In a large skillet,

melt the butter over medium high heat. Add the onion and garlic and sauté for 5 minutes or until soft. Stir in the flour and black pepper and cook until bubbly, then whisk in the warm cream mixture. Cook and stir for 3 minutes or until thickened. Remove from the heat and stir in the basil. Pour this sauce over the vegetables and toss. Spoon into the pie shell.

4 Preheat the oven to 400°F. Roll out the remaining pastry into a 12-inch circle, place on top of the pie, and flute. Cut a few steam vents. In a cup, whisk the remaining tablespoon of cream and the egg yolk; brush on the crust. Bake the pie for 30 minutes or until golden brown and bubbly. Cool for 5 minutes before serving. Refrigerate any leftovers.

1/8 pie = 531 calories, 25 g fat (14 saturated), 98 mg cholesterol, 65 g carbohydrates, 15 g protein, 1,377 mg sodium, 5 g fiber

DEEP-DISH PIZZA PIE

In 1943 in Chicago, Ike Sewell and Ric Riccardo of Pizzeria Uno created an inch-thick pizza crust, topped it with fresh ingredients, and cooked it in a heavy skillet. Thus, the pan pizza or thick-crust pizza was born. Typically, the dough has a little crunch of cornmeal, and it's pressed into the pan with your fingertips. Let it rise for a few minutes in the pan before baking. Here's one of my favorites with a hearty sausage topping ... it bakes up with a light, crispy, chewy crust.

MAKES ONE 14-INCH DEEP-DISH PIZZA PIE
PREP TIME 45 MIN ◆ BAKE TIME 30 MIN

- 1 **recipe RAPID-RISE YEAST DOUGH (page 16)**
- ½ **cup yellow cornmeal**
- 2 **teaspoons minced fresh oregano leaves or 1 teaspoon dried**

DEEP-DISH PIZZA TOPPINGS
- 1 **pound Italian sausage (mild/sweet or hot, depending on your taste)**
- 8 **ounces fresh mushrooms, washed and sliced vertically**
- 2 **teaspoons minced garlic**
- ½ **teaspoon crushed red pepper flakes**
- ½ **cup freshly grated Parmesan cheese, divided**
- 1 **pound low-moisture mozzarella cheese, sliced**
- 1 **pound plum tomatoes, thinly sliced, seeded, and drained**

- 1 **small red onion, slivered (½ cup)**
- 1 **cup red bell pepper strips**
- 2 **tablespoons extra virgin olive oil**
- 1 **cup slivered fresh basil leaves**

1 Prepare the yeast dough, adding the cornmeal to the flour mixture and substituting the oregano for the rosemary. The dough is ready to use (no need to let it rise).

2 Preheat the oven to 450°F. Oil a 14- to 15-inch deep-dish pizza pan. Turn the dough out onto a lightly floured surface. Oil your fingers and knead the dough for a minute or two. Using your fingers, press the dough into the pan, making dimples in the dough with your fingertips. Let the crust rest while you prepare the toppings.

3 Remove the sausages from their casings and crumble into a large skillet. Sauté over medium-high heat for 5 minutes. Using a slotted spoon, transfer to a plate lined with paper towels. In the drippings in the skillet, sauté the mushrooms, garlic, and crushed pepper flakes until mushrooms are light brown.

4 Layer the toppings on the slightly risen dough in this order: ¼ cup of the Parmesan, the mozzarella slices, sausage, mushroom mixture, tomatoes, onion, bell pepper, and the remaining ¼ cup of Parmesan. Drizzle with the oil. Bake for 30 minutes or until the crust is golden and the topping is bubbly. Sprinkle with the basil, slice, and serve.

1/9 pizza pie = 582 calories, 31 g fat (12 saturated), 64 mg cholesterol, 46 g carbohydrates, 29 g protein, 1,311 mg sodium, 3 g fiber

PIZZA RUSTICA

In Italy, Pizza Rustica is traditional street food, often served at home as a casual appetizer. It resembles the French Country Quiche Lorraine (the word rustica *means "from the country"). A three-cheese blend is frequently used — ricotta, Romano, and mozzarella. I like to make Pizza Rustica with an authentic sweetened lattice crust cut with a fluted pastry wheel.*

MAKES ONE 10-INCH DEEP-DISH PIE
PREP TIME 45 MIN ◆ BAKE TIME 45 MIN

- 1 **recipe PÂTE SUCRÉE (page 15)**
- ⅓ **cup granulated sugar**

PIZZA RUSTICA FILLING
- 1 **tablespoon extra virgin olive oil**
- ¾ **cup chopped green bell pepper**
- ¾ **cup chopped onion**
- 6 **ounces salami, cut into thin slivers (1½ cups)**
- 4 **large eggs**
- 1 **pound whole-milk ricotta**
- 1½ **cups (6 ounces) shredded low-moisture mozzarella**
- ¼ **cup freshly grated Romano cheese**
- 1 **tablespoon chopped fresh marjoram leaves or 1 teaspoon dried**

- ½ **teaspoon ground white pepper**
- 2 **tablespoons light cream**

1 Prepare the pastry dough, substituting the granulated sugar for the confectioners' sugar. Divide the dough into 2 equal parts, shape each piece into a 6-inch disk, and refrigerate one disk. Roll out the other pastry disk on a lightly floured surface into a 17-inch circle and fit into a 10-inch deep-dish pie plate, leaving a 1½-inch overhang. Chill.

2 Preheat the oven to 350°F. In a small skillet, heat the oil over medium-high heat. Add the bell pepper and onion and sauté for 5 minutes or until crisp-tender. Spoon over the bottom of the chilled crust and sprinkle with the salami.

3 In a large bowl, with an electric mixer on HIGH, whip the eggs until fluffy. Stir in the ricotta, mozzarella, Romano, marjoram, and white pepper. Pour over the vegetables and salami in the shell.

4 On a lightly floured surface, roll out the remaining dough disk into a 9-inch square, ⅛ inch thick. Using a fluted pastry wheel, cut into 12 strips, ¾ inch wide. Place 6 strips on top of the filling. Diagonally crisscross the remaining 6 strips to form a lattice top (see Lattice Crust, page 14). Flute and seal, then brush with the cream. Bake for 45 minutes or until the crust is golden and the filling is puffy.

1/8 pizza pie = 582 calories, 34 g fat (18 saturated), 250 mg cholesterol, 45 g carbohydrates, 24 g protein, 646 mg sodium, 2 g fiber

✦ *Deep-Dish Pizza Pie in a homemade yeast crust that's patted into the pan*

SHEPHERD'S PIE

This deep-dish pie of bite-size chunks of cooked lamb crowned with mashed potatoes was originally created as a way to use the rest of Sunday's lamb roast. By substituting beef sirloin for the lamb, you can turn it into a steak and potato pie.

MAKES ONE 12-INCH DEEP-DISH PIE
PREP TIME 30 MIN ✦ BAKE TIME 35 MIN

- 3 **pounds all-purpose potatoes (about 6 large), peeled and cut into chunks**
- 1½ **teaspoons salt, divided**
- ⅓ **cup milk**
- 5 **tablespoons unsalted butter (not margarine), melted, divided**
- 4 **large carrots, peeled and sliced ¼ inch thick (2 cups)**
- 1 **large yellow onion, slivered (1½ cups)**
- 1 **tablespoon minced garlic**
- ½ **cup all-purpose flour**
- 1 **tablespoon snipped fresh rosemary leaves or 1 teaspoon dried**
- ½ **teaspoon freshly ground black pepper**
- 4 **cups beef stock or broth**
- 6 **cups bite-size pieces cooked boneless lamb**
- 1 **cup green peas (fresh or frozen), cooked and drained**

1 Place the potatoes in a large pot, cover with water, and add ½ teaspoon of the salt. Bring to a boil over medium-high heat and simmer for 10 minutes or until the potatoes are tender. Drain and return the potatoes to the pot. Mash with the milk and 2 tablespoons of the butter. Cover the pot to keep the potatoes warm.

2 Preheat the oven to 375°F. In a deep 12-inch cast-iron skillet or 5-quart Dutch oven, heat 2 tablespoons of the remaining butter over medium-high heat. Add the carrots, onion, and garlic and cook for 5 minutes or until the carrots are crisp-tender. Stir in the flour, rosemary, pepper, and the remaining 1 teaspoon of salt and cook 3 minutes more. Gradually add the stock and cook 5 more minutes or until the gravy thickens. Stir in the lamb and peas and remove from the heat.

3 Cover and bake for 15 minutes. Remove the pie from the oven. Spoon or pipe the mashed potatoes around the edge and drizzle with the remaining tablespoon of butter. Return the pie to the oven and bake, uncovered, 20 minutes more or until the filling is bubbling and the potatoes are golden.

1/9 pie = 596 calories, 22 g fat (9 saturated), 162 mg cholesterol, 48 g carbohydrates, 49 g protein, 549 mg sodium, 4 g fiber

STEAK 'N' TATER PIE Substitute 2 pounds uncooked boneless beef sirloin, cut into ½-inch cubes, for the lamb. Add the beef to the Dutch oven with the carrots, onion, and garlic (Step 2). Cook for 8 minutes or until the beef and onions are browned.

HAM 'N' POTATO GRATIN DAUPHINOIS

Near the French-Italian border lies a mountainous French region called the Dauphiné — famous for its creamy potato gratin. Potatoes simmer in milk and seasonings, then are layered with cream and garlic. We've created a meat 'n' potatoes pie by adding cooked bites of ham. Slivered onions and a little wine turn the dish into Ham 'n' Potatoes Lyonnaise.

MAKES ONE 13 x 9-INCH GRATIN
PREP TIME 30 MIN ✦ BAKE TIME 40 MIN

- 2 **large cloves garlic, peeled and halved**
- 6 **cups milk**
- 1 **teaspoon salt, divided**
- 3 **5-inch sprigs fresh thyme**
- 3 **pounds all-purpose potatoes (about 6 large), peeled and sliced ⅛ inch thick**
- 2 **cups slivered baked ham**
- 1 **cup light cream or milk**
- 1 **large egg, slightly beaten**
- 1 **tablespoon all-purpose flour**
- ½ **teaspoon ground white pepper**
- ½ **teaspoon ground nutmeg**
- 1½ **cups (6 ounces) shredded Gruyère cheese**

1 Preheat the oven to 400°F and generously butter a 13 x 9 x 3-inch baking dish. Rub the inside of the dish well with one of the garlic cloves.

2 In a large pan, bring the milk, ½ teaspoon of the salt, the thyme, and the remaining garlic clove to a simmer over medium heat. Add the potatoes and simmer for 20 minutes or until just barely tender, stirring occasionally. Drain, then discard the garlic clove and thyme sprigs (it's fine if some leaves remain).

3 Spread the ham over the bottom of the prepared baking dish and arrange the potato slices in diagonal rows on top (see right). In a small saucepan, whisk together the cream, egg, flour, the remaining salt, the pepper, and nutmeg. Bring this mixture just to a simmer over medium heat, then pour over the potatoes and bake, uncovered, for 25 minutes. Sprinkle with the cheese and bake 15 minutes more or until the potatoes are tender and the top is golden.

1/9 gratin pie = 422 calories, 19 g fat (11 saturated), 97 mg cholesterol, 41 g carbohydrates, 22 g protein, 772 mg sodium, 2 g fiber

HAM 'N' POTATOES LYONNAISE Sprinkle 2 cups of thin onion strips and 3 tablespoons dry white wine over the potatoes before adding the cream mixture (Step 3).

Arrange the potato slices in diagonal rows in the dish, first in one direction, then in the opposite.

◆ *Shepherd's Pie, crowned with fluffy mashed potatoes*

TOURTIÈRE DE FLEUR-ANGE

My search for a traditional tourtière, the Christmas holy day pork pie, led me to this recipe from Fleur-Ange Vanier Rochon in A Taste of Quebec *by Julian Armstrong. Fleur-Ange is the mother-in-law of prize-winning chef Marcel Kretz. Marcel says, "She makes the best tourtière I have ever eaten." The secret: Use ground pork for the meat and a careful hand with the seasonings.*

MAKES TWO 9-INCH PIES
PREP TIME 1 HR ✦ BAKE TIME 35 MIN

2 recipes BUTTERY CRUST or CRISP
   FLAKY CRUST (page 15)

   TOURTIÈRE PORK FILLING
2 pounds ground pork loin
1 cup water
1 cup chopped celery
½ cup chopped celery leaves
2 large onions, chopped (2 cups)
2 large garlic cloves, chopped
½ cup chopped fresh parsley
1 tablespoon chopped fresh savory or
   1 teaspoon dried, or to taste
2 teaspoons salt
1 teaspoon freshly ground black
   pepper
   Pinch ground cinnamon
   Pinch ground cloves

1 large egg yolk
1 tablespoon milk

1 Butter two 9-inch pie plates. Using half of the chilled pastry, roll out and shape both bottom crusts, leaving a 1½-inch overhang. Chill the pie shells.

2 In a large saucepan, bring the pork, water, celery and leaves, onions, garlic, parsley, savory, salt, pepper, cinnamon, and cloves to a simmer over medium heat. Cook, uncovered, stirring occasionally, for 30 minutes or until the flavors are well blended, adding a little more water if needed to keep the mixture from drying out. Drain off any fat, adjust seasonings if you wish, and let cool.

Using a pointed knife, cut vents in the shape of a tree in the center, then cut out stars with a small cutter and place all around the edge

3 Preheat the oven to 400°F. On a lightly floured surface, roll out the remaining pastry into 2 large rounds, ⅛ inch thick, and trim each to a 12-inch circle. Cut vents in the center of each in the shape of a Christmas tree, just as Mme. Rochon suggests. Cover each pie with a top crust, seal the edges with a little water, and then flute them. With a small star cutter, cut out little stars from the scraps of pastry and "glue" around the tree with a little water. In a cup, whisk the egg yolk and milk and brush on the pies. Bake the pies for 35 minutes or until the crust is golden brown. Serve the pies hot or cold, with pickles or relish. Store any leftover pie in the refrigerator.

⅛ pie = 442 calories, 22 g fat (10 saturated), 112 mg cholesterol, 44 g carbohydrates, 19 g protein, 463 mg sodium, 2 g fiber

CHICKEN & CHEESE QUESADILLA

The stuffed tortilla turnovers called quesadillas are popular street food in Mexico. Some are made from masa (corn) tortillas and fried; others, from flour tortillas and baked on a griddle. Stuffings range from spiced vegetables to meats, poultry, and cheese. Many quesadillas are spiked with chilies then cooled with guacamole. I like to make over-sized quesadilla pies on large flour tortillas, without folding them. Before serving, crown with shredded lettuce, tomatoes, and salsa.

MAKES ONE 8-INCH PIE
PREP TIME 30 MIN ✦ BAKE TIME 15 MIN

2 8-inch flour tortillas

   CHICKEN-CHEESE FILLING
1 cup (4 ounces) shredded Cheddar
   cheese
1 cup (4 ounces) shredded Monterey
   Jack cheese
2 tablespoons vegetable oil
1 pound boneless, skinless chicken
   breasts, cut into strips (4 × 1 × ½
   inch)
1 cup chopped green onions
1 cup chopped green pepper
2 teaspoons minced garlic
½ small jalapeño pepper, seeds
   discarded, minced (optional)
1 large avocado, peeled, seeded, and
   sliced lengthwise ¼ inch thick
1 cup chunky salsa (medium to
   hot), plus extra for topping if you
   wish
1 cup shredded lettuce
1 cup seeded, chopped ripe tomatoes
1 tablespoon sliced ripe pitted olives

1 Preheat the oven to 350°F and oil a large baking sheet. Place 1 tortilla in the center of the sheet. In a small bowl, toss the two cheeses; sprinkle the tortilla with half of the cheese mixture. Set aside the rest of the cheese.

2 In a large nonstick skillet, heat the oil over medium-high heat. Add the chicken, onions, green pepper, garlic, and the jalapeño pepper, if using, and sauté for 8 minutes or until the juices of the chicken run clear when pierced with a fork. Using a slotted spoon, spread the chicken mixture on the tortilla, covering the cheese. Top with the avocado, the 1 cup of salsa, and the remaining cheese. Cover with the second tortilla, pressing it down lightly to form a sandwich.

3 Bake the quesadilla for 15 to 18 minutes or until the cheese melts, the tortillas are crisp, and the filling is heated through. Transfer the quesadilla to a platter and top with the lettuce, tomatoes, and olives. Serve piping hot, with additional salsa if you wish.

¼ pie = 595 calories, 36 g fat (15 saturated), 123 mg cholesterol, 27 g carbohydrates, 47 g protein, 848 mg sodium, 4 g fiber

SAUSAGE & PEPPER CALZONES

Stuff a pizza the way they do in Naples and you have an individual pizza pie in the shape of a turnover. Calzones are stuffed with everything from spicy sausages to grilled vegetables, shredded salami or chicken, and, almost always, mozzarella cheese.

MAKES EIGHT CALZONES
PREP TIME 45 MIN ✦ BAKE TIME 12 MIN

1 recipe **RAPID-RISE YEAST DOUGH**, made with 3½ cups all-purpose flour and fresh rosemary (page 16)

SAUSAGE & PEPPER FILLING
3 **tablespoons olive oil, divided**
1 **pound Italian sausage (mild/sweet or hot), sliced ¼ inch thick**
1½ **cups green bell pepper strips**
2 **cups red onion strips**
1 **tablespoon minced garlic**
2 **cups bottled marinara sauce**
2 **tablespoons canned tomato paste**
1 **tablespoon chopped fresh marjoram or 1 teaspoon dried**
2 **cups (8 ounces) shredded low-moisture mozzarella cheese**
½ **cup grated Parmesan cheese**

1 Generously dust a pizza peel or wooden board with flour. Mix the dough, increasing the flour to 3½ cups by kneading an additional ½ cup flour into the dough in Step 2. Cover and let the dough rise at room temperature while you make the filling.

2 In a medium-size nonstick skillet, heat 1 tablespoon of the oil over medium-high heat. Add the sausage and cook until brown and cooked through. Using a slotted spoon, transfer the sausage to a plate lined with paper towels to drain. Discard all but 1 tablespoon of the drippings in the skillet. Add the peppers, onions, and garlic to the skillet and sauté for 5 minutes or until peppers are soft. Stir in the sausage; remove from the heat.

3 Place a pizza stone or baking sheet on the middle shelf of the oven and preheat to 425°F. In a small bowl, mix the marinara sauce, tomato paste, and marjoram. Cut the dough into 8 equal pieces. On the floured pizza peel or board, pat out each piece of dough into a 6-inch circle, ¼ inch thick. Spread each circle with 3 to 4 tablespoons of sauce.

4 Spoon about ⅔ cup of the sausage filling onto the lower half of each calzone, in a semicircle, to within ½ inch

of the edge. Cover the filling with ¼ cup of the mozzarella. Fold over the top half of each calzone; seal with the tines of a fork. Make steam vents on the tops of the calzones with your thumb and pointed scissors (see right). Drizzle the calzones with the remaining 2 tablespoons of oil and sprinkle with the Parmesan. Bake the calzones on the pizza stone in batches for 12 minutes or until golden.

1 calzone = 578 calories, 27 g fat (5 saturated), 21 mg cholesterol, 52 g carbohydrates, 26 g protein, 801 mg sodium, 5 g fiber

Spoon on the filling, to within ½ inch of the edge, then fold over the top half and seal with the tines of a fork; make a vent with your thumb and snip a few smaller vents

POTATOES ANNA

French Chef Adolphe Duglère created these potatoes to accompany roast meat and poultry. He dedicated the recipe to Anna Deslions, a woman of fashion in France during the late 1800s. The classic version requires a special round two-handled casserole with an interlocking lid, plus the skill of flipping the potato pie back into the pan to brown the second side. My version is baked in a tart pan with a removable bottom and requires no flipping or turning.

MAKES ONE 11-INCH TART
PREP TIME 30 MIN ✦ BAKE TIME 40 MIN

1 **cup (4 ounces) shredded Swiss cheese**
3 **tablespoons minced fresh parsley, divided**
8 **large russet potatoes**
½ **teaspoon salt**
½ **teaspoon freshly ground black pepper**
¼ **teaspoon ground nutmeg**
½ **cup (1 stick) unsalted butter (not margarine), melted**

1 Preheat the oven to 425°F and generously butter an 11-inch tart pan with a removable bottom. In a small bowl, toss the cheese with 2 tablespoons of the parsley and set aside.

2 Peel the potatoes and slice ¼ inch thick into a bowl of ice water (you need 8 cups of potatoes). Soak them for 15 minutes (soaking them longer makes them watery). Transfer potatoes to paper towels and pat dry. In a cup, mix the salt, pepper, and nutmeg; sprinkle over the potatoes, gently tossing until well coated.

3 Arrange one third of the potato slices in a circular design in the pan, overlapping them slightly as you go. Brush with one third of the butter and sprinkle with half of the cheese. Gently press down the pie with your hands. Repeat the layering: one third more potatoes, one third more butter, and the remaining cheese. Press down, top with the remaining potatoes, and drizzle with the remaining butter. Once again, gently press down the pie with your hands.

4 Place the tart pan on a baking sheet and bake for 40 minutes or until the potatoes are tender, golden brown, and crusty on top. Remove the tart ring, leaving the tart on the bottom of the pan. Place on a platter and sprinkle with the remaining tablespoon of parsley.

1/8 pie = 287 calories, 16 g fat (10 saturated), 44 mg cholesterol, 31 g carbohydrates, 7 g protein, 181 mg sodium, 2 g fiber

POTATOES ANNETTE Peel the potatoes and cut into julienne strips, 4 × ¼ inch; proceed as for Potatoes Anna.

SHRIMP & SPRING ONION QUICHE

A traditional egg custard turns shrimp, spring onions, and Swiss cheese into a quiche that's perfect for a spring supper. As the custard cooks, it slowly bakes into a puffy golden pie that's hearty enough to make a meal, along with a fresh fruit salad.

MAKES ONE 9-INCH DEEP-DISH QUICHE
PREP TIME 45 MIN ✦ BAKE TIME 30 MIN
STANDING TIME 5 MINUTES

½ **recipe PÂTE BRISÉE (page 15)**

SHRIMP & ONION FILLING
1 **pound uncooked medium-size shrimp (about 25)**
1 **tablespoon unsalted butter (not margarine)**
½ **cup thinly sliced green onions (white and green parts)**
2 **cups (8 ounces) shredded Swiss cheese**
2 **tablespoons all-purpose flour**
3 **large eggs**
1 **large egg white**
1 **tablespoon fresh tarragon leaves or 1 teaspoon dried**

1 **teaspoon salt**
¼ **teaspoon white pepper**
1¼ **cups milk**

1 Preheat the oven to 400°F and set out a 9-inch deep-dish pie plate. Roll, shape, and flute the pie shell. Prick the shell all over with a fork. Partially prebake the shell for 10 minutes or just until set (see Blind-Baking, page 12). Cool the shell on a wire rack.

2 Meanwhile, shell and devein the shrimp. In a large nonstick skillet, melt the butter over medium-high heat. Add the shrimp and green onions and sauté for 3 minutes or just until the shrimp turn opaque (do not overcook).

3 Spread the shrimp mixture over the bottom of the partially baked shell. Toss the cheese with the flour and sprinkle over the shrimp.

4 In a medium-size bowl, whisk the eggs, egg white, tarragon, salt, and pepper until frothy. Whisk in the milk until blended. Pour this mixture over the cheese mixture in the partially baked shell. Bake for 30 minutes or until puffed and golden. Let the quiche stand on a wire rack for 5 minutes before serving.

1/9 quiche= 324 calories, 18 g fat (11 g saturated), 197 mg cholesterol, 17 g carbohydrates, 21 g protein, 505 mg sodium, 1 g fiber

ZUCCHINI GARDEN QUICHE

This vegetable quiche does triple-duty — perfect as a weekend brunch, ideal for Sunday supper, and totable as a buffet vegetable dish. This is a wonderful recipe from Food Stylist Delores Custer who frequently serves it at her country cottage.

MAKES ONE 9-INCH DEEP-DISH QUICHE
PREP TIME 45 MIN ✦ BAKE TIME 50 MIN

TWO-CHEESE CRUST
½ **cup (2 ounces) shredded Cheddar cheese**
2 **tablespoons grated Parmesan cheese**
1 **cup packaged biscuit mix**
¼ **cup unsalted butter (not margarine), at room temperature**
3 **tablespoons boiling water**

ZUCCHINI-CHEESE FILLING
½ **cup water**
2 **teaspoons salt, divided**
1½ **pounds zucchini, cut into circles ¼-inch thick (3 cups)**
2 **large eggs, separated**
1½ **cups sour cream**
2 **tablespoons all-purpose flour**
2 **tablespoons snipped fresh chives**
¼ **teaspoon freshly ground black pepper**
⅛ **teaspoon cream of tartar**
½ **cup dried herb-seasoned bread crumbs**

2 **tablespoons unsalted butter (not margarine), melted**

1 Preheat the oven to 400°F and butter a 9-inch deep-dish pie plate. In a small bowl, toss the Cheddar and Parmesan cheeses, then measure ¼ cup into a medium-size bowl. Set aside the remaining cheese mixture.

2 To the ¼ cup of cheese mixture, add the biscuit mix and toss. Using your fingers or a pastry blender, cut in the ¼ cup butter. Sprinkle with the boiling water and stir with a fork just until a dough forms. Press the dough over the bottom and up the sides of the pie plate. Flute the edges of the shell and chill.

3 Meanwhile, in a large saucepan, bring the water and 1 teaspoon of the salt to a boil over high heat. Add the zucchini and cook for 5 minutes. Drain, then cool.

4 In a medium-size bowl, with an electric mixer on HIGH, beat the egg

yolks until light yellow and thick. Reduce the speed to LOW and blend in the sour cream, flour, chives, the remaining 1 teaspoon of salt, and the pepper. In a small clean bowl, with the mixer on HIGH, beat the egg whites and cream of tartar with clean beaters until glossy stiff peaks form. Lightly fold the whites into the egg yolk mixture (some whites should still be visible).

5 Spread half of the zucchini over the bottom of the chilled crust, then top with half of the egg mixture. Repeat with the remaining zucchini and egg mixture. In a small bowl, toss the reserved cheese mixture with the bread crumbs and melted butter. Sprinkle on the quiche. Bake for 10 minutes, then reduce the oven temperature to 325°F. Bake the pie 40 minutes more or until a kitchen knife inserted in the center comes out clean.

1/9 quiche = 437 calories, 31 g fat (16 g saturated), 106 mg cholesterol, 33 g carbohydrates, 9 g protein, 846 mg sodium, 2 g fiber

◆ *Shrimp & Spring Onion Quiche, garnished with a few cooked shrimp and sprigs of fresh tarragon*

CARAMELIZED VIDALIA ONION TART

Vidalia onions are large pale yellow onions (a Granex hybrid) that are sweet and juicy. To earn the name Vidalia, an onion must be grown in a particular part of southeast Georgia. The popular onion was the inspiration for this tart created by Food Stylist Elizabeth Duffy. Since Vidalias are only in season in late spring and early summer, Bermuda or Spanish onions may be substituted when necessary. Serve this tart as the perfect complement to steaks, roast beef, or roast pork.

MAKES ONE 10-INCH TART
PREP TIME 30 MIN ✦ BAKE TIME 30 MIN

1 recipe FRESH HERB PASTRY (page 16) made with fresh rosemary

VIDALIA ONION FILLING

½ **cup golden raisins**
½ **cup red wine vinegar**
2 **pounds Vidalia onions (preferred), or Bermuda or Spanish onions, (about 4), peeled**
1 **teaspoon salt, or to taste, divided**
½ **teaspoon white pepper, divided**
2 **tablespoons extra virgin olive oil, divided**
1 **teaspoon minced garlic**
½ **cup water**
2 **large eggs**
⅓ **cup sour cream**
3 **tablespoons unsalted butter (not margarine), at room temperature**

1 Preheat the oven to 400°F and butter a 10-inch tart pan with a removable bottom. Roll, shape, trim, and prick the tart shell all over with a fork. Completely prebake the shell for 15 minutes or until golden (see Blind-Baking, page 12). Cool on a rack. (Leave the oven on.)

2 Meanwhile, in a small saucepan, simmer the raisins and vinegar over medium-low heat for 10 minutes or until the liquid has evaporated. Set aside.

3 Cut 1 pound of the onions in half vertically. Trim the ends, leaving the center core intact. Starting from the outside of each onion half, slice into wedges, ¼ inch wide. Season with ½ teaspoon of the salt and ¼ teaspoon of the pepper. In a large skillet, heat 1 tablespoon of the oil over medium-high heat. Add the onions and sauté for 5 minutes, or until golden. Set aside.

4 Chop the remaining onions into ¼-inch dice. Heat the remaining tablespoon of oil over medium heat. Add the diced onions and the garlic and sauté for 2 minutes or until the onions are translucent. Add the water and cook 3 minutes more or until all of the water has evaporated and the onions are very soft. Transfer the onions to a food processor or blender and process for 30 seconds. With the machine running, add the eggs, sour cream, and the remaining ½ teaspoon of the salt and ¼ teaspoon of the pepper. Process 30 seconds more.

5 To assemble, sprinkle the tart shell with two thirds of the raisins, then pour over the onion custard mixture. Starting at the outside edge, arrange the onion wedges in a pinwheel design on the top of the tart. Sprinkle with the remaining raisins and dot with the butter. Bake the tart for 15 minutes until golden. Serve warm.

1/10 tart = 402 calories, 25 g fat (4 saturated), 80 mg cholesterol, 40 g carbohydrates, 6 g protein, 359 mg sodium, 1 g fiber

SUMMER TOMATO PIE

Around 1595, the word tomatl *first appeared in print as the English name for the tomato, which was often called the "love apple." In Italy, the name was* pomodoro, *or "golden apple," since the first tomatoes to reach Europe were yellow varieties.*

MAKES ONE 9-INCH DEEP-DISH PIE
PREP TIME 30 MIN ✦ BAKE TIME 42 MIN

½ **recipe FRESH HERB PASTRY (page 16) made with fresh rosemary**

TOMATO FILLING

1¾ **pounds ripe plum tomatoes**
¾ **cup slivered fresh basil leaves, divided**
1 **small red onion, slivered**
¼ **cup garlic olive oil**
3 **tablespoons red wine vinegar**
½ **teaspoon freshly ground black pepper**
¾ **cup seasoned dried bread crumbs**
¼ **cup freshly grated Parmesan cheese**

2 **cups (8 ounces) shredded low-moisture mozzarella cheese, divided**

1 Preheat the oven to 400°F and butter a 9-inch deep-dish pie plate. Roll, shape, and flute the pie shell. Prick it all over with a fork. Completely prebake the shell for 15 minutes or until golden (see Blind-Baking, page 12). Cool on a rack. Keep the oven temperature at 400°F.

2 Cut the tomatoes crosswise into ¼-inch-thick slices (you need 5 cups). Place in a medium-size bowl with ½ cup of the basil and the onion. In a cup, whisk the oil, vinegar, and pepper. Toss with the tomato mixture, then let stand for 15 minutes. In a small bowl, toss the bread crumbs and Parmesan. Toss with the tomato mixture.

3 Arrange half of the tomato mixture in the baked shell. Sprinkle with 1 cup of the mozzarella and top with the remaining tomato mixture, plus any juice which has collected. Cover the pie with foil and bake for 20 minutes or until heated through. Sprinkle with the remaining 1 cup of mozzarella and ¼ cup of basil. Bake the pie, uncovered, for 7 minutes or until the cheese is melted.

1/8 pie = 369 calories, 23 g fat (9 saturated), 33 mg cholesterol, 29 g carbohydrates, 13 g protein, 349 mg sodium, 3 g fiber

◆ *Caramelized Vidalia Onion Tart*

TEENY TINY PIES

♥

Great tastes really do come in small packages, especially with teeny tiny pies. They are large enough to give several tastes of homemade goodness, yet small enough to let you eat a whole pie in just a few bites.

Imagine tiny savory snacking pies that can really fill you up, without blowing your diet! There are tiny empanada crescents, teeny puff pies filled with cheese, and totable hamburger pies. Plus plenty of sweet tiny pies too. Choose from fruit-filled ruffled pies and crisp fried pies, juicy turnovers, and fancy tartlets.

✦ *Lemon Custard Curd Tartlets topped with strawberries, grapes, and blueberries (at left, see recipe, page 58) and Tex-Mex Beef Empanadas (at right, see recipe, page 52)*

CRAB BARQUETTES

For traditional barquettes, choose the smooth-sided molds in a boat shape. They're the easiest to work with, since the baked shells slide out more readily than from the fluted molds. This recipe works well in any tiny mold.

MAKES 16 THREE-INCH BARQUETTES
PREP TIME 30 MIN ✦ BAKE TIME 23 MIN

1 recipe SPICY MUSTARD PASTRY (page 16)

CRAB FILLING

2 packages (8 ounces each) cream cheese, at room temperature
1 tablespoon milk
1 tablespoon Worcestershire sauce
½ teaspoon hot pepper sauce
12 ounces fresh crabmeat or 2 cans (6 ounces each), rinsed, drained, and picked through for shells and cartilage
⅓ cup minced green onions
**   Paprika**

1 Preheat the oven to 400°F and butter 16 three-inch boat-shaped barquette molds or other tiny molds (see page 11). Place the molds on a baking sheet. On a lightly floured board, roll out the pastry, ⅛ inch thick. Cut out the pastry into shapes to match the molds, about 2 inches larger all around. Re-roll the scraps of pastry as you go. Fit the pastry into the molds, making sure to press the pastry down into all the corners. Cut off any excess pastry by running a sharp knife across the tops of the molds. Prick the shells all over with a fork.

2 Place molds on a baking sheet and partially prebake for 8 minutes or until set (see Blind-Baking, page 12). Reduce oven temperature to 375°F.

3 In a medium-size bowl, with an electric mixer on HIGH, beat the cream cheese, milk, Worcestershire, and hot pepper sauce until smooth. Stir in the crabmeat and green onions.

4 Spoon a generous amount of filling into each partially baked shell, mounding it in the center. Sprinkle with paprika. Bake for about 15 minutes or until the filling is golden and puffy. Transfer the barquettes to a rack. Using a small spatula, carefully slide out the tiny pies.

1 barquette = 278 calories, 20 g fat (11 g saturated), 81 mg cholesterol, 16 g carbohydrates, 8 g protein, 283 mg sodium, 1 g fiber

SHRIMP BARQUETTES Add 1 teaspoon Dijon mustard to the cream cheese mixture (Step 3). Substitute 1½ cups minced cooked shelled and deveined shrimp for the crabmeat. Use either fresh or frozen shrimp.

SCALLOP BARQUETTES Substitute 1½ cups minced cooked scallops (fresh or frozen) for the crabmeat (Step 3). Add 3 slices diced crisp-cooked bacon with the onions.

GRUYÈRE BARQUETTES

The Swiss introduced us to the popular cheese called Gruyère, with its rich, sweet, nutty flavor. It's the main ingredient in this spicy filling that puffs up during baking. Create perfect party pies by trying all the different fillings.

MAKES 16 THREE-INCH BARQUETTES
PREP TIME 30 MIN ✦ BAKE TIME 23 MIN

1 recipe FRESH HERB PASTRY (page 16)

SALAMI FILLING

¾ cup light cream
2 large eggs
3 tablespoons minced fresh chives
1 teaspoon Dijon mustard
¼ teaspoon freshly ground black pepper
2 cups (8 ounces) shredded Gruyère cheese
6 ounces thinly sliced Genoa salami, minced (1 cup)

1 Preheat the oven to 400°F and butter 16 three-inch boat-shaped barquette molds or other tiny molds (see page 11). Place the molds on a baking sheet. On a lightly floured board, roll out the pastry, ⅛ inch thick. Cut out the pastry into shapes to match the molds, about 2 inches larger all around. Re-roll the scraps of pastry as you go. Fit the pastry into the molds, making sure to press the pastry down into all the corners. Cut off any excess pastry by running a sharp knife across the tops of the molds. Prick the shells all over with a fork.

2 Place molds on a baking sheet and partially prebake for 8 minutes or until set (see Blind-Baking, page 12). Reduce oven temperature to 375°F.

3 In a medium-size bowl, whisk the cream and eggs. Stir in the remaining ingredients. Spoon a generous amount of filling into each baked shell, mounding it in the center. Bake for about 15 minutes or just until the filling is golden and puffy. Using a small spatula, carefully slide out the tiny pies.

1 barquette = 294 calories, 21 g fat (10 g saturated), 74 mg cholesterol, 16 g carbohydrates, 10 g protein, 386 mg sodium, 1 g fiber

BLACK FOREST HAM BARQUETTES Substitute 1 cup (6 ounces) minced Black Forest ham for the salami (Step 3). Stir in 2 tablespoons finely chopped drained dill pickle.

PEPPERONI BARQUETTES Substitute 2 cups (8 ounces) shredded provolone cheese for the Gruyère (Step 3). Substitute 1 cup (6 ounces) minced pepperoni for the salami.

✦ Gruyère Barquettes garnished with fans of cornichon pickles and salami cornucopia (front row), Crab Barquettes with curls of green onion tops (second row), Shrimp Barquettes with baby shrimp and dill sprigs (third row), and Black Forest Ham Barquettes with cherry tomatoes and sprigs of fresh thyme (back row)

TEX-MEX BEEF EMPANADAS

Small half-moon pies large enough to be a substantial snack, and easy to shape and bake. These tiny empanadas are so unique and tasty that folks always want more than one. Create other snacking pies by varying the filling.

MAKES 48 THREE-INCH EMPANADAS
PREP TIME 45 MIN ✦ BAKE TIME 15 MIN

1 recipe CREAM CHEESE PASTRY (page 15), or FRESH HERB PASTRY made with fresh thyme (page 16), or CRISP FLAKY CRUST (page 15)

TEX-MEX BEEF FILLING

2 tablespoons vegetable oil
1 pound ground beef sirloin
½ cup minced yellow onion
½ cup minced green bell pepper
¾ to 1 teaspoon ground cumin
½ cup beef broth
1 tablespoon cornstarch
1 cup canned crushed tomatoes
⅓ cup dark raisins, finely chopped in food processor
⅓ cup finely chopped pecans
3 large egg yolks
2 tablespoons water

1 Pick a pastry recipe. Divide the dough into 2 equal pieces and flatten each piece into a 6-inch disk. Wrap the pastry tightly in plastic wrap and refrigerate for 30 minutes.

2 In a large skillet, heat the oil over medium-high heat. Stir in the beef sirloin, onion, bell pepper, and cumin. Sauté for 5 minutes or until the meat

loses its red color. Pour the broth into a cup and whisk in the cornstarch until dissolved, then stir into the meat mixture. Add the tomatoes, raisins, and pecans. Simmer uncovered for 3 minutes or until the mixture boils and thickens. Set aside.

3 Preheat the oven to 375°F and butter 3 baking sheets. On a lightly floured surface, roll out the chilled pastry dough, one disk at a time, ⅛ inch thick. Using a 3-inch fluted round cutter, cut the dough into 48 circles, re-rolling the scraps as you go (see below, left).

4 For each pie, spoon 1 heaping tablespoon of the filling onto one half of each pastry circle, leaving a ½-inch border. Brush the inside edges with a little water. Bring the pastry up over the filling, making a half-moon pie (see below, center).

5 Using the back of the prongs of a fork, press the edges together tightly to seal (see below, right).

6 Place the pastries about 1 inch apart on the baking sheets. In a cup, whisk the egg yolks with the water. Brush the top of each empanada with this mixture. Bake for 15 minutes or until golden-

brown and crisp. These are best served piping-hot, but they're delicious at room temperature too.

1 empanada = 102 calories, 7 g fat (1 g saturated), 36 mg cholesterol, 7 g carbohydrates, 4 g protein, 59 mg sodium, .5 g fiber

SPINACH AND CHEESE EMPANADAS Omit the Tex-Mex Filling. Thaw and drain one 10-ounce package frozen chopped spinach and place in a medium-size bowl. Stir in ½ cup ricotta cheese, 1 beaten large egg, ½ teaspoon salt, ¼ teaspoon cayenne pepper, and ¼ teaspoon ground nutmeg.

SPICY CHICKEN AND GREEN ONION EMPANADAS Omit the Tex-Mex Filling. In a large bowl, mix 1½ cups finely chopped cooked chicken, ½ cup mayonnaise, ¼ cup minced green onions, 1 tablespoon fresh lemon juice, ½ teaspoon salt, and ¼ teaspoon cayenne pepper. Fold in 1 beaten large egg.

SAUSAGE ITALIANO EMPANADAS Prepare the Tex-Mex Filling as directed, substituting 1 pound ground Italian sausage (hot or medium-hot) for the beef sirloin and ⅓ cup slivered fresh basil leaves for the cumin (Step 2). Omit the raisins and pecans.

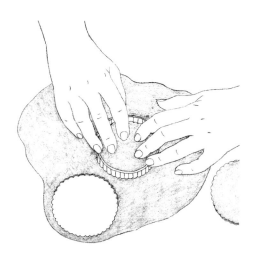

Cut out pastry circles

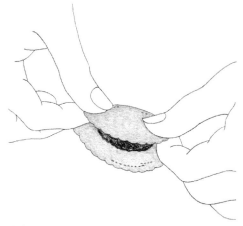

Fold pastry and bring up over the filling

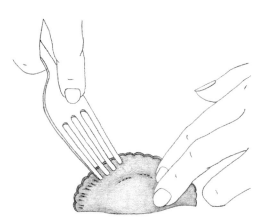

Seal with the back of the prongs of a fork

NACHO PIES

The ingredients found in cheesy nacho dip inspire these pick-me-up pies. They make great buffet pies.
A simple addition of meat, poultry, or seafood quickly turns them into a hearty snack or light supper.

MAKES 16 THREE-INCH PIES
PREP TIME 30 MIN ◆ BAKE TIME 20 MIN

1 recipe PEPPERY APPETIZER PASTRY (page 16)

NACHO FILLING
1 tablespoon unsalted butter
¼ cup minced green onions
2 cups (8 ounces) shredded Monterey Jack pepper cheese
2 tablespoons all-purpose flour
3 large eggs
1 cup milk
¼ teaspoon salt
Paprika

1 Preheat the oven to 400°F and butter 16 three-inch tiny fluted tartlet pans. On a lightly floured board, roll out the pastry, ⅛ inch thick. Using a 5-inch round cutter or a sharp knife, cut out 16 circles, re-rolling the scraps of pastry as you go. Fit the pastry into the tart pans and prick them all over with a fork. Then run a sharp knife or rolling pin across the tops to cut off the excess pastry.

2 Place the tart pans on a baking sheet and partially prebake the shells for 8 minutes or until set (see Blind-Baking, page 12). Remove shells from the oven. Reduce the oven temperature to 375°F.

3 In a small nonstick skillet, melt the butter over medium heat. Add the green onions and sauté for 5 minutes or just until soft. Transfer to a medium-size bowl and toss with the cheese and flour. Then spread the cheese mixture in the 16 pie shells, dividing the mixture evenly.

4 In the same bowl, whisk the eggs with the milk and salt. Pour about 1½ tablespoons of the egg mixture over the onion-cheese mixture in each pie shell. Sprinkle with paprika. Bake for 12 minutes, or until the filling is lightly brown and puffy. Serve the pies hot or at room temperature.

1 nacho pie = 242 calories, 16 g fat (8 g saturated), 86 mg cholesterol, 17 g carbohydrates, 8 g protein, 207 mg sodium, 1 g fiber

BEEF NACHO PIES Add 1½ cups finely chopped cooked roast beef to the onion-cheese mixture (Step 3).

CHICKEN 'N' CHEESE NACHO PIES Add 1½ cups finely chopped cooked chicken to the onion-cheese mixture (Step 3).

SEAFOOD NACHO PIES Add 1½ cups drained, flaked crabmeat to the onion-cheese mixture (Step 3). Use either fresh or canned crabmeat and pick through for shells and cartilage.

◆ *Tex-Mex Beef Empanadas*

◆ *Little Pizzas with Goat Cheese, topped with plum tomato slices, slivers of red onion, mushroom slices, arugula leaves, and fresh basil*

LITTLE PIZZAS WITH GOAT CHEESE

Garden-fresh individual pizzas, topped with creamy goat cheese, vine-ripened tomatoes, peppery arugula, and fresh basil.

MAKES 12 LITTLE PIZZAS
PREP TIME 30 MIN ✦ BAKE TIME 12 MIN

1 recipe RAPID-RISE YEAST
DOUGH made with fresh rosemary
(page 16), or 1 pound frozen
bread dough, thawed

TOMATO-ARUGULA TOPPING
8 ounces goat cheese (chèvre), thinly
sliced into 24 pieces
9 large ripe plum tomatoes, thinly
sliced into 36 rounds
3 tablespoons extra virgin olive oil,
divided
1 medium-size red onion, slivered
1 cup sliced fresh mushrooms
1 teaspoon minced garlic
Crushed red pepper flakes

1 cup packed arugula leaves
½ cup slivered fresh basil leaves

1 Put a pizza stone or baking sheet in the oven. Preheat the oven to 450°F. Dust a pizza peel or wooden pastry board with cornmeal or flour. Cut the dough into 12 equal pieces.

2 On the pizza peel or board, shape each piece of dough into a 7-inch circle, stretching from the center out, by going around and around with the heels of your hands. Top each little pizza with 2 slices of goat cheese and 3 plum tomato slices.

3 In a medium-size nonstick skillet, heat 1 tablespoon of the oil over medium-high heat. Add the onion, mushrooms, and garlic and sauté for 5 minutes. Spoon onto the pizzas. Sprinkle each pizza with a few red pepper flakes. Drizzle the pizzas with the remaining 2 tablespoons of oil. Bake the pizzas on the hot pizza stone or baking sheet for 12 minutes or until the crust is crisp. Top each pizza with a couple of leaves of arugula and a few slivers of basil.

1 little pizza = 278 calories, 14 g fat (5 g saturated), 15 mg cholesterol, 30 g carbohydrates, 9 g protein, 286 mg sodium, 2 g fiber

MUSHROOM TARTLETS

Even in their teeny tiny size, these fresh mushroom tartlets make a hearty snack, terrific hors d'oeuvres, or first course. For heartier snackin' pies, add any leftover cooked meat or seafood to the basic mushroom filling.

MAKES 16 THREE-INCH TARTLETS
OR 8 FIVE-INCH TARTS
PREP TIME 45 MIN ✦ BAKE TIME 18 MIN

1 recipe PEPPERY APPETIZER
PASTRY (page 16)

HERB MUSHROOM FILLING
2 tablespoons unsalted butter
1 pound fresh mushrooms, washed,
patted dry, and chopped (6 cups)
½ cup minced green onions
2 teaspoons minced garlic
1 tablespoon chopped fresh
marjoram or 1 teaspoon dried
¾ teaspoon salt
½ teaspoon freshly ground black
pepper
¼ cup dry Marsala wine or beef broth
¾ cup soft fresh white bread crumbs
¼ cup light cream
⅓ cup herb-seasoned dry bread
crumbs
⅓ cup minced fresh parsley

1 Preheat the oven to 400°F and butter 16 three-inch tiny fluted tartlet pans or 8 five-inch fluted tart pans with removable bottoms. On a lightly floured board, roll out the pastry, ⅛ inch thick.

Using a round cutter 2 inches wider in diameter than the pans, cut out enough circles to fit your pans, re-rolling the scraps of pastry as you go. Shape the pastry into the pans, lightly pressing it over the bottom and up the sides. Run a sharp knife or rolling pin across the tops of the pans to cut off excess pastry. Prick the shells all over with a fork.

2 Partially prebake for 8 minutes for 3-inch shells, 10 minutes for 5-inch shells, or until golden (see Blind-Baking, page 12). Cool the shells on a wire rack while you make the filling. Reduce the oven temperature to 375°F.

3 In a large skillet, melt the butter over medium-high heat. Add the mushrooms and sauté for 3 minutes or until almost translucent. Add the green onions, garlic, marjoram, salt, and pepper. Sauté for 1 minute more. Add the Marsala and let simmer, uncovered, until most of the liquid evaporates. Stir in the fresh bread crumbs and the cream, tossing just until the mixture holds together (do not overmix).

4 Spoon a generous amount of filling into each shell, mounding it in the center. In a small bowl, toss the dry bread crumbs with the parsley. Sprinkle the crumbs generously on top of the tartlets. Bake until the filling is golden and puffy, about 10 minutes for tartlets, 15 minutes for tarts. Serve hot.

1 tartlet = 200 calories, 12 g fat (6 g saturated), 36 mg cholesterol, 20 g carbohydrates, 4 g protein, 208 mg sodium, 1 g fiber

CHICKEN-MUSHROOM TARTS
Prepare 2 recipes of the pastry and shape 24 three-inch tartlet shells or 12 five-inch tart shells. (Freeze extra pastry to use later, see page 12.) Add 2 cups chopped cooked chicken to the mushroom mixture with the onions (Step 3).

SAUSAGE-MUSHROOM TARTS
Prepare 2 recipes of the pastry and shape 24 three-inch tiny shells or 12 five-inch tart shells. (Freeze extra pastry to use later, see page 12.) Add 2 cups drained browned country sausage (1 pound uncooked), to mushrooms with the onions (Step 3).

HAMBURGER PICNIC TOTING PIES

These teeny-tiny pies stuffed with a scrambled sirloin mixture make perfect picnic pies. They pack safely in an ice chest, tote easily without being crushed, and stay fresh for hours. They're small enough to hold in your hand ... their half-moon shapes make them easy to eat. No plates or utensils are needed.

MAKES 20 FIVE-INCH PIES
PREP TIME 45 MIN ✦ BAKE TIME 12 MIN

1 recipe FRESH HERB PASTRY
made with fresh thyme (page 16)

SAVORY BEEF FILLING
1 tablespoon vegetable oil
1 pound ground beef sirloin
½ cup minced onion
1 teaspoon minced garlic
1 8-ounce can tomato sauce
½ cup slivered fresh basil leaves
½ teaspoon salt
½ teaspoon freshly ground black pepper
¼ cup milk

1 Preheat the oven to 425°F and butter 2 baking sheets. Mix and chill pastry.

2 In a large skillet, heat the oil over medium-high heat. Add the beef sirloin, onion, and garlic and sauté for 7 minutes. Add the tomato sauce, basil, salt, and pepper and simmer uncovered for 15 minutes. Let cool for 10 minutes.

3 On a lightly floured surface, roll out the pastry, ⅛ inch thick. Using a 5-inch fluted cutter, cut into rounds, re-rolling the scraps to get 20 rounds.

4 For each pie, spoon about 2 heaping tablespoons of filling onto one half of a dough circle, leaving a 1-inch border.

✦ BAKER'S TIP ✦

Picnic pies freeze perfectly. Prepare and bake the pies. Let them cool, then pack and freeze them in plastic freezer bags. To thaw the frozen pies, place them directly on the middle rack in a 350°F oven for 10 minutes. Or microwave the frozen pies on high for 30 seconds.

Brush the inside edges with a little milk. Bring the dough up and over the filling, making a half-moon pie. Flute the pie closed with your fingertips. Cut three small slanted slits in the top of each pie. Brush the top with a little milk.

5 Place pies 1 inch apart on the baking sheets. Bake for 12 minutes or just until lightly brown (do not overbake).

1 toting pie = 205 calories, 13 g fat (6 g saturated), 33 mg cholesterol, 14 g carbohydrates, 8 g protein, 207 mg sodium, 1 g fiber

COCK-A-LEEKIE TOTING PIES. Prepare as for Hamburger Picnic Toting Pies, using fresh rosemary instead of thyme to make the Fresh Herb Pastry. Replace the beef sirloin, onion, tomato sauce, and basil with 1 pound ground white-meat chicken, ⅓ cup minced green onions, ½ cup chicken broth, and ⅓ cup minced fresh parsley (Step 2).

TINY 'TATER ONION TARTS

These crustless potato and onion tarts are substantial enough to build a picnic around. Tote them inside an ice chest, right inside the tart pans they're baked in. Serve with a marinated tomato salad, slices of sourdough bread, and fresh pears.

MAKES 8 FIVE-INCH TARTS
PREP TIME 30 MIN ✦ BAKE TIME 30 MIN

1½ cups slivered yellow onions
1½ cups (6 ounces) shredded Gruyère cheese
½ cup all-purpose flour
1 teaspoon chopped fresh rosemary
½ teaspoon salt
½ teaspoon freshly ground black pepper
5 strips thick-sliced bacon, diced
1 teaspoon minced garlic
6 medium-size russet baking potatoes (2 pounds), peeled and thinly sliced (4 cups)
1½ cups milk
Paprika

1 Preheat the oven to 375°F and butter 8 five-inch fluted tart pans, with or without removable bottoms. Place the pans on a baking sheet. In a medium-size bowl, toss the onions with the cheese and set aside. In a large bowl, mix the flour, rosemary, salt, and pepper.

2 In a small skillet, sauté the bacon and garlic over medium heat until the bacon is crisp, then stir into the flour mixture. Add the potato slices and toss gently with your hands until the potatoes are thoroughly coated.

3 Line each tart pan with a thin layer of the potato-bacon mixture. Sprinkle with about 2 tablespoons of the onion-cheese mixture, then 1½ tablespoons of the milk. Repeat one time. Sprinkle generously with the paprika.

4 Cover each tart with foil and bake for 15 minutes. Remove the foil and bake 15 minutes more or until the potatoes are tender and tops are golden and crusty.

1 tiny tart = 277 calories, 11 g fat (6 g saturated), 33 mg cholesterol, 34 g carbohydrates, 12 g protein, 297 mg sodium, 2 g fiber

BROCCOLI AND 'TATER TARTS Prepare as for Tiny 'Tater Onion Tarts, adding 1 cup coarsely chopped cooked broccoli florets to the flour mixture with the potatoes (Step 2).

+ *Apple Fried Pies, drizzled with Vanilla Icing*

APPLE FRIED PIES

Travel through the southern states and you'll find many pies are fried — not baked. Choose cooking apples such as Jonathan, McIntosh, or Rome Beauty. When shaping pies for frying, seal them tightly, with the bottom side of the prongs of a fork.

MAKES 16 FIVE-INCH PIES
PREP TIME 45 MIN + FRY TIME 4 MIN
COOL TIME 30 MIN

1 recipe **CRISP FLAKY CRUST**
   (page 15)

   APPLE RAISIN FILLING
8 **cups very thin slices peeled apples**
   (about 2 pounds apples)
½ **cup golden raisins**
½ **cup apple cider or apple juice**
⅔ **cup packed light brown sugar**
½ **teaspoon ground cinnamon**

   Cooking oil for frying pies

   VANILLA ICING
2 **cups sifted confectioners' sugar**
5 **to 6 teaspoons milk**
1 **teaspoon vanilla extract**

1 On a lightly floured surface, roll out the pastry, ⅛ inch thick. Using a 5-inch fluted cutter, cut into 16 circles, re-rolling the scraps as you go.

2 In a medium-size saucepan, bring the apples, raisins, and cider to a boil over high heat. Reduce the heat and let simmer, uncovered, for 5 minutes or until the apples are tender. Stir in the brown sugar and cinnamon and cook 3 minutes more or until most of the liquid has been absorbed. Cool the filling for 15 minutes.

3 Place about 2 tablespoons of the filling on one half of each circle, leaving a 1-inch border. Brush the edges with a little water. Bring the dough up over the filling, making a half-moon pie.

Seal the edges with the back of the prongs of a fork.

4 In a large deep skillet or Dutch oven, heat an inch of cooking oil to 375°F. Cook 3 or 4 pies at a time — fry for 4 minutes or until light brown, turning the pies once. Cool the pies on racks for about 15 minutes.

5 In a small bowl, stir all ingredients for the Vanilla Icing until smooth. Using a teaspoon, drizzle the icing back and forth in a zigzag design over the warm pies. Great served warm or at room temperature.

1 fried pie = 291 calories, 11 g fat (5 g saturated), 16 mg cholesterol, 47 g carbohydrates, 2 g protein, 81 mg sodium, 2 g fiber

LEMON CUSTARD CURD TARTS

During my first trip to London, afternoon tea arrived with hot scones and a rich buttery lemony creation called Lemon Curd. The authentic version takes real culinary expertise to prepare. This adaptation is easier and makes a divine tart filling. It's also a great beginning for other fabulous fruit tarts. Make them into individual tarts or tiny two-bite tartlets (see photo, pages 48 – 49).

MAKES 8 FIVE-INCH TARTS
OR 16 THREE-INCH TARTLETS
PREP TIME 30 MIN ✦ BAKE TIME 12 MIN
COOL / CHILL TIME 1¾ HR

1 recipe PÂTE BRISÉE (page 15),
    or BUTTERY CRUST (page 15),
    or CREAM CHEESE PASTRY
    (page 15)

LEMON CUSTARD CURD FILLING
½   cup (1 stick) unsalted butter (not
    margarine), at room temperature
1   cup sugar
¼   teaspoon salt
3   large eggs
1   large egg yolk
2   tablespoons grated lemon zest
½   cup fresh lemon juice

1   recipe Tart Glaze made with
    currant jelly (page 20)
2   cups fresh raspberries

1 Preheat the oven to 400°F. Set out 8 five-inch fluted tart pans with removable bottoms or 16 three-inch tiny fluted tartlet pans. Pick a pastry recipe and shape the shells. Prick the shells all over with a fork. Completely prebake the shells for 12 minutes for 5-inch shells, 10 minutes for 3-inch shells, or until golden (see Blind-Baking, page 12).

2 In a medium-size bowl, with an electric mixer on HIGH, cream the butter, sugar, and salt until light yellow. Transfer this mixture to a heavy medium-size saucepan.

3 In the same bowl, with the mixer on HIGH, beat the eggs and egg yolk until thick and light yellow, then blend in the lemon zest and lemon juice. Fold into the butter mixture in the saucepan. Whisk constantly over medium heat for 5 minutes or until the mixture becomes thick and creamy. Cool for 20 minutes.

4 Spoon the filling into the tart shells until almost full (about ¼ cup each). Lay a piece of plastic wrap directly on the filling of each tart to prevent a skin from forming. Chill for 45 minutes or just until set. While the filling cools, make the Tart Glaze. Then, arrange the raspberries, pointed ends up, on top of the tarts. Spoon the glaze over the berries and any filling peeking out. Chill at least 1 hour more or until serving time.

1 five-inch tart = 501 calories, 29 g fat (17 g saturated), 177 mg cholesterol, 57 g carbohydrates, 7 g protein, 250 mg sodium, 3 g fiber

STRAWBERRY LIME TARTS Make the filling (Steps 2 and 3), replacing the lemon zest and lemon juice with 2 tablespoons grated lime zest and ½ cup fresh lime juice. To decorate, replace the raspberries with 2 cups fresh strawberries, hulled and thinly sliced lengthwise (Step 4). Artistically arrange the fruits in concentric circles, starting at the center and fanning out to the edge. Prepare the Tart Glaze using strawberry jelly instead of currant jelly.

ORANGE CURD TARTS Make the filling (Steps 2 and 3), replacing the lemon zest and lemon juice with 2 tablespoons grated orange zest and ½ cup fresh orange juice. To decorate, replace the raspberries with 2 large navel oranges, peeled and thinly sliced crosswise (Step 4). Prepare the Tart Glaze using apple jelly instead of currant.

PINK GRAPEFRUIT AND RASPBERRY CURD TARTS Make the filling (Steps 2 and 3) replacing the lemon zest and lemon juice with 2 tablespoons grated grapefruit zest and ½ cup fresh pink grapefruit juice. Decorate the tarts with the raspberries as in the master recipe. Prepare the Tart Glaze using strawberry jelly instead of currant jelly.

OTHER FRUIT TOPPINGS For variety, replace the raspberries in the master recipe with other fruits (see photo, facing page). A few fruits that we've found work well: sliced fresh blackberries, fresh blueberries, seedless red grapes, thin slices of peeled kiwi, paper-thin slices of unpeeled lemons or oranges, thin slices of unpeeled nectarines, orange sections, thin slices of peeled star fruit, sliced strawberries.

✦ *BAKER'S TIP* ✦

To slice berries for decorating tarts, use a serrated fruit knife. Remove the stems and hulls from the berries. Hold the berry, stem-side down, on a flat surface. Slice down vertically, sawing gently back-and-forth.

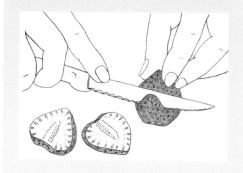

✦ Lemon Custard Curd Tarts (front to back) — topped with star fruit and nectarines, sliced fresh red-ripe strawberries and fresh mint, orange and kiwi slices, fresh blueberries dusted with confectioners' sugar, and fresh raspberries

APPLE-BERRY DUMPLINGS

Wrap up apples and fresh raspberries in a pocket of rich pastry dough. Then pack in an extra punch of flavor —
a red-hot cinnamon sauce that glazes the dumplings as they bake. Top each dumpling with a couple of pastry leaves and
serve with pride. Create other fruit-pocket pies by substituting peaches for the apples in the master recipe.

MAKES 6 DUMPLINGS
PREP TIME 45 MIN ✦ BAKE TIME 1 HR

1 recipe CREAM CHEESE PASTRY (page 15)

RED-HOT CINNAMON SAUCE
1¾ **cups water**
1 **cup red-hot candies (sold in the candy section of the supermarket)**
½ **cup granulated sugar**
½ **teaspoon ground cinnamon**
2 **cinnamon sticks**

APPLE-BERRY FILLING
6 **small McIntosh or Jonathan apples**
¾ **cup packed light brown sugar**
½ **cup toasted pecans, finely chopped**
½ **teaspoon ground cinnamon**
1 **cup (1 cup) fresh raspberries**

Vanilla ice cream (optional)

1 Make the pastry. Pat into two disks — ⁴/₅ of the pastry in one, remaining pastry in the second. Wrap in plastic wrap and refrigerate for 30 minutes. Preheat the oven to 375°F. Bring all of the sauce ingredients to a boil in a medium-size saucepan over high heat. Cook, uncovered, for 5 minutes. Remove the cinnamon sticks. Let cool.

2 Peel the apples. Then core them by carefully inserting an apple corer firmly into the stem end of each. Twist and pull to remove the core. Don't worry if you cut through the bottom of the apple — any juices escaping during baking will add extra flavor to the pastry.

3 On a lightly floured surface, roll out the larger disk of pastry into a 27 × 18-inch rectangle, ⅛ inch thick. Using a sharp pointed knife, cut into six 9-inch squares. Place 1 apple in the center of each pastry square. In a cup, toss the brown sugar, pecans, and cinnamon together. Spoon 1 heaping tablespoon of this mixture into the cavity of each apple (see below, left) and sprinkle 2 tablespoons over the top.

4 Sprinkle about 8 berries around the base of each apple. Using a pastry brush, moisten the edges of each pastry square with water (see below, center). Bring all four corners up over the apple, pleating the pastry around the apple and pinching it at the top to seal (see below, right). Place the dumplings in a 13 × 9 × 2-inch baking pan, sealed-ends up. Pour half of the sauce over the dumplings. Bake the dumplings, uncovered, for 50 minutes or until the pastry is crisp and golden brown and the apples are tender, basting frequently with more sauce.

5 To make the leaves, roll out the second disk of pastry, ¼ inch thick. Using a leaf cutter or the sharp point of a knife, cut out 12 leaves about 2 inches long. Score the veins of the leaves with a knife (see below). Tightly roll up a 1-inch cylinder of foil, about 12 inches long, and place on a baking sheet. Drape the leaves over the foil and brush with some sauce. Bake at 375°F for about 10 minutes or until crisp. Attach 2 leaves to the top of each dumpling with a toothpick. Serve dumplings with the remaining sauce, plus scoops of vanilla ice cream, if you wish.

1 dumpling = 809 calories, 33 g fat (2 g saturated), 109 mg cholesterol, 123 g carbohydrates, 7 g protein, 337 mg sodium, 5 g fiber

RUBY PEACH-BLUEBERRY DUMPLINGS. Substitute 6 peeled, halved, and pitted medium-size ripe peaches for the apples (Step 3). For each dumpling, stand up 2 peach halves in the center of a pastry square, forming the whole peach, and sprinkle with the filling. Replace the raspberries with fresh blueberries. Wrap the pastry tightly.

TRACING PATTERN Use pattern as a guide to cut out pastry leaves. Score with the tip of a knife

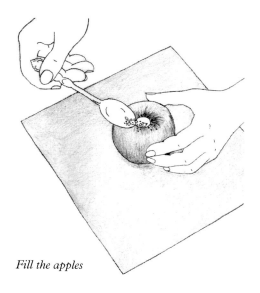

Fill the apples

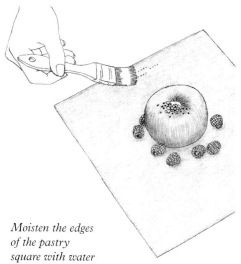

Moisten the edges of the pastry square with water

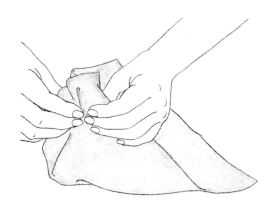

Bring all 4 corners of the pastry up over the apple, pleating the pastry and pinching at the top to seal

◆ *Apple-Berry Dumpling with Red-Hot Cinnamon Sauce*

KOLACHES

Originally from Czechoslovakia, these little fruit-filled buns are now being made by their Czech descendants in the Midwest, using a flaky sour cream pastry. The pies bake into small square pockets of pastry with bright fruit filling peeking out.

MAKES 4 DOZEN KOLACHES
PREP TIME 45 MIN ◆ BAKE TIME 8 MIN

1 **recipe SOUR CREAM PASTRY (page 15)**

KOLACHE FILLING
1 **cup apricot preserves**
1 **cup raspberry preserves**
¼ **cup milk**
½ **cup sifted confectioners' sugar**

1 Preheat the oven to 425°F and butter 2 baking sheets. On a lightly floured surface, roll out the pastry, ⅛ inch thick. Using a sharp pointed knife, cut into 3½-inch squares, re-rolling the scraps of pastry as you go. You need 48 squares.

2 Spoon 2 teaspoons of either the apricot or raspberry preserves into the center of each square. Moisten the

corners with a little milk so they adhere. Make little pockets by bringing all four corners to the center of each square.

3 Bake the Kolaches for 8 minutes or until golden. Cool on racks. Sprinkle the tops with a fine dusting of sugar.

1 kolache = 95 calories, 3 g fat (2 g saturated), 8 mg cholesterol, 16 g carbohydrates, 1 g protein, 36 mg sodium, .5 g fiber

TINY STRAWBERRY RUFFLED PIES

These little pies are pinched tightly enough on the edges to look ruffled, sealing in the filling at the same time.
They're stuffed with fruit preserves, sealed by hand, and then decorated with fun pastry cutouts before baking (see facing page).

MAKES 20 LITTLE PIES
PREP TIME 45 MIN ✦ BAKE TIME 15 MIN

1 recipe SOUR CREAM PASTRY (page 15), or CINNAMON BUTTERY CRUST (page 15), or WHIPPED PASTRY (page 15)

STRAWBERRY FILLING
2½ **cups low-sugar chunky strawberry preserves**
2 **tablespoons fresh lemon juice**
¼ **teaspoon almond extract**
⅓ **cup light cream**
¼ **cup sugar**

1 Preheat the oven to 400°F and butter 2 baking sheets. Pick a pastry recipe. On a lightly floured surface, roll out the dough, ⅛ inch thick. Using a fluted 5-inch cutter, cut pastry into 20 rounds, re-rolling the scraps as you go.

2 In a small bowl, blend the preserves with the lemon juice and almond extract. Spoon about 2 tablespoons of the preserves mixture on one half of each dough circle, mounding it near the center and leaving a ½-inch border along the edge (see below, left). Brush the inside edges with a little cream.

3 For each pie, gently bring the dough up over the filling, making a half-moon pie (see below, center).

4 With your fingertips, flute the pie tightly shut, making a ruffled edge (see below, right). Using a sharp pointed knife, cut 3 small slanted slits in the top of each pie. Decorate the pies if you wish (see facing page).

5 Place the pies on the baking sheets, brush each with a little cream, and sprinkle with a little sugar. Bake for 15 minutes or until lightly brown, then transfer to racks. Delicious served warm.

1 ruffled pie = 194 calories, 8 g fat (5 g saturated), 20 mg cholesterol, 29 g carbohydrates, 2 g protein, 117 mg sodium, 1 g fiber

PICK-A-FRUIT RUFFLED PIES
Substitute 2½ cups of another fruit preserves, such as blackberry, blueberry, damson plum, pineapple, or red raspberry, for the strawberry preserves

(Step 2). Omit the almond extract and add ½ teaspoon ground nutmeg.

PEACH RUFFLED PIES Substitute low-sugar chunky peach preserves for the strawberry preserves (Step 2). Omit the almond extract and add 1 teaspoon pumpkin pie spice.

APRICOT-CRUNCH PIES Substitute 2½ cups low-sugar chunky apricot preserves for the strawberry preserves (Step 2). Stir in ¼ cup finely chopped toasted almonds and ½ teaspoon ground nutmeg.

EASY APPLE RUFFLED PIES Substitute one 15-ounce can apple pie filling for the strawberry preserves (Step 2). Omit the almond extract and add 1 teaspoon pumpkin pie spice.

YOUR FAVORITE FRUIT FILLINGS FROM A CAN Substitute a filling made from your favorite canned fruit for the strawberry preserves mixture (Step 2). See chart on the facing page for easy-to-make choices.

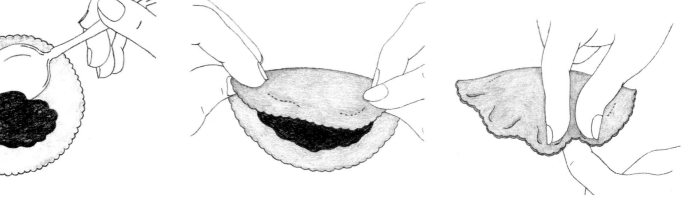

Fill the little pie

Fold the pastry up over the filling to make a half-moon pie

Ruffle the edges to seal

✦ PASTRY CUTOUT DECORATIONS ✦

*Dress up tiny pies with pastry cut outs. Pick a pastry and make
a double recipe. Use half the dough to make the pies, the remaining dough
for the cutout decorations. Don't worry if you have some pastry left over.
Just freeze any extra, then thaw and use later (see page 12).*

1 Before you plan to bake, collect some tiny cookie cutters about 1 to 1½ inches
long. Look for them in specialty bake shops in various shapes — leaves, flowers,
fruits, hearts, stars, and any other shapes that catch your eye.

2 Preheat the oven as directed in your pastry recipe (400°F for ruffled pies). Butter
2 baking sheets. Shape the pies as directed, fill with your favorite flavor of fruit
filling, and then seal the pies. Using a sharp pointed knife, cut 2 to 3 small slits in each pie (do not brush with cream).

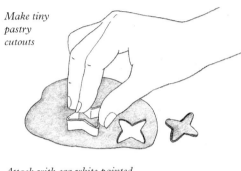

*Make tiny
pastry
cutouts*

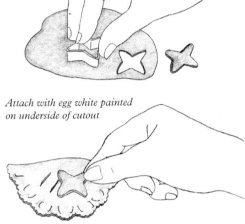

*Attach with egg white painted
on underside of cutout*

3 On a lightly floured surface, roll out the remaining pastry, ⅛ inch thick. Using one or several little cutters, cut out 20 pastry decorations.

4 In a small bowl, whisk 2 large egg whites with 1 tablespoon of water. Brush the tops of the little pies and the bottom of the pastry cutouts with this mixture. Attach one decoration to the top of each pie, pressing down slightly.

5 Carefully brush the tops of the little pies and the decorations with a little cream, then sprinkle with a little sugar. Bake as your recipe directs.

FRUIT FILLINGS FROM A CAN

*Instead of the Strawberry Filling (Step 2 for Ruffled Pies), make
a filling from one of your favorite canned fruits. Pour off the syrup into a small
saucepan. Whisk in the cornstarch and flavorings. Stirring constantly, bring the
mixture to a boil over medium-high heat and boil for 1 minute to thicken.
Cool the syrup mixture, then fold in the fruit.*

CANNED FRUIT	CORNSTARCH	FLAVORINGS
Dark Sweet Cherries two 15-ounce cans	¼ cup cornstarch	2 tablespoons fresh lemon juice ¼ teaspoon almond extract
Blueberries two 16-ounce cans	¼ cup cornstarch	2 tablespoons fresh lemon juice 1½ teaspoons ground cinnamon 1 teaspoon vanilla extract ¼ teaspoon ground nutmeg
Blackberries two 16-ounce cans	¼ cup cornstarch	2 tablespoons fresh lemon juice 1½ teaspoons ground cinnamon 1 teaspoon vanilla extract
Mandarin Oranges three 10-ounce cans	¼ cup cornstarch	2 tablespoons fresh lemon juice 1½ teaspoons ground cinnamon 1 teaspoon vanilla extract ¼ teaspoon ground nutmeg

FRUIT-BASKET TURNOVERS

Here are small triangular pies brimming with fresh juicy berries. They're tightly sealed and easy to carry and eat anywhere.
Try our other combinations of fresh fruits too. Whatever the season and for any reason, you can bake up terrific turnovers.

MAKES 12 TURNOVERS
PREP TIME 45 MIN ◆ BAKE TIME 15 MIN

1 recipe CREAM CHEESE PASTRY
(page 15), or SOUR CREAM
PASTRY (page 15)

STRAWBERRY-BLUEBERRY FILLING
4 cups fresh strawberries, hulled and
thinly sliced lengthwise
1 cup fresh blueberries
⅔ cup granulated sugar
2 tablespoons all-purpose flour
1 teaspoon ground cinnamon
⅛ teaspoon ground nutmeg
3 tablespoons light cream
Decorator's coarse sanding sugar
or granulated sugar for sprinkling

1 Pick a pastry recipe. Divide the
dough into 2 equal pieces and flatten
each piece into a 6-inch disk. Wrap each
tightly in plastic wrap and refrigerate for
30 minutes while preparing the filling.

2 In a medium-size bowl, toss the
strawberries and blueberries with the
granulated sugar, the flour, cinnamon,
and nutmeg. Let the fruit stand for
10 minutes to blend the flavors and bring
out the juices from the fruits.

3 Preheat the oven to 425°F and butter
2 baking sheets. On a lightly floured

surface, roll out the dough, one disk at a
time, ⅛ inch thick. Cut into 12 five-inch
squares, re-rolling the scraps as you go.
For a more decorative edge, cut the
pastry with a zigzag pastry wheel (see
below, left).

4 Mound about 2 tablespoons of the
filling near the center of each dough
square (see below, center). Brush the
edges of each turnover with a little cream.

5 Bring one corner of the dough up
over the filling to the opposite corner,
making a triangular pie. Make sure the
filling doesn't run out to the edges. Seal
the edges by pressing them closed with
the back edge of the tines of a fork.

6 Using a sharp pointed knife, cut three
small slanted slits in the top of each
turnover to allow the steam to escape as
the pies bake (see below, right). Brush
each pie with cream and sprinkle with a
little of the decorator's sanding sugar.

7 Bake for 15 minutes or until lightly
brown. Transfer turnovers to a rack
to cool. These turnovers are delicious
either warm or at room temperature.

1 turnover = 299 calories, 14 g fat (1 g saturated),
57 mg cholesterol, 40 g carbohydrates, 5 g protein,
164 mg sodium, 2 g fiber

APPLE-RAISIN-WALNUT
TURNOVERS Substitute 2 pounds
peeled, cored, and thinly sliced Rome
Beauty apples (4 cups) for the
strawberries and blueberries. Add
½ cup golden raisins and ½ cup finely
chopped toasted walnuts. (Step 2).

BLUEBERRY-RASPBERRY
TURNOVERS Substitute 2 cups fresh
blueberries and 1 cup fresh raspberries
for the strawberries and blueberries
(Step 2).

PEAR-RASPBERRY TURNOVERS
Substitute 2 pounds peeled, cored,
and thinly sliced ripe pears (4 cups)
and 1 cup fresh raspberries for the
strawberries and blueberries (Step 2).
Use the sweetest, juiciest pears you
can find, such as red or yellow Bartlett,
Anjou, or Bosc.

RASPBERRY-PEACH TURNOVERS
Substitute 2 pounds peeled, pitted, and
thinly sliced ripe peaches (4 cups) and
1 cup fresh raspberries for the
strawberries and blueberries (Step 2).

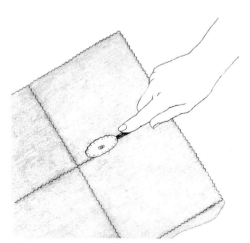

Cut pastry with a zigzag
pastry wheel

Spoon on the filling, mounding
it near the center

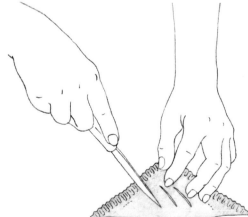

Decorate with slanted steam vents
to allow turnovers to bake up crisp

◆ *Fruit Basket Turnovers (front to back): Strawberry-Blueberry, Blueberry-Raspberry, and Raspberry-Peach —*
sprinkled with decorator's coarse sanding sugar, found in specialty bake shops

FRUIT PIES

❤

Fruit pies, every way you like them. Bake them fancy and French — into classic fresh fruit galettes on buttery puff pastry or into traditional fruit tarts filled with rich custard crème. Make them easy-as-pie by tossing two fruits together into a single crust. Or create rich creamy shortcake pizzas, blooming berry chocolate truffle tarts, and beautiful fruit designs on pat-in-the-pan shortbread. Take your pick from berries and peaches of the summer, papayas and mangoes from the islands, apples and dried fruits of the winter. Glaze them, caramelize them, or crumb them. Whatever the season, and even for no reason, bake up a fabulous fruit pie.

✦ *French Galettes (from top, clockwise) — Fresh Peach and Blueberry Galette, Apple and Cranberry Galette, and Fresh Plum Galette (see recipes, page 68)*

RHUBARB-STRAWBERRY GALETTE

In the spring, rhubarb is in the markets and ready for baking into pies, such as this creation by Food Stylist Delores Custer. Rhubarb is technically a vegetable, but as early as the 19th century, bakers were baking rhubarb into so many sweet pies that it quickly became known as the "pie plant." The deep dark red stalks are field-grown rhubarb, usually very tart, and need more sugar than the lighter pink hothouse variety.

MAKES ONE 12-INCH GALETTE
PREP TIME 30 MIN ✦ BAKE TIME 45 MIN
COOL TIME 10 MIN

1 recipe PÂTE SUCRÉE (page 15)

RHUBARB-STRAWBERRY FILLING
- 1½ pounds rhubarb stalks without leaves (6 cups)
- 1 cup fresh strawberries, hulled and sliced vertically, ½ inch thick
- 1¼ to 1½ cups granulated sugar
- 3 tablespoons all-purpose flour
- 2 tablespoons unsalted butter (not margarine), melted

Decorator's coarse sanding sugar for sprinkling (sold in gourmet food stores and bake shops)
Crème Fraîche (page 20) (optional)

1 Preheat the oven to 400°F and line a baking sheet with parchment. Make the pastry and chill it while you prepare the rhubarb. Wash the rhubarb and trim off the ends. If the stalks are thicker than 1 inch, halve the stalks lengthwise. Cut them into 1-inch pieces and place in a large bowl with the strawberries.

2 On a lightly floured board, roll out the pastry into a 16-inch circle, ⅛ inch thick. Using a paring knife, trim the circle of pastry to even the edges. Transfer the pastry circle to the parchment-lined baking sheet.

3 Toss the rhubarb-strawberry mixture with the granulated sugar and flour. Gently spoon the fruit into the center of the pastry circle, leaving a 2-inch margin. Carefully fold up the edges of the dough over the fruit, pleating them as you go. The fruit in the center will show. Brush the pleated edges with butter and sprinkle with some coarse sugar. Bake for 35 minutes. Reduce the oven temperature to 375°F and bake the galette 10 minutes more or until the rhubarb is soft and the juices are bubbling. Let the galette cool on a rack for 10 minutes. Serve warm with Crème Fraîche, if you wish.

1/12 galette = 216 calories, 7 g fat (4 g saturated), 33 mg cholesterol, 35 g carbohydrates, 2 g protein, 56 mg sodium, 1 g fiber

RHUBARB-RASPBERRY GALETTE
Substitute 1 cup fresh raspberries for the strawberries.

APPLE & CRANBERRY GALETTE

The prettiest of pies — fresh fruits swirled on crisp puff pastry, sprinkled with sugar and spice, then baked until bubbling. Whatever the season, galettes are great — apples and cranberries for fall, peaches and plums for summer (photo, pages 66–67).

MAKES ONE 12-INCH GALETTE
PREP TIME 45 MIN ✦ BAKE TIME 18 MIN
CHILL TIME 1HR

½ recipe PÂTE FEUILLETÉE (page 19)

GALETTE FRUIT TOPPING
- ½ cup dried cranberries
- ⅓ cup packed light brown sugar
- ⅓ cup granulated sugar
- 1 teaspoon ground cinnamon
- 2 tablespoons all-purpose flour
- 4 large Granny Smith apples, peeled, cored, and sliced ⅛ inch thick
- 2 tablespoons cold unsalted butter (not margarine), cut into ½-inch cubes
- 1 large egg yolk
- 1 tablespoon heavy (whipping) cream

1 The night before or the morning you plan to bake, prepare the puff pastry and chill. When ready to shape and bake the galette, preheat the oven to 400°F and line a baking sheet with parchment. Place the cranberries in a small bowl, cover with boiling water, and let stand for 15 minutes or until plump. Drain on paper towels and set aside. In another bowl, mix both of the sugars and the cinnamon.

2 On a lightly floured board, roll out the dough into a 16-inch circle, ⅛ inch thick. Using a paring knife, trim the circle of pastry to even the edges. Transfer the pastry circle to the parchment-lined baking sheet. Bring 2 inches of the edges up, then fold over to form a 1-inch-high rim that stands up straight. Flute if you wish (traditionally, galettes have a simple straight edge). Using a fork, prick the bottom of the pastry. Sprinkle with the flour and half of the sugar-cinnamon mixture.

3 Beginning at the outside edge, arrange the apple slices, on a slight slant, in concentric circles, with the cut edges toward the center. Sprinkle with the remaining sugar-cinnamon mixture and dot with the butter. In a cup, whisk the egg yolk with the cream and brush on the edge of the pastry. Bake the galette for 12 minutes. Top with the cranberries and bake 6 minutes more or until the apples are tender and pastry is puffed.

1/9 galette = 293 calories, 14 g fat (9 g saturated), 61 mg cholesterol, 41 g carbohydrates, 2 g protein, 65 mg sodium, 2 g fiber

FRESH PEACH & BLUEBERRY GALETTE Substitute 5 large peeled, pitted, and thinly sliced peaches for the apples and ¾ cup fresh blueberries for the cranberries. Do not soak the berries.

FRESH PLUM GALETTE Substitute 8 large thinly sliced deep reddish-purple plums, preferably with red flesh, for the apples. Omit the cranberries.

✦ *Rhubarb-Strawberry Galette, sprinkled with decorator's coarse sanding sugar*

Julia Child's Free-Form Fresh Apple Tart

Basic, blissful, fresh, and fabulous. This apple tart is classic French — classic Julia. I've doubled her recipe, then shaped and baked it on a large baking sheet. It makes a crisp beautiful tart that impresses the most discriminating guests. As Julia advises, "For the crispest tart, form it on foil on a pizza paddle, then slide it onto a hot pizza stone in the oven to bake."

MAKES ONE 15 X 13-INCH TART
PREP TIME 45 MIN ✦ BAKE TIME 30 MIN

1 **recipe PÂTE FEUILLETÉE (page 19) or PÂTE BRISÉE (page 15)**

JULIA'S APPLE FILLING
½ **cup sugar, divided**
3 **pounds Golden Delicious apples (about 6 large)**

APRICOT GLAZE
1 **cup apricot jam**
3 **tablespoons sugar**
3 **tablespoons dark rum**

1 The night before or the morning you plan to bake, pick a pastry, prepare the dough, and chill. When ready to shape and bake the tart, preheat the oven to 375°F and generously butter a large baking sheet (about 16 × 14 inches).

2 On a lightly floured surface, roll out the pastry into a large rectangle, ⅛ inch thick. Trim to a 16 × 14-inch rectangle. Roll up the pastry onto your rolling pin and unroll it onto the baking sheet. Using a pastry brush, lightly paint a ½-inch border of cold water all around the rectangle of dough.

3 Cut a ½-inch square out of each corner and discard. Fold ½ inch of dough over onto itself, making an edging on all four sides. Using the back of the tines of a fork, seal the inside edges all around, then the outside edges. Prick the bottom of the shell all over at ½-inch intervals, going through the dough to the baking sheet. Sprinkle the shell all over with ¼ cup of the sugar.

4 To prepare the apples, peel and halve them lengthwise. Using a melon baller, neatly dig out the core, then remove the stem with a small knife. Place the apples, cut-side down, on a work surface. Thinly slice lengthwise, ⅛ inch thick. Arrange the apples side by side in diagonal rows, in alternating directions (see photo, opposite). Overlap the slices as you go. Sprinkle with the remaining ¼ cup of sugar.

5 Bake the tart on the middle rack of the oven for 30 minutes or until the crust is lightly browned on the bottom and the apples are golden and tender. Meanwhile, in a small saucepan, boil the jam, sugar, and rum over medium heat for 3 to 5 minutes or until the glaze thickens. Strain. Using a pastry brush, paint the tart all over with the glaze.

1/12 tart = 609 calories, 31 g fat (19 saturated), 83 mg cholesterol, 79 g carbohydrates, 5 g protein, 186 mg sodium, 4 g fiber

Blushing Pear & Raspberry Tart

Buy the juiciest pears you can find, then poach them in a simple syrup. Arrange them with fresh raspberries in a flaky puff pastry tart shell and brush with a rosy currant glaze. Bake it crisp and bubbly, just as French bakers have for centuries.

MAKES ONE 11-INCH TART
PREP TIME 45 MIN ✦ BAKE TIME 20 MIN
STANDING TIME 30 MIN

½ **recipe PÂTE FEUILLETÉE (page 19)**
3 **tablespoons all-purpose flour**

CURRANT & PEAR GLAZE
1 **cup currant jelly**
3 **tablespoons sugar**
3 **tablespoons Pear William (pear brandy)**

BLUSHING PEAR FILLING
2 **pounds ripe fresh Bartlett pears**
1½ **cups sugar**
1 **cup dry wine white**
2 **teaspoons vanilla extract**
1 **teaspoon grated lemon zest**
1 **cinnamon stick, 3 inches long**
2 **tablespoons unsalted butter (not margarine), cut into pieces**
1 **cup fresh raspberries**

1 The night before or the morning you plan to bake, prepare the dough and chill. When ready to bake the tart, preheat the oven to 425°F and butter an 11-inch fluted tart pan with a removable bottom.

2 On a lightly floured surface, roll out the dough into a large circle, ⅛ inch thick. Trim to a 14-inch round. Shape and trim the shell. Prick the bottom of the shell all over with a fork. To make the glaze, boil the jelly, sugar, and Pear William in a small saucepan over medium heat for 3 to 5 minutes or until thickened. Brush the inside of shell with some of the glaze. Sprinkle with the flour.

3 Peel, core, and slice the pears lengthwise, ¼ inch thick. In a large skillet, mix the sugar, wine, vanilla, lemon zest, and cinnamon stick. Stir over medium-high heat until the mixture boils and the sugar dissolves. Add the pears and butter and cook for 5 minutes or until pears are just barely tender and plump. Using a slotted spoon, transfer to paper towels to drain. Remove the cinnamon stick and reserve the glaze.

4 Arrange the pears in a flower design and sprinkle with the raspberries. Brush with the remaining glaze. Bake for 20 minutes or until the pears are tender.

1/10 tart = 499 calories, 15 g fat (9 saturated), 40 mg cholesterol, 87 g carbohydrates, 3 g protein, 78 mg sodium, 4 g fiber

Create a pinwheel of pear slices, standing up more slices in the center to form a flower.

◆ *Julia Child's Free-Form Fresh Apple Tart on Pâte Feuilletée*

Rosy Nectarine & Berry Croustade

A croustade is technically an edible container that can be filled with various foods, from meat to vegetables to fruits. French pâtissiers create croustades from rich puff pastry, fill them with fresh fruits, and decorate them with pastry cutouts. They proudly showcase these works of pastry art in their shops for all to admire and take home to enjoy.

MAKES ONE 14-INCH CROUSTADE
PREP TIME 45 MIN ✦ BAKE TIME 50 MIN
STANDING TIME 1 HR

1 recipe **PÂTE FEUILLETÉE**
(page 19)

NECTARINE-BERRY FILLING
3 **pounds ripe fresh nectarines**
   (9 large)
1 **cup fresh blueberries**
⅓ **cup sugar, plus extra for sprinkling**
¼ **cup all-purpose flour**
1 **teaspoon grated lemon zest**
1 **tablespoon peach brandy (optional)**
2 **tablespoons unsalted butter (not**
   margarine), cut into pieces

1 **large egg**
2 **teaspoons cold water**

1 The night before or the morning you plan to bake, prepare the dough, shape into 2 disks, one slightly larger than the other. Wrap and chill. When ready to make the croustade, preheat the oven to 400°F. Line 2 large baking sheets with parchment paper. Butter both parchment paper liners.

2 On a lightly floured surface, roll out the smaller pastry disk into a circle, ⅛ inch thick. Trim to a 16-inch circle, preferably with a fluted pastry cutter. Roll out the larger disk and trim to a 19-inch circle. Re-roll the scraps and cut out decorations such as hearts or flowers. Transfer the pastry circles and the decorations to the buttered parchment-lined baking sheets, cover with plastic wrap, and refrigerate.

3 Peel, pit, and slice the nectarines ¼ inch thick. Place in a large bowl and toss with the blueberries, the ⅓ cup of sugar, the flour, and lemon zest, plus the brandy, if you wish. Spoon the filling into the center of the 16-inch circle and spread it out to 2 inches from the edge. Dot with the butter and top with the 19-inch circle. Moisten the edges with ice water. Fold over about 1 inch of the bottom pastry circle and press to seal. Decorate the croustade with the cutouts, gluing them to the pastry with ice water.

4 In a cup, whisk the egg with the water. Lightly brush the croustade with this egg glaze and sprinkle with a little extra sugar. Bake the croustade for 50 minutes or until the pastry is puffed and golden brown. Transfer to a wire rack and cool for about 1 hour. Best served warm. Store in the refrigerator.

1/12 croustade = 538 calories, 34 g fat (21 saturated), 106 mg cholesterol, 55 g carbohydrates, 6 g protein, 189 mg sodium, 4 g fiber

APPLE & RASPBERRY CROUSTADE
Substitute 3 pounds of Granny Smith apples, peeled, cored, and sliced ¼ inch thick, and 1 cup fresh raspberries for the fruit. Substitute 1 tablespoon Calvados for the brandy, if desired.

Clafoutis aux Cerises

From the Limousin district in central France comes this famous cherry flan, made with fresh sweet cherries and a delicate but rich creamy custard. This recipe is similar to the original one, but it's flavored with a little cherry brandy.

MAKES ONE 12-INCH CLAFOUTIS
PREP TIME 30 MIN ✦ BAKE TIME 45 MIN

½ **recipe PÂTE SUCRÉE (page 15)**

CHERRY FILLING
½ **cup all-purpose flour**
1 **teaspoon baking powder**
¼ **teaspoon salt**
3 **large egg yolks**
⅓ **cup granulated sugar**
1 **cup milk**
¼ **cup light cream**
1 **tablespoon cherry brandy**
1 **tablespoon vanilla extract**
4 **large egg whites**
1 **pound fresh sweet Bing cherries,**
   pitted and halved (3 cups)
   Sifted confectioners' sugar

1 Preheat the oven to 325°F and butter a 12-inch round flan dish. Roll, shape, and trim the flan shell and prick it all over with a fork. Partially prebake the shell for 10 minutes or just until set (see Blind-Baking, page 12). Cool on a rack.

2 In a small bowl, mix the flour, baking powder, and salt. In a large bowl, with an electric mixer on HIGH, beat the egg yolks and granulated sugar until thick and light yellow. Blend in the milk, cream, brandy, and vanilla. Reduce the speed to LOW, add the flour mixture, and beat just until smooth.

3 In a small bowl, with the mixer on HIGH, beat the egg whites with clean beaters until soft glossy peaks form. Fold the whites into the batter. Spread the cherries in a single layer in the flan shell. Carefully pour the batter over the cherries.

4 Bake the clafoutis for 35 minutes or until the clafoutis is puffed and a knife inserted in the center comes out clean. Dust with confectioners' sugar and serve immediately. Store in refrigerator.

1/12 clafoutis = 203 calories, 8 g fat (4 saturated), 88 mg cholesterol, 23 g carbohydrates, 5 g protein, 129 mg sodium, 1 g fiber

CLAFOUTIS WITH RED GRAPES
Substitute 1 pound halved, seedless red grapes for the Bing cherries.

◆ *Rosy Nectarine & Berry Croustade, decorated with flowers, fruits, and leaves cut from puff pastry*

APPLE-RASPBERRY PIE-IN-THE-SKY

Select the best pie apples you can find — some red, sweet, and tart, others crisp and green. Slice them, spice them, and stack them with raspberries in a cinnamon-spiced crust. Then quickly pleat the edges, covering the filling only about three inches. After baking, you'll have a fresh fruit pie that's open in the center, showing off the filling, as clear as a "pie in the sky."

MAKES ONE 10-INCH DEEP-DISH PIE
PREP TIME 40 MIN ✦ BAKE TIME 65 MIN
CHILL / STANDING TIME 2½ HR

1 recipe CRISP FLAKY CRUST
   (page 15)
1 teaspoon ground cinnamon
2 tablespoons heavy cream, divided

APPLE-RASPBERRY FILLING

1½ pounds sweet-tart red apples,
   such as Cortland, Gravenstein,
   Jonathan, McIntosh, or Pippin,
   peeled, cored, and sliced ¼ inch
   thick (4½ cups)
1 pound green or yellow apples, such
   as Granny Smith, Rhode Island
   Greening, or Golden Delicious,
   peeled, cored, and sliced ¼ inch
   thick (3 cups)
3 tablespoons fresh lemon juice
2 cups fresh raspberries
2 tablespoons Calvados (apple
   brandy)

¾ cup packed light brown sugar
⅔ cup granulated sugar, plus extra
   for sprinkling
⅓ cup cornstarch
1 tablespoon pumpkin pie spice
½ teaspoon salt
2 tablespoons unsalted butter (not
   margarine), cut into pieces

1 Butter a 10-inch deep-dish pie plate. Mix the crust, adding the cinnamon to the flour mixture. Chill the dough for 30 minutes.

2 Preheat the oven to 400°F. On a lightly floured surface, roll the pastry into a 20-inch circle, ⅛ inch thick. Fit into the pie plate, letting the edges hang over 3 inches. Brush 1 tablespoon of the cream over the shell. Refrigerate.

3 In a large bowl, toss the apples with the lemon juice. Gently stir in the raspberries and the Calvados. In a small bowl, mix the brown sugar, the ⅔ cup of granulated sugar, cornstarch, pumpkin pie spice, and salt. Toss with the fruit.

4 Pile the fruit high into the pie shell (the filling will decrease in height considerably during baking). Dot with the butter. Fold over the crust toward the center, leaving some of the fruit exposed. Pinch the folded pastry into a Rustic Pleat, (see page 13). Brush the ruffle with the remaining tablespoon of cream and sprinkle with a little extra sugar.

5 Bake the pie for 20 minutes; lower the oven temperature to 375°F and bake 45 minutes more or until the apples are tender when tested with a fork. As the edges brown, cover with strips of foil. Let the pie cool on a rack for at least 2 hours before serving.

1/10 pie = 507 calories, 20 g fat (10 saturated), 35 mg cholesterol, 80 g carbohydrates, 4 g protein, 239 mg sodium, 4 g fiber

---

DOUBLE-FRUIT PIES-IN-THE-SKY

For other juicy fresh fruit pies, try these options: Follow the Apple-Raspberry Pie-in-the-Sky recipe, varying the fruits, sugars, and thickener. Omit the pumpkin pie spice and Calvados, and replace with the flavorings and seasonings suggested.

MAKES ONE 10-INCH DEEP-DISH PIE

FRESH FRUIT PIE	FRUIT NEEDED	SUGARS	THICKENER	FLAVORINGS/SEASONINGS
Double-the-Berries	4 cups fresh blackberries 4 cups fresh raspberries ½ cup granulated sugar	⅔ cup packed light brown sugar	⅓ cup cornstarch	1 teaspoon grated lemon zest 1 teaspoon ground cinnamon 2 tablespoons blackberry liqueur
Pear & Bing Cherry	2 pounds pears (Anjou or Bosc), peeled, cored, and sliced ¼ inch thick (6 cups) 1½ pounds fresh Bing cherries, pitted and halved (4½ cups)	1 cup granulated sugar	⅓ cup cornstarch	¼ teaspoon ground mace 2 tablespoons Pear William (pear brandy)
Peach & Raspberry	2 pounds ripe fresh peaches, peeled, pitted and sliced ¼ inch thick (6 cups) 3 cups fresh raspberries	¾ cup packed light brown sugar ¾ cup granulated sugar	¼ cup flour ¼ cup cornstarch	½ teaspoon ground nutmeg 2 tablespoons Framboise (raspberry brandy)
Damson Plum & Apricot	2 pounds ripe fresh plums, pitted and sliced ¼ inch thick (6 cups) 1 pound ripe fresh apricots, pitted and sliced ¼ inch thick (3 cups)	1⅓ cups granulated sugar	⅓ cup cornstarch	1 teaspoon grated lemon zest ½ teaspoon ground nutmeg 2 tablespoons Curaçao (orange liqueur)
Pear & Red Grape	3 pounds ripe fresh pears (Anjou or Bosc), peeled, cored, and sliced ¼ inch thick (9 cups) 2 cups seedless red grapes	¾ cup packed light brown sugar ⅓ cup granulated sugar	¼ cup cornstarch 2 tablespoons quick-cooking tapioca	2 teaspoons grated lemon zest 2 tablespoons Crème de Cassis (black currant liqueur)

✦ *Apple-Raspberry Pie-in-the-Sky in a cinnamon-spiced crispy crust with a pleated ruffle edge*

APRICOT & CREAM PIE

Fresh apricots can usually only be found in the markets from late May through July. If you've never made a pie with them, you're in for a big treat. Look for the sweetest ones, which are plump, ripe, and semi-firm with a golden hue and a red blush. If it's not apricot season, substitute mangoes for the apricots, or use fresh peaches and blueberries.

MAKES ONE 9-INCH DEEP-DISH PIE
PREP TIME 30 MIN ✦ BAKE TIME 1 HR
COOL / CHILL TIME 2¼ HR

½ recipe PÂTE SUCRÉE (page 15)
1 tablespoon cold heavy (whipping) cream

FRESH APRICOT FILLING
1 cup sugar
⅓ cup all-purpose flour
¼ teaspoon ground nutmeg
2 cups light cream
4 large egg yolks
1 tablespoon unsalted butter (not margarine), cut into small pieces
1 tablespoon vanilla extract
2½ pounds ripe fresh apricots, peeled, pitted, and sliced ¼ inch thick (6 cups)

1 Preheat the oven to 350°F and butter a 9-inch deep-dish pie plate. Roll, shape, and flute the pie shell. Brush the shell with the cream and refrigerate.

2 In a medium-size saucepan, mix the sugar, flour, and nutmeg. Slowly whisk in the cream until smooth. Cook over medium heat, whisking constantly, for 8 minutes or just until the mixture comes to a full boil and thickens. Remove the custard from the heat.

3 In a small bowl, with an electric mixer on HIGH, beat the egg yolks until light yellow and frothy. Stir about 1 cup of the hot cream mixture into the egg yolks, then return this mixture to the saucepan. Cook and stir over low

✦ *BAKER'S TIP* ✦

To peel peaches and apricots easily, drop the whole fruit into boiling water for about 1 minute. Using a slotted spoon, transfer the fruit to a bowl of cold water. Slip the skins off with your fingers. Use a knife to remove any clinging spots.

heat for 2 minutes or until thickened (do not let boil). Remove the custard from the heat and stir in the butter and vanilla. Cool for 15 minutes.

4 Spread the apricot slices in the pie shell and pour the custard over the top. Bake for 1 hour or until the crust is golden and the filling is set in the center. Cool the pie on a wire rack for 1 hour, then refrigerate for at least 1 hour before serving. Store in the refrigerator.

1/9 pie = 420 calories, 21 g fat (12 saturated), 173 mg cholesterol, 47 g carbohydrates, 7 g protein, 97 mg sodium, 3 g fiber

MANGO CREAM PIE Substitute 3 large mangoes (about 3 pounds), peeled, pitted, and sliced ¼ inch thick, plus 1 cup dried pitted cherries for the apricots.

PEACH 'N BLUEBERRY CREAM PIE Substitute 2 pounds ripe peaches, peeled, pitted, and sliced ¼ inch thick, plus 2 cups blueberries for the apricots.

HOLLY'S PEACH CRUMB PIE

Celebrate the peach season with a hot-from-the-oven peach pie. This recipe comes via Drama Professor Holly Hill. It uses two layers of streusel crumbs, one on the bottom and one on the top. She serves it warm, with scoops of vanilla ice cream.

MAKES ONE 9-INCH DEEP-DISH PIE
PREP TIME 30 MIN ✦ BAKE TIME 50 MIN
COOL TIME 30 MIN

1 recipe CRISP FLAKY CRUST (page 15)

STREUSEL CRUMB TOPPING
½ cup all-purpose flour
½ cup packed light brown sugar
½ cup (1 stick) cold unsalted butter (not margarine)

FRESH PEACH FILLING
3 pounds ripe fresh peaches, peeled, pitted, and sliced ¼ inch thick (9 cups)
½ cup granulated sugar
¾ teaspoon ground nutmeg
1 large egg

2 tablespoons light cream
1 teaspoon vanilla extract

Vanilla ice cream (optional)

1 Preheat the oven to 400°F and butter a 9-inch deep-dish pie plate. Roll, shape, flute, and chill the pie crust.

2 In a medium-size bowl, mix the flour and brown sugar. Using your fingers or a pastry blender, cut in the butter until coarse crumbs form. Spread half of the crumbs over the bottom of the shell.

3 In a large bowl, toss the peaches with the sugar and nutmeg. Spoon the peaches over the crumbs in the pie shell, mounding them in the center.

4 In a medium-size bowl, with an electric mixer on HIGH, beat the egg, cream, and vanilla until light yellow and frothy. Pour over the peaches. Sprinkle the remaining crumb mixture on top.

5 Bake the pie for 50 minutes or until the peaches are tender and the top is crisp. Cool on a rack for 30 minutes. Serve warm with generous scoops of ice cream, if you wish. Store any leftover pie in the refrigerator.

1/9 pie = 425 calories, 21 g fat (11 saturated), 67 mg cholesterol, 59 g carbohydrates, 4 g protein, 83 mg sodium, 3 g fiber

IT'S THE BERRIES PEACH PIE Reduce the peaches to 2 pounds and add 2 cups fresh blueberries.

Apricot & Cream Pie

STRAWBERRY FRANGIPANE TART

Traditional French frangipane is a rich almond crème pâtissière, *or pastry cream, that is used for filling tarts and pastries. This one is flavored with fresh orange and rum as well, then topped with a spectacular "chrysanthemum" of strawberries.*

MAKES ONE 11-INCH TART
PREP TIME 30 MIN ✦ BAKE TIME 25 MIN
COOL / CHILL TIME 1½ HR

½ **recipe BUTTERY CRUST (page 15)**

FRANGIPANE FILLING
1 **cup blanched almonds**
¼ **teaspoon ground cinnamon**
6 **tablespoons (¾ stick) unsalted butter (not margarine), at room temperature**
½ **cup sifted confectioners' sugar**
3 **large eggs**
½ **teaspoon grated orange zest**
¾ **cup fresh orange juice**
1 **tablespoon light rum or ½ teaspoon rum flavoring**

4 **cups fresh strawberries, hulled**
1 **cup strawberry jelly**
2 **tablespoons granulated sugar**

1 Preheat the oven to 450°F and butter an 11-inch tart pan. Roll, shape, and flute the shell (do not bake). In a food processor or blender, process the almonds and cinnamon until the nuts are finely ground but not powdery.

2 In a medium-size bowl, with an electric mixer on HIGH, cream the butter. Beat in the confectioners' sugar, then add the eggs one at a time, beating until thick and light yellow. Beat in the almonds, then beat in the orange zest, orange juice, and rum.

3 Pour the filling into the unbaked shell. Bake for 10 minutes. Reduce the oven temperature to 350°F. Bake 15 minutes more or until a knife inserted in the center comes out clean. Cool for 15 minutes, then chill 15 minutes.

4 Pick out the best berry and stand it in the center of the tart, pointed end up. Cut half of the berries vertically in half. Slice the remaining berries vertically ¼ inch thick. Starting at the edge, arrange the berries, slightly on a slant, in alternating circles of sliced berries and halved berries (cut-side down) until you reach the center berry and the tart is covered with berries.

5 In a small saucepan, boil the jelly and granulated sugar over medium heat for 3 to 4 minutes or until the glaze thickens. Drizzle the glaze over the tart and chill for 1 hour. Store any leftover tart in the refrigerator.

1/10 tart = 465 calories, 24 g fat (9 g saturated), 106 mg cholesterol, 55 g carbohydrates, 8 g protein, 88 mg sodium, 3 g fiber

CRANBERRY FRANGIPANE TART

Canadian TV Host and Food Stylist Nathan Fong shares his favorite frangipane tart, which is topped with fresh cranberries.

MAKES ONE 12-INCH TART
PREP TIME 30 MIN ✦ BAKE TIME 1 HR
CHILL / COOL TIME 1½ HR

NATHAN'S TART CRUST
1½ **cups all-purpose flour**
3 **tablespoons sugar**
7 **tablespoons shortening**
5 **tablespoons unsalted butter (not margarine), chilled**
6 **tablespoons ice water**

FRANGIPANE FILLING
1½ **cups blanched almonds**
¾ **to 1 cup granulated sugar**
½ **cup (1 stick) unsalted butter (not margarine), melted**
1 **large egg**
1 **teaspoon vanilla extract**
3 **cups fresh cranberries**

STREUSEL TOPPING
6 **tablespoons all-purpose flour**
6 **tablespoons packed light brown sugar**
2 **teaspoons ground cinnamon**

3 **tablespoons unsalted butter (not margarine), melted**

CINNAMON WHIPPED CREAM (OPTIONAL)
1 **cup cold heavy (whipping) cream**
3 **tablespoons granulated sugar**
¼ **teaspoon ground cinnamon**

1 In a food processor, mix the flour, sugar, shortening, and butter until coarse crumbs form. Add the water and process until a dough forms. Shape the pastry into a 6-inch disk and chill 1 hour.

2 Preheat the oven to 375°F and butter a 12-inch tart pan with a removable bottom. Roll out and shape the tart shell.

3 In the food processor, process the almonds and sugar until the almonds are finely ground. Add the melted butter, egg, and vanilla and process until a smooth paste forms. Spread evenly in the tart shell and top with the cranberries.

4 In a small bowl, combine all of the ingredients for the topping and sprinkle evenly over the cranberries. Bake on the middle rack of the oven for 1 hour or until the berries are tender. Cover the pie with a foil tent if it browns too fast. Cool on a rack for 30 minutes.

5 Meanwhile, if you wish to serve the tart with the Cinnamon Whipped Cream, beat the cream in a small bowl with the mixer on HIGH until it begins to thicken. Add the sugar and cinnamon and whip until peaks form (do not overbeat). Chill until ready to serve. Serve the tart warm or at room temperature with spoonfuls of cream, if you wish. Store any leftover tart in the refrigerator.

1/10 tart = 598 calories, 39 g fat (15 g saturated), 71 mg cholesterol, 62 g carbohydrates, 78 g protein, 15 mg sodium, 2 g fiber

◆ *Strawberry Frangipane Tart*

BETH'S SHORTCAKE PIZZA PIE

Mom never measured anything to make her shortcakes. She just worked butter into the flour mixture until it looked right, then added cream until it came together in a soft dough. I've now figured out measurements and often bake the dough in one large open-faced pie, perfect for a small dinner party. Shape it ahead and let it bake during dinner. It's best served warm.

MAKES ONE 14-INCH PIZZA PIE
PREP TIME 30 MIN ✦ BAKE / BROIL
TIME 13 MIN

1 recipe MOM ALLEN'S
   SHORTCAKE DOUGH (page 19)
1 tablespoon heavy or light cream
1 tablespoon sugar

   SUMMER FRUIT TOPPING
⅔ cup apricot preserves
3 tablespoons sugar, divided
2 tablespoons peach-flavored brandy
1½ pounds ripe fresh peaches, peeled,
   pitted, and sliced ¼ inch thick
   (4½ cups)
1½ pounds ripe fresh Damson plums,
   pitted and sliced ¼ inch thick
   (4½ cups)
2 cups fresh blueberries
1 recipe Crème Fraîche (page 20)
   (optional)

1 Preheat the oven to 425°F and line a
14- to 15-inch deep-dish pizza pan
with foil. Generously butter the foil. Mix, lightly knead, and pat the dough into the pizza pan, pushing it up the sides. Flute the edges, making a rim, ½ inch high. Brush with the cream and sprinkle with the sugar. Bake the shortcake for 10 to 13 minutes or just until the "pizza crust" is light golden and set. Transfer the pan to a wire rack and preheat the broiler.

2 Meanwhile, make the filling: in a small saucepan, melt the apricot preserves with 1 tablespoon of the sugar over medium heat. Cook for 4 to 5 minutes or until the glaze thickens. Remove the glaze from the heat and stir in the brandy.

3 Decoratively arrange the fruit on top of the shortcake. First, set aside about 6 slices each of the peaches and plums and 10 berries. Alternately arrange the remaining peach and plum slices in a pinwheel, and slightly on a slant, around the outside edge of the pie (see photo, opposite). Fill in the empty spaces with the blueberries. Finish with a flower design in the center, using the reserved peaches, plums, and berries. Paint the fruit with the apricot glaze. Sprinkle with the remaining 2 tablespoons of sugar. Broil the pie, about 8 inches from the heat, for 3 minutes or just until glazed.

1/10 pizza pie = 450 calories, 17 g fat (10 saturated), 72 mg cholesterol, 12 g carbohydrates, 5 g protein, 274 mg sodium, 4 g fiber

BERRY PATCH SHORTCAKE PIZZA
Substitute 4 cups sliced strawberries and 3 cups raspberries for the peaches and plums. Toss the strawberries and raspberries with the blueberries and scatter on the top, completely covering the pizza with fruit (Step 3).

CHRISTINE KOURY'S STRAWBERRY TRUFFLE TART

The creamy chocolate truffle confections coated in cocoa were so named because they resemble the rare black truffle from the Périgord region in France, in both their irregular shape and color. A chocolate truffle filling gives this fresh strawberry tart a regal, elegant flavor. It was created by Food Editor Christine Smith Koury.

MAKES ONE 10-INCH TART
PREP TIME 30 MIN ✦ BAKE TIME 20 MIN
COOL / CHILL TIME 1½ HR

1 recipe CHRIS'S BUTTER PASTRY
   (page 15)

   STRAWBERRY TRUFFLE FILLING
½ cup heavy (whipping) cream
6 ounces bittersweet or semisweet
   chocolate, chopped (about 1 cup)
½ cup seedless strawberry fruit
   spread (in preserves department)
6 cups fresh strawberries

1 cup strawberry jelly, melted

1 Preheat the oven to 375°F and generously butter a 10-inch fluted tart pan with a removable bottom. Mix, shape, and trim the tart shell, then freeze
it for 15 minutes. Prick the shell all over with a fork and completely prebake the shell for 20 minutes or until golden (see Blind-Baking, page 12). Cool the tart shell on a wire rack.

2 Meanwhile, in a small saucepan, bring the cream to a boil over medium-high heat. Place the chocolate in a medium-size bowl and pour over the boiling cream. Let the chocolate stand for 1 minute or until melted, then stir until smooth. Refrigerate the chocolate mixture, stirring occasionally, for at least 30 minutes or until thickened.

3 Spread the chocolate filling over the bottom of the cooled baked shell. Turn the fruit spread into a small bowl
and stir until smooth. Spread over the chocolate filling.

4 Pick through the berries and set aside about 2 cups of them (the biggest, prettiest ones). Cut the remaining berries in half vertically. Starting at the outside edge of the tart, arrange a circle of halved berries, cut-side down, tips pointing toward the center. Arrange a second circle of berries, resting the bottom of the berries on the tips of those in the outside circle. Repeat with a third circle. Stand the whole berries in the center. Paint the melted jelly over the berries. Chill for 1 hour before serving.

1/10 tart = 390 calories, 18 g fat (9 saturated), 41 mg cholesterol, 58 g carbohydrates, 3 g protein, 35 mg sodium, 3 g fiber

◆ *Beth's Shortcake Pizza Pie*

MICHELLE'S ISLAND FRUIT TART

The pick of island fruits swirl on top of a rich shortbread crust and rum-laced custard cream to make this spectacular tart. Michelle Gurdon from the island of Jamaica created it to serve at her family's barbecues featuring typical Caribbean fare.

MAKES ONE 12-INCH TART
PREP TIME 45 MIN ✦ BAKE TIME 15 MIN
COOL / CHILL TIME 2¼ HR

1 recipe **PAT-IN-THE-PAN CRUST (page 18)**

TROPICAL FRUIT FILLING
2 **cups light cream**
½ **cup sugar**
2½ **tablespoons cornstarch**
3 **large egg yolks**
⅓ **cup flaked coconut**
2 **tablespoons unsalted butter (not margarine), cut into pieces**
1 **tablespoon dark rum**
2 **teaspoons vanilla extract**
5 **large kiwi, peeled and sliced into semicircles, ⅛ inch thick (2 cups)**
2 **small papayas (preferably red strawberry papayas), peeled, seeded, and sliced ¼ inch thick**
2 **large mangoes, peeled, pitted, and cut into ½-inch dice**
3 **tablespoons fresh pomegranate seeds or fresh red currants**

GUAVA GLAZE
½ **cup guava jelly**
2 **tablespoons sugar**
1 **tablespoon dark rum**

1 Preheat the oven to 350°F and butter a 12-inch fluted tart pan with a removable bottom. Mix, shape, and trim the pastry shell, then prick the shell all over with a fork. Completely prebake for 15 minutes or until golden (see Blind-Baking, page 12). Cool on a wire rack.

2 In a medium-size saucepan, whisk the cream, sugar, and cornstarch over medium-high heat for 5 minutes or just until the mixture comes to a boil and thickens. Remove from the heat.

3 In a medium bowl, with an electric mixer on HIGH, beat the egg yolks until light yellow and thick. Whisk about 1 cup of the hot cream mixture into the egg yolks, then return this mixture to the

saucepan. Cook and stir over low heat for 3 minutes (do not boil). Remove from heat and stir in the coconut, butter, rum, and vanilla. Pour into the tart shell. Cool for 15 minutes.

4 Decorate the tart. Place three quarters of the kiwi semicircles around the outside edge, cut-edge out (see photograph, opposite). Make a pinwheel with the papaya slices and spoon the mango pieces in between. Finish with a flower made with the remaining kiwi and the pomegranate seeds. In a small saucepan, cook all of the glaze ingredients over medium heat for 4 to 5 minutes or until the glaze thickens. Using a pastry brush, paint the tart with the glaze. Chill for at least 2 hours. Store any leftover tart in the refrigerator.

1/12 tart = 498 calories, 28 g fat (17 saturated), 127 mg cholesterol, 59 g carbohydrates, 5 g protein, 115 mg sodium, 3 g fiber

PINEAPPLE CREAM PIE

This is a dream of a pie. But it really needs a sweet ripe pineapple. Look for a full plump one with dark green leaves and no dark spots. When ripe, the fruit should feel slightly soft to the touch and heavy in your hand, indicating that it's full of juice. Sniff the bottom of the pineapple — it should have a sweet aroma.

MAKES ONE 9-INCH DEEP-DISH PIE
PREP TIME 45 MIN ✦ BAKE TIME 15 MIN
CHILL TIME 2 HR

½ recipe **PÂTE BRISÉE (page 15)**

PINEAPPLE CREAM
1¼ **cups sugar**
⅓ **cup cornstarch**
¼ **cup all-purpose flour**
¼ **teaspoon salt**
2½ **cups milk**
4 **large egg yolks**
2 **tablespoons unsalted butter (not margarine), cut into small pieces**
1 **tablespoon vanilla extract**
1 **teaspoon grated lemon zest**
1 **large ripe fresh pineapple, peeled, cored, eyes removed, cut into 1-inch wedges, ¼ inch thick (4 cups)**

1 recipe **Decorator's Whipped Cream (page 20)**
1 recipe **Candied Lemon Zest (page 21)**

1 Preheat the oven to 400°F and butter a 9-inch deep-dish pie plate. Roll, shape, and flute the pie shell, then prick all over with a fork. Completely prebake the shell for 15 minutes or until golden (see Blind-Baking, page 12), then cool.

2 In a medium-size saucepan, mix the sugar, cornstarch, flour, and salt. Whisk in the milk until smooth. Cook over medium heat, whisking constantly, for 8 minutes or just until the mixture comes to a full boil and thickens. Remove from the heat.

3 In a medium-size bowl, with an electric mixer on HIGH, beat the egg yolks until light yellow and thick ribbons form. Stir about 1 cup of the hot custard into the egg yolks, then return this mixture to the saucepan.

4 Cook and stir the custard over low heat for 2 minutes or until thickened (do not let boil). Remove from the heat. Stir in the butter, vanilla, and lemon zest. Gently fold in the pineapple. Spoon into the baked shell. Chill for at least 2 hours or until set. Pipe or spoon the whipped cream on the pie. Sprinkle with the zest.

1/9 pie = 565 calories, 24 g fat (14 saturated), 164 mg cholesterol, 85 g carbohydrates, 7 g protein, 179 mg sodium, 2 g fiber

✦ *Michelle's Island Fruit Tart in a fluted Pat-in-the-Pan Crust*

CARAMELIZED ROSY ORANGE & GRAPEFRUIT TART

A duo of citrus fruits makes a colorful tart that's perfect for a dramatic presentation, similar to tarts created by France's finest pastry chefs. I often use ruby red grapefruit and navel oranges, but sometimes substitute tangelos for the oranges.

MAKES ONE 13-INCH TART
PREP TIME 45 MIN ✦ BAKE / BROIL TIME
22 MIN ✦ STANDING TIME 1 HR

- ½   recipe PÂTE FEUILLETÉE
      (page 19)
- 1   tablespoon light cream
- ¼   cup chopped almonds, toasted

CARAMELIZED TART FILLING
- ⅓   cup plus 2 tablespoons sugar,
      divided
- 1   teaspoon grated orange zest
- 6   large navel oranges, peeled,
      sectioned, and seeded (3 cups)
- 2   large pink grapefruit, peeled,
      sectioned, and seeded (2 cups)
- 3   tablespoons Grand Marnier
- ⅓   cup currant jelly
- 1   tablespoon fresh lemon juice

1 The night before or the morning you plan to bake, prepare the dough and chill. When ready to shape and bake the tart, preheat the oven to 400°F and generously butter a large baking sheet (about 15 × 14-inches).

2 On a lightly floured surface, roll out the pastry into a large circle, ⅛ inch thick, and trim to a 15-inch round. Transfer the pastry to the baking sheet and flute the edge to make a rim, 1 inch high. Prick the bottom of the shell all over, going through the dough to the baking sheet. Sprinkle with the almonds.

3 In a small bowl, toss the ⅓ cup of sugar and the orange zest and set aside. In a large bowl, gently toss the orange and grapefruit sections with the Grand Marnier. Arrange the fruits in a circular design on top of the tart. Sprinkle with the orange sugar. Bake the tart for 20 minutes or until the pastry is golden and filling is bubbling. Remove tart from the oven. Preheat the broiler.

4 Meanwhile, in a small saucepan, stir the jelly, the remaining 2 tablespoons of sugar, and the lemon juice over medium heat and boil for 4 minutes or until the glaze thickens. As soon as the tart comes out of the oven, paint it with the glaze. Then broil the tart for 2 minutes or until the fruit glistens.

1/12 tart = 324 calories, 17 g fat (10 saturated), 42 mg cholesterol, 40 g carbohydrates, 3 g protein, 94 mg sodium, 1 g fiber

WINTER FRUIT PIE

Food Stylist Delores Custer used the fruits of winter to create this delicious pie. Choose tart red baking apples, such as Cortland or Rome Beauty. For the pears, select a winter variety, such as Bosc, with its golden brown skin, creamy texture, and ability to hold its shape during baking. Tart cranberries and dried cherries round out the flavors in this wintry fruit blend.

MAKES ONE 9-INCH PIE
PREP TIME 45 MIN ✦ BAKE TIME 45 MIN

- 1   recipe PÂTE BRISÉE (page 15)
- 2   tablespoons light cream, divided

WINTER FRUIT FILLING
- 1   pound ripe fresh pears (Bosc,
      Anjou, or Bartlett), peeled, cored,
      and sliced ¼ inch thick (2 cups)
- ¾   pound sweet-tart red baking
      apples, such as Cortland,
      Jonathan, McIntosh, or Rome
      Beauty, peeled, cored, and sliced
      ¼ inch thick (2 cups)
- 1   cup dried pitted red sour cherries
- 1   cup fresh or dried cranberries
- 1   teaspoon grated lemon zest
- 3   tablespoons fresh lemon juice
- ½   cup granulated sugar
- ½   cup packed light brown sugar
- ¼   cup all-purpose flour
- ½   teaspoon ground cinnamon
- ½   teaspoon salt

- 2   tablespoons unsalted butter (not
      margarine), cut into pieces

1 Preheat the oven to 375°F and set out a 9-inch pie plate and a baking sheet. Divide the pastry into 2 disks, one slightly larger than the other. On a lightly floured surface, roll out each disk into a large circle, ⅛ inch thick. Trim the larger piece to a 15-inch circle and the smaller piece to an 11-inch circle. Fit the larger round into the pie plate, leaving a 1½-inch overhang. Brush the shell with 1 tablespoon of the cream and refrigerate. Transfer the remaining pastry circle to the baking sheet and refrigerate.

2 In a large bowl, toss the pears, apples, cherries, cranberries, lemon zest, and lemon juice. In a small bowl, mix both of the sugars, the flour, cinnamon, and salt. Toss with the fruits, then spoon the filling into the pie shell and dot with the butter.

3 To decorate, cut out about 7 designs at random from the remaining dough circle with a ¾- to 1-inch decorative cutter, such as an apple or a flower (stay 1 inch inside the edge). Lay the dough circle on top of the pie. Seal the edges together with a little ice water, then flute. Brush the top crust with the remaining tablespoon of cream. Bake for 45 minutes or until the filling is bubbling.

1/9 pie = 438 calories, 17 g fat (10 saturated), 44 mg cholesterol, 70 g carbohydrates, 4 g protein, 264 mg sodium, 3 g fiber

Use a decorative cutter to create a design on the top crust; the cutout areas double as steam vents

• *Caramelized Rosy Orange & Grapefruit Tart in a Pâte Feuilletée tart shell*

CHOCOLATE, WITH LOVE

♥

Many things are coming up chocolate — especially pies. Take a taste of this traditional chocolate silk pie, filled with a velvety deep chocolate cream and topped with a golden meringue. Discover other chocolate creations too — layered with bananas, marbled with vanilla custard, or lined with a black cookie bottom and filled with rum custard.

Chocolate pies can be fudgy, rich, and decadent. They can be piled into a meringue shell and have a little crunch, or they can be soft and cookie-like. Another is filled with mile-high scoops of ice cream, while others are laden with nuts. Whichever ones you indulge in, serve chocolate pies with love.

♦ *Chocolate Silk Pie in a Buttery Crust*
(see recipe, page 88)

CHOCOLATE SILK PIE

The filling is deep chocolate, thick, and rich ... the texture is silky and luxurious. It's a typical cream pie, since it's thickened with both flour and eggs. Top with a golden meringue (see photo, pages 86 – 87), or whipped cream and shaved chocolate.

MAKES ONE 9-INCH DEEP-DISH PIE
PREP TIME 1 HR ✦ BAKE TIME 27 MIN
COOL / CHILL TIME 4¼ HR

½ recipe BUTTERY CRUST
(page 15)

CHOCOLATE SILK FILLING
1⅓ cups sugar
⅓ cup cornstarch
¼ cup all-purpose flour
¼ teaspoon salt
1½ cups milk
1 cup light cream
4 ounces unsweetened chocolate, melted (page 21)
4 large egg yolks
2 tablespoons unsalted butter (not margarine), softened
1 tablespoon vanilla extract

MERINGUE TOPPING
5 large egg whites
½ teaspoon cream of tartar
1 cup sugar

1. Preheat the oven to 400°F and set out a 9-inch deep-dish pie plate. Roll, shape, and flute the pie shell. Prick it all over with a fork. Completely prebake the shell for 15 minutes or until golden (see Blind-Baking, page 12). Cool on a rack. Reduce the oven temperature to 350°F.

2. In a medium-size saucepan, mix the sugar, cornstarch, flour, and salt. Slowly whisk in the milk and cream until smooth. Whisk constantly over medium heat for 8 minutes or until the mixture boils and thickens. Whisk in the melted chocolate. Remove from the heat.

3. In a small bowl, with an electric mixer on HIGH, beat the egg yolks until light yellow and thick. Stir 1 cup of the hot milk mixture into the egg yolks, then return this mixture to the saucepan. Cook and stir over low heat for 2 minutes or until thickened (do not let boil).

4. Remove the filling from the heat and stir in the butter and vanilla. Pour the filling into the baked shell. Lay a piece of plastic wrap directly on the filling to prevent a skin from forming. Let stand while you make the meringue.

5. In a medium-size bowl, with an electric mixer on HIGH, beat the egg whites and cream of tartar until fluffy. Gradually beat in the sugar until the meringue stands in glossy soft peaks. To attach the meringue, lightly score the filling with the prongs of a fork. Cover the hot filling with the meringue, sealing it well at the edges. Make peaks with the back of a spoon as you go. Bake 12 to 15 minutes or until lightly browned. Cool for 15 minutes. To set, chill for at least 4 hours. Store in the refrigerator.

1/9 pie = 574 calories, 29 g fat (12 g saturated), 159 mg cholesterol, 78 g carbohydrates, 9 g protein, 199 mg sodium, 1 g fiber

CHOCOLATE MARBLE PIE

Take a creamy vanilla custard and flavor half of it chocolate. Then swirl it into a buttery pie shell and top with whipped cream.

MAKES ONE 9-INCH DEEP-DISH PIE
PREP TIME 1 HR ✦ BAKE TIME 15 MIN
COOL / CHILL TIME 4¼ HR

½ recipe PÂTE BRISÉE (page 15)

MARBLE FILLING
1⅓ cups sugar
¼ cup all-purpose flour
¼ cup cornstarch
¼ teaspoon salt
2¾ cups milk
4 large egg yolks
2 tablespoons unsalted butter (not margarine), softened
1 tablespoon vanilla extract
2 ounces semisweet chocolate, melted (page 21)

1 recipe Decorator's Whipped Cream (page 20)
1 ounce semisweet chocolate, shaved (page 21)

1. Preheat the oven to 400°F and set out a 9-inch deep-dish pie plate. Roll, shape, and flute the pie shell. Prick the shell all over with a fork. Completely prebake the shell for 15 minutes or until golden (see Blind-Baking, page 12). Cool the shell on a wire rack.

2. In a medium-size saucepan, mix the sugar, flour, cornstarch, and salt. Slowly whisk in the milk until smooth. Cook over medium heat, whisking constantly, for 8 minutes or just until the mixture comes to a full boil and thickens. Remove from the heat.

3. Meanwhile, in a small bowl, with an electric mixer on HIGH, beat the egg yolks until light yellow and thick. Stir about 1 cup of the hot milk mixture into the egg yolks, then return this mixture to the saucepan. Cook and stir over low heat for 2 minutes or until thickened (do not let boil). Remove from the heat and stir in the butter and vanilla.

4. Divide the filling equally between 2 bowls. Fold the melted chocolate into the filling in one bowl. Cool both fillings for 15 minutes. Alternately spoon the vanilla and chocolate fillings into the baked shell. With the tip of a knife, swirl through the filling to create a marbled effect. Cover the pie with plastic wrap and chill for 1 hour.

5. Pipe or spoon the Decorator's Whipped Cream in a ring around the outside edge of the pie. Sprinkle with the shaved chocolate. To set, chill for at least 3 hours more. Store in the refrigerator.

1/9 pie = 467 calories, 28 g fat (15 g saturated), 171 mg cholesterol, 46 g carbohydrates, 8 g protein, 209 mg sodium, 1 g fiber

BLACK BOTTOM PIE

In the early 1900s, this chocolate black bottom pie, topped with a rum custard and whipped cream, began appearing.

MAKES ONE 9-INCH DEEP-DISH PIE
PREP TIME 30 MIN ✦ BAKE TIME 10 MIN
CHILL TIME 3½ HR

1 recipe **GINGERSNAP CRUMB
CRUST (page 17), or CHOCOLATE
COOKIE CRUMB CRUST (page 17), or
GRAHAM CRACKER CRUMB
CRUST (page 17)**

RUM CUSTARD FILLING
2 **cups cold milk**
1 **envelope (¼ ounce) plain gelatin**
¾ **cup sugar**
¼ **teaspoon salt**
4 **large egg yolks**
1 **tablespoon vanilla extract**
2 **ounces unsweetened chocolate,
   melted (page 21)**
1 **cup cold heavy (whipping) cream**
1 **to 2 tablespoons light rum
   or 1 teaspoon rum extract**
1 **ounce unsweetened chocolate,
   shaved (page 21)**

1 Preheat the oven to 350°F and butter
a 9-inch deep-dish pie plate. Pick a
crust. Press the crumbs over the bottom
and up the sides of the pie plate. Bake for
10 minutes or until set. Cool on a rack.

2 Meanwhile, pour the milk into a
medium-size saucepan and sprinkle
the gelatin over the top. Let stand for
3 minutes or until gelatin is softened. Stir
in the sugar and salt. Stir over medium
heat just until the mixture thickens (do
not let boil). Remove from the heat.

3 Meanwhile, in a small bowl, with an
electric mixer on HIGH, beat the egg
yolks until light yellow and thick. Stir
1 cup of the hot milk mixture into the
egg yolks, then return this mixture to the
saucepan. Cook and stir over low heat for
2 minutes or until thickened (do not let
boil). Remove from heat. Stir in vanilla.

4 Divide the custard equally between
2 bowls. Fold the melted chocolate
into the custard in one bowl, then spoon
into the bottom of the baked crust to
make the chocolate layer. Refrigerate
for 30 minutes or until soft-set.

5 In a small bowl, with an electric
mixer on HIGH, whip the cream.
Fold half of the whipped cream and
the rum into the remaining vanilla
custard (refrigerate the remaining
cream). Spread this rum custard over
the chocolate layer, cover with plastic
wrap, and chill at least 3 hours more.
To serve, pipe or spoon the remaining
whipped cream on top of the pie and
sprinkle with the shaved chocolate. Store
any leftover pie in the refrigerator.

*1/9 pie = 439 calories, 29 g fat (10 g saturated), 142 mg
cholesterol, 43 g carbohydrates, 6 g protein, 198 mg
sodium, 1 g fiber*

CHOCOLATE BANANA CREAM PIE

This pie is layered with deep chocolate cream and rings of bananas, then topped with whipped cream and chocolate curls.

MAKES ONE 9-INCH DEEP-DISH PIE
PREP TIME 1 HR ✦ BAKE TIME 15 MIN
COOL / CHILL TIME 4 HR

½ **recipe PÂTE SUCRÉE (page 15)**

CHOCOLATE BANANA FILLING
¾ **cup sugar**
7 **tablespoons cornstarch**
¼ **teaspoon salt**
1 **cup light cream**
¾ **cup milk**
4 **ounces semisweet chocolate,
   melted (page 21)**
3 **large egg yolks**
2 **tablespoons unsalted butter (not
   margarine), softened**
1 **tablespoon vanilla extract**
1 **teaspoon banana extract**
4 **large ripe bananas, divided**

1 **recipe Decorator's Whipped
   Cream (page 20)**
1 **3-ounce bar bittersweet chocolate,
   curled (page 20), optional**

1 Preheat the oven to 400°F and set out
a 9-inch deep-dish pie plate. Roll,
shape, and flute the pie shell. Prick the
shell all over with a fork. Completely
prebake the shell for 15 minutes or until
golden (see Blind-Baking, page 12). Cool
the shell on a wire rack.

2 In a medium-size saucepan, mix
the sugar, cornstarch, and salt.
Slowly whisk in the cream and milk until
smooth. Cook over medium heat,
whisking constantly, for 8 minutes or
just until the mixture comes to a full
boil and thickens. Whisk in the melted
chocolate. Remove from the heat.

3 Meanwhile, in a small bowl, with an
electric mixer on HIGH, beat the egg
yolks until light yellow and thick. Stir
about 1 cup of the hot cream mixture
into the egg yolks, then return this
mixture to the saucepan. Cook and stir

over low heat for 2 minutes or until
thickened (do not let boil). Remove from
the heat. Stir in the butter, vanilla, and
banana extract. Pour half of the filling
into the baked shell.

4 Thinly slice 2 of the bananas and
layer over the filling in the shell.
Gently spoon over the remaining filling.
Cover the pie with plastic wrap and chill
for 4 hours or until serving time.

5 Right before serving, thinly slice the
remaining 2 bananas. Arrange them
in a ring around the edge of the pie,
overlapping them as you go. Spoon the
Decorator's Whipped Cream into the
center of the ring of bananas. Sprinkle
with the chocolate curls, if you wish.
Store any leftover pie in the refrigerator.

*1/9 pie = 547 calories, 30 g fat (16 g saturated), 179 mg
cholesterol, 66 g carbohydrates, 7 g protein, 185 mg
sodium, 2 g fiber*

◆ *Chocolate Angel Pie, topped with dollops of whipped cream and curls of chocolate*

CHOCOLATE ANGEL PIE

A pie book wouldn't be complete without an angel pie. A classic since the early 1900s,
this pie has a crisp hard meringue shell and a rich chocolate crème filling.

MAKES ONE 9-INCH DEEP-DISH PIE
PREP TIME 45 MIN ♦ BAKE TIME 1 HR
COOL / CHILL TIME 4 HR

MERINGUE SHELL

4 **large egg whites, at room**
   temperature
¼ **teaspoon cream of tartar**
   Pinch of salt
¾ **cup granulated sugar**
1 **teaspoon vanilla extract**
⅓ **cup finely chopped walnuts**

CHOCOLATE CRÈME

½ **cup milk**
2 **teaspoons vanilla extract**
¼ **teaspoon mint extract**
⅛ **teaspoon salt**
9 **ounces semisweet chocolate,**
   melted (page 21)
2 **cups cold heavy (whipping)**
   cream, divided
2 **tablespoons sifted confectioners'**
   sugar

1 **3-ounce bar bittersweet chocolate,**
   curled (page 20)

1 Preheat the oven to 275°F and butter a 9-inch deep-dish pie plate. To make the Meringue Shell, in a large bowl, with an electric mixer on HIGH, beat the egg whites, cream of tartar, and salt together until soft peaks form. Gradually add the granulated sugar, 2 tablespoons at a time, and continue beating until the meringue stands up in glossy stiff peaks when the beaters are lifted. Beat in the vanilla.

2 Gently spoon the meringue into the pie plate, building up the sides as high as possible. Sprinkle the walnuts over the bottom and sides. Bake for 1 hour. Peek in the oven after 15 minutes. If the meringue is sinking down the sides, gently push it into place with the back of a spoon. Turn off the oven when the meringue is dry and light toasty brown. Leave the meringue in the closed oven for 30 minutes. Transfer to a rack to cool.

3 In a small saucepan, heat the milk and stir in the vanilla, mint extract,

and salt. Remove from the heat and whisk in the melted chocolate. Pour into a medium-size bowl and set aside to cool.

4 Meanwhile, in a small bowl, with an electric mixer on HIGH, whip 1½ cups of the cream. Fold into the cooled chocolate mixture. Spoon the chocolate crème into the cooled meringue shell, mounding it in the center. Swirl the filling into peaks with the back of a spoon. Cover loosely with plastic wrap and chill for at least 3 hours.

5 Right before serving, whip the remaining ½ cup cream with the confectioners' sugar until stiff peaks form. Spoon the cream in the center of pie, making peaks with the back of a spoon. Sprinkle the top of the pie generously with the chocolate curls. Store any leftover pie in the refrigerator.

1/10 pie = 415 calories, 27 g fat (11 g saturated),
70 mg cholesterol, 43 g carbohydrates, 5 g protein,
101 mg sodium, 0 g fiber

CHOCOLATE ORANGE TRUFFLE TART

The aroma, silky texture, and deep flavor of truffle candies inspired this pie.
When showered with candied orange zest, this tart is very impressive — yet very easy.

MAKES ONE 12-INCH TART
PREP TIME 30 MIN ♦ BAKE TIME 15 MIN
COOL / CHILL TIME 3½ HR

1 **recipe PAT-IN-THE-PAN CRUST**
   (page 18)

CHOCOLATE ORANGE TRUFFLE
FILLING

½ **cup milk**
1 **teaspoon vanilla extract**
⅛ **teaspoon salt**
8 **ounces semisweet or bittersweet**
   chocolate, melted (page 21)
2 **teaspoons grated orange zest**
   (page 21)
2 **cups cold heavy (whipping)**
   cream
¼ **cup sifted confectioners' sugar**
   Candied Orange Zest (page 21)
   Fresh mint leaves (optional)

1 Preheat the oven to 350°F and butter a 12-inch tart pan with a removable bottom. Pat the crust over the bottom and up the sides. Prick the bottom and sides all over with a fork. Completely prebake the shell for 15 minutes or until golden (see Blind-Baking, page 12). Cool the shell on a wire rack.

2 Meanwhile, in a small saucepan, heat the milk, then stir in the vanilla and salt. Remove from the heat and whisk in the melted chocolate. Stir in the grated orange zest. Set aside to cool completely.

3 In a small bowl, with an electric mixer on HIGH, whip the cream until fluffy. Add the sugar and continue whipping until soft peaks form. Gently

fold the cream into the cooled chocolate mixture and spoon into the tart shell. Refrigerate the tart for at least 3 hours.

4 Generously sprinkle the Candied Orange Zest on top of the tart and garnish the center with a cluster of fresh mint leaves if you wish. Store any leftover pie in the refrigerator.

1/12 tart = 541 calories, 35 g fat (19 g saturated),
98 mg cholesterol, 57 g carbohydrates, 5 g protein,
149 mg sodium, 1 g fiber

**CHOCOLATE MARNIER MOUSSE
TART** Stir in 1 tablespoon Grand Marnier with the orange zest (Step 2).

MOCHA MOUSSE TART Stir 1 tablespoon dry instant coffee into the milk with the vanilla and salt (Step 2).

MAIDA HEATTER'S
SALTED ALMOND CHOCOLATE PIE

In the world of desserts, Maida Heatter is known as one of the best dessert makers of our time, as well as a chocolate lover. This chocolate pie, marbled with marshmallows and almonds, is her dreamy version of an old favorite called Chocolate Mallow.

MAKES ONE 9-INCH PIE
PREP TIME 30 MIN ✦ BAKE TIME 15 MIN
COOL / FREEZE TIME 4 HR

1 recipe MAIDA HEATTER'S CHOCOLATE WAFER CRUMB CRUST (page 17)

SALTED ALMOND CHOCOLATE FILLING

2 cups miniature marshmallows (about 4 ounces), divided
8 ounces milk chocolate, chopped
½ cup light cream
⅓ cup roasted salted almonds, plus 2 tablespoons for garnish (look in nut section of supermarket)
1 cup cold heavy (whipping) cream

1 Preheat the oven to 300°F and set out a freezer-proof 9-inch pie plate. Press the crumb mixture over the bottom and up the sides of the pie plate. Bake for 15 minutes or until set. Turn off the oven and let the crust remain in the oven for 15 more minutes. Cool on a wire rack and freeze the crust until ready to fill.

2 Meanwhile, in a medium-size heavy saucepan, place 1½ cups of the marshmallows and the chocolate, then pour over the light cream. Cook, stirring frequently, over medium heat, until the marshmallows and chocolate are melted and the mixture is smooth. Pour into a large bowl and cool completely (the mixture will thicken slightly as it cools).

3 Meanwhile, coarsely chop the ⅓ cup almonds into uneven pieces. Stir into the cooled chocolate.

4 In a small chilled bowl, with an electric mixer on HIGH, whip the heavy cream until soft peaks form. Gradually, in about four additions, fold the whipped cream and the remaining ½ cup marshmallows into the cooled chocolate mixture just until combined.

Do not over-mix or the filling will lose its fluffy texture and be hard to spread.

5 Spoon the filling into the crust and smooth out with a spatula. Freeze for at least 3 hours. Store in the freezer.

1/9 pie = 363 calories, 35 g fat (18 g saturated), 90 mg cholesterol, 33 g carbohydrates, 5 g protein, 230 mg sodium, 1 g fiber

> **✦ BAKER'S TIP ✦**
>
> **Can't find roasted salted almonds?** *Toast them yourself. Buy whole almonds with their skins still on. Preheat the oven to 375°F. Spread the almonds in a single layer in a shallow baking pan. Sprinkle with salt to taste. Toast for about 8 minutes, turning and shaking the almonds 2 to 3 times. Cool the almonds in the pan, then coarsely chop them.*

GERMAN CHOCOLATE PIE

All the ingredients and flavors of the popular German Chocolate Cake — baked in a coconut crust.

MAKES ONE 9-INCH DEEP-DISH PIE
PREP TIME 30 MIN ✦ BAKE TIME 55 MIN
COOL / CHILL TIME 4½ HR

1 recipe TOASTED COCONUT CRUMB CRUST (page 17)

GERMAN CHOCOLATE FILLING

3 ounces German-sweet chocolate, chopped
½ cup corn syrup
2 tablespoons unsalted butter (not margarine)
¾ cup light cream
½ cup milk
¼ cup cornstarch
3 large eggs
⅔ cup granulated sugar
⅛ teaspoon salt

2 teaspoons vanilla extract
½ cup coarsely chopped pecans

1 Preheat the oven to 350°F and butter a deep-dish 9-inch pie plate. Press the coconut-crumb mixture over the bottom and up the sides of the pie plate. Cover with plastic wrap and refrigerate for 30 minutes or until set.

2 Meanwhile, in a heavy saucepan, cook the chocolate, corn syrup, and butter over medium heat, stirring, until the chocolate and butter are melted and the mixture is smooth. Remove from the heat and set on a wire rack to cool.

3 Meanwhile, in a small bowl, whisk the cream, milk, and cornstarch until smooth. In a medium-size bowl, with an electric mixer on HIGH, beat the eggs, sugar, and salt until light yellow and thick. Reduce the mixer to LOW. Beat in the cream mixture, then the cooled chocolate mixture and the vanilla.

4 Pour the filling into the chilled crust and sprinkle the pecans on top. Bake for 55 minutes or until a knife inserted halfway between the crust edge and the center of the pie comes out clean. Cool on a rack for 30 minutes, then chill for 4 hours or until serving time. Store any leftover pie in the refrigerator.

1/9 pie = 558 calories, 34 g fat (17 g saturated), 132 mg cholesterol, 61 g carbohydrates, 6 g protein, 128 mg sodium, 2 g fiber

◆ *Maida Heatter's Salted Almond Chocolate Pie in a Chocolate Wafer Crumb Crust, topped with an extra dollop of whipped cream*

MISSISSIPPI MUD PIE

From the homes along the Mississippi River comes this rich deep-dark chocolate pie. As the legend goes, its name comes from the way the pie looks when baked — cracked on the top, soft on the inside. It resembles a mud pie that has dried in the sun.

MAKES ONE 12-INCH PIE
PREP TIME 30 MIN ✦ BAKE TIME 45 MIN
COOL TIME 1 HR

1 recipe CHOCOLATE COOKIE CRUMB CRUST (page 17)
½ teaspoon ground cinnamon

FUDGE MUD FILLING
2 cups sifted all-purpose flour
1 teaspoon baking powder
½ teaspoon salt
¾ cup chopped pecans, toasted
1 cup (2 sticks) unsalted butter (not margarine), at room temperature
1½ cups granulated sugar
4 large eggs
4 ounces semisweet chocolate, melted (page 21)
2 teaspoons vanilla extract

CHOCOLATE GLAZE
¾ cup sifted confectioners' sugar
1 ounce semisweet chocolate, melted (page 21)
2 to 3 tablespoons light cream

1 Preheat the oven to 350°F and butter a 12-inch fluted quiche dish with 2-inch sides. In a small bowl, make and shape the crust, mixing the cinnamon with the crumbs. Bake the crust for 10 minutes or until set. Cool on a rack.

2 Into a medium-size bowl, sift the flour, baking powder, and salt. Toss with the pecans and set aside.

3 In a large bowl, with an electric mixer on HIGH, cream the butter and granulated sugar until light yellow. Beat in the eggs, one at a time. Blend in the chocolate and the vanilla. Using a spoon, stir in the flour-pecan mixture just until the flour disappears (do not overmix). Spoon the batter into the crust.

4 Bake the pie for 35 minutes or until a pick inserted in the center comes out almost clean (do not overbake). When the pie is ready to come out of the oven, it will look slightly dry and cracked on top, but will still be moist on the inside. Cool the pie on a wire rack for 1 hour.

5 Make the Chocolate Glaze by beating the confectioners' sugar and chocolate in a small bowl. Slowly stir in the cream, beating until smooth and adding a little more cream if necessary to make a thick glaze. Quickly drizzle the glaze over the cooled pie in a swirl design. Delicious served warm. Store in the refrigerator.

1/12 pie = 533 calories, 38 g fat (15 g saturated), 131 mg cholesterol, 76 g carbohydrates, 7 g protein, 291 mg sodium, 2 g fiber

Swirl the chocolate glaze over the top of the pie

JOE'S CHOCOLATE FUDGE PIE

This recipe comes from the pages of MAIDA HEATTER'S BEST DESSERT BOOK EVER. As Maida says, "It has a crisp pie crust and a chocolate-fudge filling that is about halfway between a dense fudge sauce and fudge candy ... it's ecstasy."

MAKES ONE 9-INCH PIE
PREP TIME 30 MIN ✦ BAKE TIME 40 MIN
COOL TIME 1 HR

½ recipe BUTTERY CRUST (page 15)

FUDGE FILLING
½ cup (1 stick) unsalted butter (not margarine)
4 ounces unsweetened chocolate
4 large eggs
1½ cups granulated sugar
¼ cup milk
1 tablespoon light corn syrup
¼ to ½ teaspoon ground nutmeg
¼ teaspoon salt
1 teaspoon vanilla extract

WHIPPED CREAM (OPTIONAL)
2 cups cold heavy (whipping) cream

1 teaspoon vanilla extract
¼ cup sifted confectioners' sugar

1 Preheat the oven to 400°F and butter a 9-inch pie plate. Roll, shape, and flute the pie shell. Prick the shell all over with a fork. Partially prebake the shell for 10 minutes or just until set (see Blind-Baking, page 12). Cool on a wire rack. Lower the oven temperature to 350°F.

2 In a medium-size heavy saucepan, melt the butter and chocolate over low heat, stirring until smooth. Remove from the heat and set aside to cool.

3 In a medium-size bowl, with an electric mixer on HIGH, beat the eggs until light yellow and thick. Beat in the sugar, milk, corn syrup, nutmeg, salt, and vanilla until well blended. Beat in the cooled chocolate mixture and pour the filling into the shell. Bake the pie for about 30 minutes or until a kitchen knife gently inserted halfway between the crust and the center of the pie comes out almost, but not completely, clean (do not overbake). Cool on a rack for 1 hour.

4 If you wish to serve the pie with whipped cream: In a small bowl with an electric mixer on HIGH, beat the cream and vanilla until frothy. Add the confectioners' sugar and beat until stiff peaks form. Spoon dollops of cream on top of the pie. Store in the refrigerator.

1/9 pie = 474 calories, 28 g fat (11 g saturated), 148 mg cholesterol, 54 g carbohydrates, 7 g protein, 164 mg sodium, 1 g fiber

BANANA SPLIT CHOCOLATE PIZZA PIE

Ruth Short shares a recipe for one of her favorite pies. "It looks like a pizza but tastes like a banana split." She spreads the brownie crust with strawberry cream cheese, then tops it with fruits, nuts, and swirls of hot fudge.

MAKES ONE 14-INCH PIZZA PIE
PREP TIME 30 MIN ✦ BAKE TIME 15 MIN
COOL / CHILL TIME 1¾ HR

1 **20-ounce package brownie mix**
2 **large eggs**
⅓ **cup cooking oil**
⅓ **cup water**
12 **ounces strawberry or plain cream cheese, at room temperature**
¾ **cup sifted confectioners' sugar**
2 **cups fresh strawberries, hulled and sliced vertically (8 whole berries reserved)**
2 **large bananas, thinly sliced**
3 **tablespoons fresh lemon juice**
2 **cups wedges fresh pineapple, about 1 × ½-inch**
1 **cup hot fudge ice cream topping, warmed**
2 **tablespoons chopped walnuts**

1 Preheat the oven to 375°F and butter a 14-inch deep-dish pizza pan. Line the pan with parchment paper. To keep the batter from overflowing, let the paper stand 1-inch higher than the sides of pan.

2 In a large bowl, stir the brownie mix, eggs, oil, and water until well blended. Spread the batter in the pan and bake for 15 to 20 minutes or until a pick inserted in the center comes out almost clean. Cool the pie in the pan on a rack for 15 minutes, then turn the pie upside down onto the rack and peel off the paper. Cool upside down for 1 hour, then slide, top-side down, onto a platter.

3 To decorate, mix the cream cheese and sugar in a small bowl until smooth. Spread on top of the pie. Mound the whole strawberries in the center and the sliced berries around the edge. Toss the bananas with the lemon juice, then arrange in alternating circles with the pineapple on top of pizza (see right, top). Drizzle with the fudge sauce (see right, bottom). Sprinkle with the walnuts. Chill for at least 30 minutes. Refrigerate.

1/16 pizza pie = 416 calories, 19 g fat (8 g saturated), 50 mg cholesterol, 59 g carbohydrates, 5 g protein, 240 mg sodium, 1 g fiber

Arrange the strawberries around the edge and the bananas and pineapple in alternating circles

Drizzle with the hot fudge sauce and then sprinkle the walnuts over the pie

CHOCOLATE SUPREME PIE

Art Director Lynn Yost shares one of her favorite chocolate pies. She makes the filling quickly in a blender using only six ingredients, including either coffee-flavored Kahlúa liqueur or almond flavoring. Chocolate-dipped almonds top it off.

MAKES ONE 9-INCH PIE
PREP TIME 30 MIN ✦ BAKE TIME 15 MIN
CHILL TIME 4 HR

½ **recipe WHIPPED PIE PASTRY (page 15), or BUTTERY CRUST (page 15), or CRISP FLAKY CRUST (page 15)**

SUPREME CHOCOLATE FILLING
2 **cups (12 ounces) mini semisweet chocolate chips**
2 **large eggs**
1 **tablespoon sugar**
2 **teaspoons Kahlúa (coffee liqueur) or ½ teaspoon almond extract**
½ **teaspoon salt**
1¼ **cups cold heavy (whipping) cream or milk**

½ **cup blanched whole almonds, chocolate dipped (optional)**

1 Preheat the oven to 400°F and butter a 9-inch pie plate. Pick a pastry. Roll, shape and flute the shell. Prick it all over with a fork. Completely prebake the shell for 15 minutes or until golden (see Blind-Baking, page 12). Cool on a wire rack.

2 In a food processor or blender, process the chocolate chips until finely chopped. Add the eggs, sugar, Kahlúa, and salt and process until frothy.

3 In a small saucepan, bring the cream to a boil over medium-high heat. With the processor motor running, slowly pour in the cream and process until smooth. Pour filling into the baked shell and chill for 4 hours. Top with the almonds if you wish. Store in refrigerator.

1/9 pie = 375 calories, 26 g fat (10 g saturated), 68 mg cholesterol, 35 g carbohydrates, 5 g protein, 218 mg sodium, 1 g fiber

> ✦ **CHOCOLATE-DIPPED ALMONDS** ✦
>
> *To dip enough almonds to create a border on a 9-inch pie, begin with ½ cup blanched whole almonds and 3 ounces bittersweet chocolate. Melt the chocolate (see page 21). One by one, dip the pointed ends of the almonds into the chocolate and cool on a rack.*

✦ *Lone Star Chocolate Pecan Pie in a Buttery Crust with a pointed scalloped edging*

LONE STAR CHOCOLATE PECAN PIE

In my home state of Texas, pecan orchards are plentiful. The long thin paper-shell pecans make some of the best pies.
This pecan filling is flavored with chocolate and has a layer of melted tiny chocolate chips on the bottom.

MAKES ONE 9-INCH DEEP-DISH PIE
PREP TIME 30 MIN ✦ BAKE TIME 50 MIN
COOL TIME 2¼ HR

½ recipe **BUTTERY CRUST** **(page 15)**
¾ **cup (4½ ounces) mini semisweet chocolate chips**

CHOCOLATE PECAN FILLING
3 **large eggs, at room temperature**
½ **teaspoon salt**
½ **cup granulated sugar**
½ **cup packed light brown sugar**
1 **cup light corn syrup**
4 **ounces semisweet chocolate, melted (page 21)**
½ **cup finely chopped pecans**
3 **tablespoons unsalted butter, melted**
1 **teaspoon vanilla extract**
1¼ **cups whole pecan halves**

Lone Star pattern

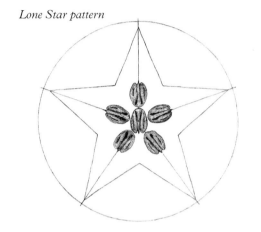

1 Preheat the oven to 350°F and set out a 9-inch deep-dish pie plate. Roll, shape, and flute the pie shell, then refrigerate for 15 minutes. Line the chilled shell with the chocolate chips.

2 Meanwhile, in a medium-size bowl, whisk the eggs and salt just until frothy. Do not overbeat. Whisk in both sugars, the corn syrup, and melted chocolate. Stir in the chopped pecans, butter, and vanilla. Pour into the pie shell.

3 Bake the pie for 20 minutes. Meanwhile, arrange whole pecans in a 7-inch star pattern on a flat surface, filling in the design completely with pecans. Remove the pie from the oven and transfer the star, one pecan at a time, onto the top of the pie (work fast). Bake 30 minutes more or until the pie is just set in the center. Let pie cool on a rack at room temperature for at least 2 hours. Store in the refrigerator.

1/12 pie = 510 calories, 26 g fat (6 g saturated), 80 mg cholesterol, 68 g carbohydrates, 5 g protein, 193 mg sodium, 1 g fiber

LARRY FORGIONE'S PENNSYLVANIA DUTCH CHOCOLATE NUT PIE

Larry Forgione, acclaimed chef and owner of An American Place in New York City, offers this basic, very good pie.
He adapted this pie recipe from one he tasted while traveling through the Pennsylvania Dutch country.

MAKES ONE 9-INCH PIE
PREP TIME 30 MIN ✦ BAKE TIME 45 MIN

½ recipe **CRISP FLAKY CRUST** **(page 15)**

CHOCOLATE NUT FILLING
¾ **cup sugar, plus additional for sprinkling**
¼ **cup water**
2 **large eggs**
¼ **cup unsweetened cocoa powder**
1 **tablespoon plus 2 teaspoons all-purpose flour**
½ **cup coarsely chopped walnuts or pecans**
3 **ounces semisweet chocolate, at room temperature, grated**
½ **cup plus 2 tablespoons dark corn syrup**

1 Preheat the oven to 425°F and set out a 9-inch pie plate. Roll, shape, and flute the pie shell. Prick the shell all over with a fork. Completely prebake the shell for 15 minutes or until golden (see Blind-Baking, page 12). Cool on a rack. Reduce the oven temperature to 350°F.

2 In a heavy medium-size saucepan, combine the ¾ cup sugar and the water and bring to a boil. Brush down the sides of the pan with a wet pastry brush and cook, without stirring, until the syrup reaches 234° to 236°F on a candy thermometer. (A little of the syrup dropped in cold water will form a soft ball.) Immediately remove from the heat.

3 Meanwhile, in a heatproof bowl, with an electric mixer on HIGH, beat the eggs until foamy. Reduce the speed to

MEDIUM and gradually beat the hot sugar syrup into the eggs. Continue beating about 10 minutes or until mixture is cool.

4 Onto a piece of waxed paper, sift together the cocoa and flour. Gently but thoroughly fold the mixture into the cooled egg mixture, a tablespoon at a time. Fold in the walnuts and chocolate, then stir in the corn syrup.

5 Pour the filling into the baked pie shell. Bake for 30 to 40 minutes or until the filling is puffed and slightly cracked on top. Transfer the pie to a rack, sprinkle with a little additional sugar, and let cool slightly. The pie will fall a little, but that's just fine. Store in refrigerator.

1/8 pie = 377 calories, 19 g fat (6 g saturated), 68 mg cholesterol, 49 g carbohydrates, 6 g protein, 120 mg sodium, 1 g fiber

CHOCOLATE RASPBERRY HEART PIE

Not a cookie, not a candy, not a cake — but a cookie-candy-brownie pie. Bake the batter in two pans — a round one lined with pie pastry and a square one lined with foil. Cut and shape into a heart and frost, then top with juicy red raspberries.

MAKES ONE 12-INCH HEART PIE
PREP TIME 1 HR ✦ BAKE TIME 25 MIN
COOL TIME 2 HR

½ recipe BUTTERY CRUST
   (page 15)

CHOCOLATE HEART BROWNIE
1 cup (2 sticks) unsalted butter (not margarine)
3 ounces bittersweet chocolate
2 ounces unsweetened chocolate
1½ cups sifted all-purpose flour
1 teaspoon salt
4 large eggs
2 cups granulated sugar
1½ tablespoons vanilla extract
2 cups chopped walnuts

FUDGY FRENCH BUTTERCRÈME
½ cup (1 stick) unsalted butter (not margarine), at room temperature
4 cups sifted confectioners' sugar
¼ teaspoon salt
¼ cup light cream, plus 1 tablespoon if needed
2 teaspoons vanilla extract
6 ounces unsweetened chocolate, melted and cooled (page 21)

4 cups fresh raspberries

1 Preheat the oven to 325°F. Line one 8-inch square baking pan with a double-layer of foil, leaving a 1-inch overhang. Butter one 8-inch round baking pan with a removable bottom. Mix, shape, and flute the pastry in the round pan, then refrigerate. In a small saucepan, melt the butter and both chocolates, then cool. Onto a piece of waxed paper, sift the flour and salt.

2 In a large bowl, with an electric mixer on HIGH, beat the eggs until foamy. Blend in the granulated sugar, then the cooled chocolate mixture and the vanilla. With a spoon, stir in the flour mixture, then the walnuts.

3 Divide the batter evenly between the 2 pans. Bake for 25 minutes or just until a pick inserted in the center comes out almost clean. (Do not overbake.) Cool for 30 minutes. Transfer the round brownie in its shell from pan onto a rack. Lift the square brownie out of its pan onto the rack by grasping the edges of the foil. Peel away foil. Cool completely.

4 While the brownies cool, make the Fudgy French Buttercrème. In a large bowl, combine butter, confectioners' sugar, salt, cream, and vanilla. Pour in the cooled chocolate and stir to blend. Using an electric mixer on HIGH, beat frosting until very smooth and thick, adding a little more cream if necessary to reach spreading consistency.

5 On a large serving plate, place the square brownie pie, with one point at the bottom. Cut the round brownie into 2 equal semicircles. Place the semicircles at the top of the square brownie, with the cut sides against the two edges of the square and the pastry edges on the outside. "Glue" the cut edges of the semicircles to the square with a little buttercrème, forming a heart. Frost the sides of the square brownie (but not the pastry sides of the semicircles). Frost the top of the heart. Completely cover the top with the raspberries, pointed ends up.

1/24 heart pie = 470 calories, 28 g fat (10 g saturated), 78 mg cholesterol, 54 g carbohydrates, 5 g protein, 152 mg sodium, 6 g fiber

TOLL HOUSE COOKIE PIE

Here's my favorite version of the famous Toll House Cookie. The mini chocolate chips melt as the pie bakes, creating a marbled effect. Delicious when served warm with a scoop of ice cream.

MAKES ONE 14-INCH PIE
PREP TIME 30 MIN ✦ BAKE TIME 25 MIN

TOLL HOUSE COOKIE PIE
2 cups sifted all-purpose flour
1 teaspoon baking powder
¾ teaspoon salt
¾ cup (1½ sticks) unsalted butter (not margarine), at room temperature
½ cup granulated sugar
½ cup packed light brown sugar
2 large eggs
⅓ cup milk
1 tablespoon vanilla extract

1½ cups (9 ounces) mini semisweet chocolate chips
1 cup chopped pecans

CHOCOLATE DRIZZLE
½ cup (3 ounces) mini semisweet chocolate chips, melted (page 21)
Coffee ice cream (optional)

1 Preheat the oven to 350°F and butter a 14-inch round deep-dish quiche dish or pizza pan with 2-inch sides. Onto a piece of waxed paper, sift the flour, baking powder, and salt.

2 In a large bowl, with an electric mixer on HIGH, cream the butter and both sugars until light. Beat in the eggs, one at a time, then the milk. Stir in the flour mixture just until it disappears, then blend in the vanilla. Fold in the chocolate chips and pecans. Evenly spread the batter in the pan.

3 Bake for 25 minutes or until a pick inserted in the center comes out almost clean. Drizzle the melted chips over the cookie pie. Serve wedges of the warm cookie pie right from the pan, with coffee ice cream if you wish.

1/16 cookie pie = 336 calories, 19 g fat (6 g saturated), 51 mg cholesterol, 43 g carbohydrates, 4 g protein, 149 mg sodium, 1 g fiber

♦ *Chocolate Raspberry Heart Pie in a fluted Buttery Crust*

To assemble:

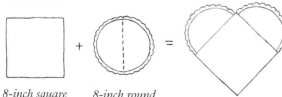

8-inch square   8-inch round   Completed
(no crust)   (with crust)   heart pie
                    cut in half

ROCKY ROAD SUNDAE PIE

This pie is reminiscent of the chunky "rocky" candy made of marshmallows, nuts, and chocolate. To cut the fat and calories, use nonfat or low-fat ice cream to make the Rocky Road Filling and omit the nuts.

MAKES ONE 10-INCH DEEP-DISH PIE
PREP TIME 30 MIN ◆ BAKE TIME 10 MIN
FREEZE TIME 2½ HR OR OVERNIGHT

1 recipe CHOCOLATE COOKIE
   CRUMB CRUST (page 17)

ROCKY ROAD FILLING

1 pint coffee ice cream
3 pints chocolate ice cream, divided
1 cup miniature marshmallows
   (about 2 ounces)
¾ cup chopped toasted pecans
   (page 21)

HOT FUDGE SAUCE

6 ounces semisweet chocolate
½ cup cold heavy (whipping) cream
¼ cup light corn syrup
   Pinch of salt
3 tablespoons unsalted butter (not
   margarine)
1 teaspoon vanilla extract

1 Preheat the oven to 350°F and butter a freezer-proof 10-inch deep-dish pie plate. Press the crumb mixture over the bottom and up the sides of the pie plate. Bake for 10 minutes or until set. Cool.

2 Soften the coffee ice cream (see tip box at right) and spread into the cooled crust. Place in the freezer to harden for about 15 minutes. Meanwhile, soften 1 pint of the chocolate ice cream in a large bowl. Stir in the marshmallows and pecans. Spread on top of the coffee layer. Cover and freeze 15 minutes more.

3 Scoop the remaining 2 pints chocolate ice cream on top of the pie, mounding the scoops high in the center to resemble a "bed of rocks." Wrap and freeze for at least 2 hours. Store in the freezer. To slice, let the pie stand at room temperature for about 15 minutes (see Baker's Tip, page 121).

4 Meanwhile, chop the chocolate for the Hot Fudge Sauce. In a heavy saucepan, heat the cream, corn syrup, and salt over medium heat just until bubbles start to form around the edge (do not boil). Add the chocolate, butter, and vanilla and heat, stirring constantly, until smooth. To serve, spoon a little of the hot sauce onto the bottom of each dessert plate. Top with a slice of pie and drizzle more sauce over the top.

¹/₁₂ pie = 396 calories, 29 g fat (12 g saturated), 59 mg cholesterol, 55 g carbohydrates, 5 g protein, 246 mg sodium, 1 g fiber

◆ **SOFTENING ICE CREAM** ◆

Ice cream too hard to scoop out? Loosen the cover of the container and set it on an angle. Microwave the ice cream in its container on HIGH for 4 to 5 seconds.

To soften ice cream enough to spread into a pie, *microwave the ice cream on MEDIUM, right in its container. Check and stir every 20 seconds, until the ice cream softens throughout, just until it reaches spreading consistency. Watch carefully, as it should not be allowed to melt.*

◆ **STORING FUDGE SAUCE** ◆

Fudge sauce left over? *It stores well in a covered jar in the refrigerator for up to 2 weeks. To serve, spoon the sauce into a small microwave-proof bowl, cover with plastic wrap, and warm in the microwave on HIGH for 1½ to 2 minutes, stirring frequently. Or place in a small saucepan and stir over MEDIUM-LOW heat for 4 to 5 minutes.*

CHOCOLATE CHESS PIE

Chess pie is a simple pie, quickly made from few ingredients: mainly eggs, sugar, and milk or cream. Add chocolate and you have a deep chocolate, very rich, very serious pie.

MAKES ONE 9-INCH PIE
PREP TIME 30 MIN ◆ BAKE TIME 35 MIN
COOL TIME 2 HR

½ recipe BUTTERY CRUST (page 15)

CHOCOLATE CHESS FILLING

½ cup (1 stick) unsalted butter (not
   margarine), at room temperature
3 ounces bittersweet or semisweet
   chocolate, chopped
¾ cup packed light brown sugar
¾ cup granulated sugar
1 tablespoon all-purpose flour

3 large eggs
1 cup light cream
1 tablespoon vanilla extract
¼ cup blanched almonds, chopped

1 Preheat the oven to 325°F and set out a 9-inch pie plate. Roll, shape, flute, and chill the pie shell.

2 In a saucepan, melt the butter and chocolate over low heat. Set aside to cool. In a small bowl, mix both sugars and the flour; set aside. In a large bowl, whisk the eggs until frothy. Whisk in the sugar mixture, then the chocolate mixture, cream and vanilla until well blended. Pour into the unbaked pie shell.

3 Bake for 20 minutes, sprinkle with the almonds, and bake 15 minutes more or just until set and a knife inserted halfway between the edge and the center comes out clean. Cool on a rack for at least 2 hours before serving. Refrigerate.

¹/₉ pie = 523 calories, 30 g fat (14 g saturated), 141 mg cholesterol, 59 g carbohydrates, 6 g protein, 109 mg sodium, 1 g fiber

◆ *Rocky Road Sundae Pie with Hot Fudge Sauce*

CUSTARD &
CREAM
PISS

♥

*These pies come filled with delicate vanilla
custards or heavenly creams that melt in your
mouth. Some take a slice out of history, with Olde
English custard pudding pies and slip-slide
coconut custard ones. Others serve up regional and
down-home traditions — such as key lime pie,
pecan pie, and maple sugar pies. There are modern
impossible pies, plus old-fashioned pumpkin, mile-
high lemon, and new-fashioned cheesecake pies.
Enjoy the simple pleasures of these custards and
creams, served up in a pie.*

✦ *Slip-Slide Coconut Custard Pie, slipped into a crust
with a fancy leaf edging, (see recipe, page 104)*

TYLER SUGAR PIE

Rich, sweet, and representative of presidential fare. Tyler Sugar Pie, named for the tenth U.S. president, usually includes both brown and white sugars. Southern cooks often sprinkled the pie shell with a little sugar before pouring in the filling. On some plantations, toasted coconut was sprinkled on top during the last few minutes of baking. In Newfoundland, sugar pies are baked with molasses or maple sugar. Stir raisins into the filling and you have an Osgood pie (Oh-so-good) pie.

MAKES ONE 9-INCH PIE
PREP TIME 30 MIN ✦ BAKE TIME 35 MIN
CHILL TIME 2 HR

½ recipe **CRISP FLAKY CRUST (page 15)**

TWO-SUGAR CUSTARD
- ¾ **cup packed light brown sugar**
- ¾ **cup granulated sugar**
- ¾ **cup cold heavy (whipping) cream**
- 6 **tablespoons (¾ stick) unsalted butter (not margarine), cut into pieces**
- ¼ **teaspoon salt**
- 4 **large eggs**
- ½ **teaspoon maple extract**
- 2 **tablespoons flaked coconut, toasted (page 21)**

1 Preheat the oven to 375°F and butter a 9-inch pie plate. Roll, shape, and flute the pie shell. In a small bowl, toss both of the sugars together. Measure out ¼ cup of the sugar mixture and sprinkle over the bottom of the pie shell. Chill.

2 In a heavy medium-size saucepan, combine the remaining 1¼ cups of the sugar mixture, the cream, butter, and salt. Stir constantly over medium-high heat until smooth and melted, then remove from the heat. In a large heatproof bowl, with an electric mixer on HIGH, beat the eggs until thick and light yellow. Gradually beat in the hot cream mixture and the maple extract.

3 Pour the filling into the unbaked shell. Bake the pie for 30 minutes, then sprinkle with the coconut and bake 5 minutes more or until a kitchen knife inserted halfway between the edge of the pie and the center comes out clean. Chill for at least 2 hours or until serving time. Store any leftover pie in the refrigerator.

1/9 pie = 454 calories, 27 g fat (15 g saturated), 156 mg cholesterol, 50 g carbohydrates, 5 g protein, 171 mg sodium, 1 g fiber

OSGOOD PIE Prepare filling (Step 2) then add ½ cup golden raisins and ½ teaspoon of ground cinnamon.

SLIP-SLIDE COCONUT CUSTARD PIE

One of the simplest of pies there is, made from milk, sugar, eggs, and coconut. Bake the custard and the shell in separate pie plates, then gently slide the filling into the baked shell. The shell bakes crisp and never gets soggy (see photo, pages 102–103).

MAKES ONE 9-INCH PIE
PREP TIME 30 MIN ✦ BAKE TIME 55 MIN
COOL TIME 45 MIN

1 recipe **PÂTE BRISÉE (page 15)**

SLIP-SLIDE CUSTARD
- 4 **large eggs**
- ½ **cup sugar**
- ½ **teaspoon salt**
- 1 **tablespoon vanilla extract**
- ½ **teaspoon coconut extract**
- 2½ **cups milk**
- 1 **cup flaked coconut (fresh or canned)**
- ¼ **teaspoon ground nutmeg**

1 Preheat the oven to 400°F and butter two identical 9-inch pie plates. Roll half of the pastry, then shape shell with a flat edge in one of the pie plates. Prick the shell. Decorate edge with leaves cut from remaining dough (see page 13). Prebake for 15 minutes or until golden (see Blind-Baking, page 12). Cool on a rack. Reduce oven temperature to 350°F.

2 In a large bowl, with an electric mixer on HIGH, beat the eggs until foamy. Beat in the sugar, salt, vanilla, and coconut extract. In a small saucepan, over medium heat, bring the milk just to a simmer, then beat into filling. Stir in the coconut. Pour the filling into the second pie plate. Sprinkle with the nutmeg.

3 Set this pie plate with the filling in a shallow baking pan. Pour in enough boiling water to come halfway up the sides of the plate (see right, top). Bake for 40 minutes or until almost set and a knife inserted halfway between the center and the edge of the custard comes out clean. Cool for 45 minutes.

4 With a small spatula, gently lift the custard away from the pie plate. Shake to loosen the custard. Holding the plate over the baked pie shell, slip the custard into the shell (see right, bottom). Gently shake the custard to settle in place. Serve warm. Store in refrigerator.

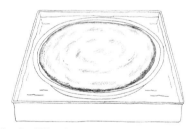

Bake the filling in a water bath. Fill the pan with water so it is halfway up the sides of the pie plate

Shake and slip-slide custard into its baked shell

1/9 pie = 358 calories, 18 g fat (11 g saturated), 133 mg cholesterol, 29 g carbohydrates, 7 g protein, 238 mg sodium, 2 g fiber

PAT-IN-THE-PAN BERRY TART

Here's one of the simplest French fruit tarts. Its crust is a buttery shortbread, its filling the rich pastry cream called Crème Pâtissière, and its topping a mix of fresh berries. Raspberries and blueberries work best, as strawberries will soften the filling.

MAKES ONE 12-INCH TART
PREP TIME 45 MIN ✦ BAKE TIME 15 MIN
CHILL TIME 3½ HR

1 recipe **PAT-IN-THE-PAN CRUST (page 18)**

VERY BERRY FILLING

½ cup granulated sugar
3 tablespoons cornstarch
2⅓ cups light cream or half-and-half
3 large egg yolks
2 tablespoons unsalted butter (not margarine), cut into pieces
2 teaspoons vanilla extract
1 to 2 teaspoons grated lemon zest (page 21)
2 cups fresh blueberries, stems removed
2 cups fresh raspberries
½ cup currant jelly, melted

Mint leaves (optional)

1 Preheat the oven to 350°F. Butter a 12-inch tart pan with a removable bottom. Mix, shape, and trim the shell, then prick it all over with a fork. Bake the shell for 15 minutes or until golden, (see Blind-Baking, page 12). Cool.

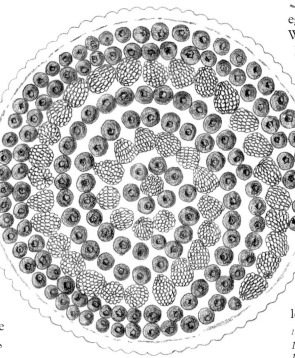

Arrange the berries in alternating spirals to create a decorative pinwheel (see photo, pages 4–5)

2 In a medium-size saucepan, mix the sugar and cornstarch. Whisk in the cream. Cook over medium-high heat for 5 minutes or until the mixture boils and thickens. Remove the custard from heat.

3 Meanwhile, in a medium bowl, with an electric mixer on HIGH, beat the egg yolks until light yellow and thick. Whisk in 1 cup of the hot cream mixture. Return this mixture to the pan and cook over low heat 3 minutes more (do not boil). Remove from the heat, stir in the butter, vanilla, and lemon zest. Pour the custard into the shell and lay a piece of plastic wrap directly on the warm filling. Chill for 30 minutes.

4 Remove the plastic wrap and arrange the berries in a pinwheel design on top of the tart, alternating the types of berry (see left). Brush with the melted jelly, then chill for at least 3 hours. Garnish the center of the tart with fresh mint leaves if you wish. Store any leftover tart in the refrigerator.

1/12 tart = 463 calories, 28 g fat (17 saturated), 131 mg cholesterol, 50 g carbohydrates, 5 g protein, 116 mg sodium, 3 g fiber

PECAN ORCHARD PIE

Wharton, Texas, lies in the heart of pecan country. Hinze's Bar-B-Que Cafe is famous — not only for its pecan-smoked barbecue, but also for Rosemary Hinze's homemade pies. Her pecan pie has a deep, rich, translucent custard filling, made with brown sugar and chock-full of pecans. All translucent custard pies contain no milk and more sugar than creamy custard pies.

MAKES ONE 9-INCH DEEP-DISH PIE
PREP TIME 30 MIN ✦ BAKE TIME 45 MIN
COOL TIME 2 HR

½ recipe **CRISP FLAKY CRUST (page 15)**

PECAN FILLING

5 large eggs
1¼ cups sugar
½ cup light corn syrup
½ cup dark corn syrup
1 tablespoon vanilla extract
1⅓ cups coarsely chopped pecans

1 Preheat the oven to 350°F and butter a 9-inch deep-dish pie plate. Roll, shape, flute, and chill the pie shell.

2 In a large bowl, lightly whisk the eggs. Stir in the sugar, both the light and the dark corn syrups, the vanilla, and pecans just until blended. Do not overmix, as this may cause the pecans to stay on the bottom of the pie and prevent them from rising to the top during baking. Pour the pie filling into the unbaked shell.

3 Bake the pie for 45 minutes or until it is puffed and golden brown. When the pie is ready to come out of the oven, the pecans will have risen to the top and the top of the pie will have cracked slightly. As the pie cools, it may settle slightly, but that's fine. Cool the pie at room temperature for at least 2 hours or until set. Store in the refrigerator.

1/9 pie = 511 calories, 23 g fat (6 g saturated), 132 mg cholesterol, 72 g carbohydrates, 7 g protein, 131 mg sodium, 2 g fiber

BOSTON CREAM PIE

Today's Boston Cream Pie is lighter than the one first baked in the 1850s. It's now three layers of a light moist cake and two of pastry cream. It's topped with a thin layer of chocolate, only about one third as much chocolate as the original used. The chocolate topping is swirled with a web of white icing and the sides are adorned with toasted almonds.

MAKES ONE 10-INCH PIE
PREP TIME 1 HR ✦ BAKE TIME 25 MIN
COOL / CHILL TIME 3 HR

PASTRY CREAM

- 2 **cups light cream**
- 2 **cups milk**
- 1 **tablespoon unsalted butter (not margarine), cut into pieces**
- 6 **large eggs**
- ½ **cup granulated sugar**
- 3½ **tablespoons cornstarch**
- 1 **teaspoon dark rum or vanilla extract**
- ½ **cup cold heavy (whipping) cream**

SPONGE LAYERS

- 7 **large eggs, separated**
- 1 **cup granulated sugar, divided**
- 1 **cup all-purpose flour**
- 2 **tablespoons unsalted butter (not margarine), melted**

ICINGS

- 6 **ounces semisweet chocolate**
- ¼ **cup water, divided**
- 1 **cup sifted confectioners' sugar**
- 1 **teaspoon light corn syrup**
- ½ **cup sliced almonds, toasted**

1 In a large saucepan, bring the cream, milk, and butter to a boil over medium-high heat. Remove from the heat. In a large bowl, with an electric mixer on HIGH, beat the eggs, granulated sugar, and cornstarch for 3 minutes or until light yellow and thick. Stir about 1 cup of the hot cream mixture into the egg mixture, then return this mixture to the saucepan. Return to a boil and cook for 1 minute. Transfer the Pastry Cream to a bowl, lay a piece of plastic wrap on the surface. Chill for at least 3 hours.

2 Meanwhile, preheat oven to 350°F and butter a 10-inch nonstick springform pan. In a large bowl, with the mixer on HIGH, beat the egg whites and ½ cup of the granulated sugar with clean beaters until soft peaks form. In another bowl, beat the yolks with the remaining ½ cup of granulated sugar for 3 minutes or until light yellow and thick.

3 Fold one third of the egg whites into the yolks, then gently fold in the remaining whites (do not overmix). Fold in the flour, then the butter. Spoon the batter into the pan. Bake for about 25 minutes or until the cake is golden and a pick inserted in the center comes out clean. Cool the cake in the pan on a rack for 30 minutes. Remove the sides of the pan, then slide the cake onto a rack and cool completely (about 2 hours).

4 Stir the rum into the chilled Pastry Cream. In a small bowl, with an electric mixer on HIGH, beat the cream until soft peaks form. Fold into the Pastry Cream. Refrigerate 1½ cups of the Pastry Cream (for icing the sides). Melt the chocolate for the icing with 3 tablespoons of the water (see page 21) and set aside.

5 Using a long serrated knife, slice the cake horizontally into 3 even layers. Place the bottom cake layer on a platter. Spread half of the remaining Pastry Cream on top of the bottom layer. Top with the second cake layer, spread with the other half of the Pastry Cream, and cover with the third cake layer.

6 To decorate, spread the melted chocolate on top. In a small bowl, whisk the confectioners' sugar, corn syrup, and the remaining tablespoon of water until smooth. Using a pastry bag fitted with a small round tip (#3 or #4), or a cone made from

parchment paper, pipe a spiral of the white icing, starting from the center of the cake (see facing page, left). Quickly score the spiral with the point of a paring knife in alternating directions, making a web design (see facing page, center). Spread sides with the reserved Pastry Cream and press in the almonds (see facing page, right).

1/16 pie = 383 calories, 21 g fat (9 g saturated), 213 mg cholesterol, 43 g carbohydrates, 9 g protein, 83 mg sodium, 1 g fiber

UPSIDE-DOWN BUTTERMILK PIE

This easy pie made from a baking mix comes out of the oven with a golden cake-like layer on top and a cream custard below.

MAKES ONE 9-INCH DEEP-DISH PIE
PREP TIME 15 MIN ✦ BAKE TIME 45 MIN
STANDING TIME 5 MIN

- 1⅓ **cups sugar**
- 1 **cup buttermilk**
- ½ **cup packaged baking mix**
- ⅓ **cup unsalted butter (not margarine), melted**
- 1 **teaspoon vanilla extract**
- 3 **large eggs, slightly beaten**

- 1 **cup fresh blackberries or raspberries**

1 Preheat the oven to 350°F and butter a 9-inch deep-dish pie plate.

2 Into a large bowl, put all of the ingredients except the blackberries and stir just until blended. With an electric mixer on HIGH, beat for 1 minute or until smooth and creamy.

3 Pour the batter into the pie plate and bake for 45 minutes or until a kitchen knife inserted in the center comes out clean. Let the pie stand on a wire rack for 5 minutes. Serve warm with the berries.

1/8 pie = 273 calories, 11 g fat (6 g saturated), 103 mg cholesterol, 41 g carbohydrates, 4 g protein, 145 mg sodium, 2 g fiber

---

✦ A CAKE OR A PIE? ✦

French Chef Sanzian, while working at the Parker House Hotel in Boston, Massachusetts, in 1855, topped an English cream cake with chocolate frosting, creating the first Boston Cream Pie. Technically, it's more a cake than a pie. But Sanzian first presented it in a metal pie tin. Therefore, it has always been called a pie.

✦ *Boston Cream Pie*

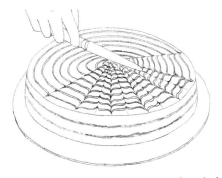

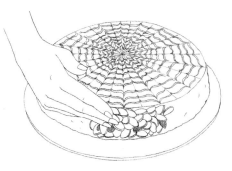

To decorate the pie, make a spiral of white icing on top of the chocolate glaze, starting at the center and piping in one continuous line out to the edge

Create a web by pulling a knife across the spiral in alternating directions — from the edge of pie to the center, then from the center back to the edge

Press almonds into the pastry cream to cover the sides completely

MARTHA WASHINGTON'S PIE

Whether at Mount Vernon or in the executive mansion, the first U.S. President and his wife entertained formally and often. Their menus were elaborate and ended with many dessert offerings — sweet pudding baked in a paste (pastry), ice creams, jellies, fruits, and nuts. This rich custard pie topped with fresh raspberry sauce is typical of the desserts of Martha Washington's day.

MAKES ONE 9-INCH DEEP-DISH PIE
PREP TIME 45 MIN ✦ BAKE TIME 15 MIN
COOL / CHILL TIME 3¼ HR

½ **recipe PÂTE SUCRÉE (page 15), or PÂTE BRISÉE (page 15)**

LEMON CREAM FILLING
1¼ **cups granulated sugar**
¼ **cup all-purpose flour**
¼ **cup cornstarch**
¼ **teaspoon salt**
2 **cups milk**
1 **cup light cream**
4 **large egg yolks**
2 **tablespoons unsalted butter (not margarine)**
1 **tablespoon vanilla extract**
1 **teaspoon grated lemon zest (page 21)**

RASPBERRY SPOON SAUCE
1 **cup fresh raspberries**
½ **cup superfine sugar**

1 Preheat the oven to 400°F and butter a 9-inch deep-dish pie plate. Pick a pastry recipe. Roll, shape, and flute the pie shell. Prick the shell all over with a fork. Completely prebake the shell for 15 minutes or until golden (see Blind-Baking, page 12). Cool on a wire rack.

2 In a medium-size saucepan, mix the granulated sugar, flour, cornstarch, and salt. Whisk in the milk and cream until the sugar mixture has completely dissolved. Cook the custard, whisking occasionally, over medium heat for 8 minutes or just until the mixture comes to a full boil and thickens. Remove the custard from the heat.

3 Meanwhile, in a small bowl with an electric mixer on HIGH, beat the egg yolks until light yellow and thick. Stir about 1 cup of the hot milk mixture into the eggs, then return this mixture to the saucepan. Cook over low heat and stir for 2 minutes or until thickened (do not let boil). Remove the custard from the heat and stir in the butter, vanilla, and lemon zest. Pour the custard filling into the baked shell. To prevent a skin from forming, lay a piece of plastic wrap directly on the filling. Cool the pie on a rack for 15 minutes. Refrigerate for at least 3 hours or until serving time.

4 Meanwhile, in a food processor or blender, process the raspberries with the superfine sugar until almost smooth. Spoon some of this Raspberry Spoon Sauce onto each dessert plate and place a serving of pie on top. Store any leftover pie and sauce in the refrigerator.

1/9 pie = 406 calories, 18 g fat (10 g saturated), 164 mg cholesterol, 52 g carbohydrates, 6 g protein, 171 mg sodium, 1 g fiber

MRS. COOLIDGE'S CUSTARD PIE

In the 1920s, Grace Coolidge, wife of the 30th U.S. President, brought warm hospitality to the White House — with carol sings at Christmas, large receptions for hundreds, and fireside teas for a few. This simple, elegant pie is reminiscent of her party tables.

MAKES ONE 8-INCH PIE
PREP TIME 30 MIN ✦ BAKE TIME 50 MIN
COOL / CHILL TIME 3 HR

½ **recipe BUTTERY CRUST (page 15)**

CUSTARD FILLING
3 **large eggs**
½ **cup sugar**
¾ **teaspoon vanilla extract**
½ **teaspoon salt**
¼ **teaspoon ground nutmeg**
2 **cups milk**

1 **recipe Decorator's Whipped Cream (page 20)**
½ **cup strawberry jelly**

1 Preheat the oven to 350°F and butter an 8-inch pie plate. Roll, shape, and flute the pie shell. Chill until ready to fill.

2 In a medium-size bowl, with an electric mixer on HIGH, beat the eggs until light yellow and thick. Beat in the sugar, vanilla, salt, and nutmeg, then the milk. Pour into the unbaked shell.

3 Bake for 50 to 55 minutes, or until a kitchen knife inserted in the center comes out clean. Lay a piece of plastic wrap on the warm filling, and chill for 3 hours or until serving time.

4 Pipe or spoon the Decorator's Whipped Cream around the edge of the pie (see right, top). Decorate the top with triangles of jelly (see right, bottom). Store any leftover pie in the refrigerator.

1/8 pie = 46 calories, 24 g fat (13 g saturated), 157 mg cholesterol, 52 g carbohydrates, 8 g protein, 234 mg sodium, 1 g fiber

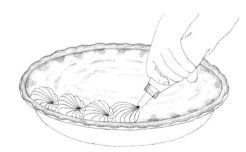

Pipe a ring of whipped cream around the edge

Decorate the center with triangles of jelly

CHESS PIE

Chess pie is "jes' pie," as one Southern folktale goes. Another story relates it to a "chest pie," or one that was stored in a pie chest with perforated tin panels. However it got its name, chess pie is simple pie, made from a basic rich egg custard and often flavored with lemon. This easy recipe makes one of the best I have tasted. It comes from Illustrator and Restaurateur Carrie Arnold at The Fort in Denver, Colorado.

MAKES ONE 8-INCH PIE
PREP TIME 15 MIN ✦ BAKE TIME 35 MIN
COOL TIME 2 HR

½ **recipe** PÂTE BRISÉE **(page 15)**

CUSTARD FILLING
1 **extra-large lemon**
¾ **cup sugar**
4 **large whole eggs**
2 **tablespoons unsalted butter (not margarine), at room temperature**

1 Preheat the oven to 350°F and butter an 8-inch pie plate. Roll, shape, and flute the pie shell. Prick the shell all over with a fork. Partially prebake the shell for 10 minutes or just until set (see Blind-Baking, page 12). Cool on a wire rack. Leave the oven set at 350°F.

2 Using a lemon zester or a sharp peeler, remove all of the thin, yellow zest of the lemon, leaving all of the white rind. Set the yellow zest aside. On a chopping board, cut the lemon lengthwise in half. Place each half cut-side down on the board. Trim away and discard all of the white rind. Cut the lemon into 1-inch chunks. Discard seeds.

3 In a food processor or blender, process the lemon sections, the lemon zest, the sugar, eggs, and butter until the mixture is well blended but not smooth. Bits of lemon should still remain. Pour the filling into the partially baked shell. Bake for 25 to 30 minutes or until a kitchen knife inserted in the center comes out clean. Cool for 2 hours. Serve at room temperature or chilled. Store any leftover pie in the refrigerator.

⅛ pie = 272 calories, 13 g fat (7 g saturated), 134 mg cholesterol, 34 g carbohydrates, 5 g protein, 111 mg sodium, 1 g fiber

✦ PUDDING PIES THROUGH HISTORY ✦

IN THE MID-1700S IN ENGLAND, "All Sorts of Puddings" were desserts of their day, as recorded in THE COMPLEAT HOUSEWIFE by Eliza Smith. These creations were actually more pies then puddings. "Put a bit of fine puff paste (PASTRY) about the brim and bottom of your dish ... put in the (orange) pudding and bake it." Often, the fancier, the better. MRS. BEETON'S COOKERY BOOK includes an Apple Amber Pudding, baked in a pie dish with thin strips of paste, decorated on the edge with overlapping leaves. In France, puff paste was spread with rich pastry crème and artistically decorated with fresh fruits.

ACROSS THE ATLANTIC in Quebec, creamy egg puddings were sweetened with maple sugar and baked into sugar pies. And throughout Canada, rich egg-cream fillings were baked into butter tarts, often laced with currants and nuts.

PRESIDENTIAL PUDDINGS baked into pies are a slice of America's history. Martha Washington baked lemon chess cakes, which were not cakes at all but chess pie fillings in shells. Her writings feature a Bake'd Almond Pudding that's more an almond custard pie than a pudding. It bakes an egg custard with "halfe a pound of blanch'd & beaten almonds and 2 or 3 spoonfulls of rose water," under a puff paste.

At Thomas Jefferson's Monticello home, Pineapple Pudding was baked two ways: either with or without a puff paste lining the dish. President John Tyler offered his guests a rich egg custard in a shell, sprinkled with toasted coconut. And Eleanor and Franklin D. Roosevelt frequently ended their White House dinner parties with pecan custard pies, topped with whipped cream rosettes and tiny leaves baked from leftover pastry.

MARLBOROUGH TART

New England settlers liked their apple pies. When apples were out of season, they made apple-custard pies from applesauce, traditionally put up during the fall harvest. This recipe comes from the pages of the AMERICAN HERITAGE COOKBOOK.

MAKES ONE 9-INCH PIE
PREP TIME 30 MIN ✦ BAKE TIME 55 MIN
COOL / CHILL TIME 2 HR

½ **recipe** BUTTERY CRUST **(page 15)**

MARLBOROUGH TART FILLING
½ **cup applesauce**
¼ **cup sugar**
⅔ **cup light cream**
1 **teaspoon grated lemon zest (page 21)**
3 **tablespoons fresh lemon juice**
¼ **cup sherry**
3 **large eggs, well beaten**

1 Preheat the oven to 400°F and butter a 9-inch pie plate. Roll, shape, and flute the pie shell. Refrigerate the shell while you make the filling.

2 In a large bowl, stir together the applesauce, sugar, cream, lemon zest, lemon juice, and sherry until blended.

3 In a medium-size bowl, with an electric mixer on HIGH, beat the eggs until light yellow and thick. Gently fold the eggs into the applesauce mixture.

4 Pour the apple filling into the chilled shell and bake for 10 minutes. Reduce the oven temperature to 325°F and bake the pie 45 minutes more or until the center is almost set. Cool the pie on a wire rack for 1 hour, then chill for at least 1 hour. Store any leftover pie in the refrigerator.

⅛ tart = 256 calories, 14 g fat (7 g saturated), 108 mg cholesterol, 26 g carbohydrates, 5 g protein, 99 mg sodium, 1 g fiber

KEY LIME PIE

This traditional recipe comes from Pastry Chef Denise Leary of the garden Roof Top Cafe on the isle of Key West, Florida. The typical key lime filling is baked in a graham cracker crust, instead of a pastry one, and topped with meringue.

MAKES ONE 9-INCH DEEP-DISH PIE
PREP TIME 30 MIN ✦ BAKE TIME 20 MIN
COOL TIME 3 HR

1 recipe **GRAHAM CRACKER CRUMB CRUST** (page 17)

KEY LIME FILLING
4 **jumbo egg yolks**
3 **cups canned sweetened condensed milk (Eagle Brand preferred)**
1 **cup key lime juice (fresh or bottled)**

MERINGUE
5 **jumbo egg whites, at room temperature**
¼ **teaspoon cream of tartar**
1 **cup sugar**

1 Preheat the oven to 350°F and butter a 9-inch deep-dish pie plate. Press the crumb mixture over the bottom and up the sides of the pie plate, then refrigerate.

2 In a large bowl, with an electric mixer on HIGH, beat the egg yolks until light yellow and thick. Reduce the speed to MEDIUM. Beat in the condensed milk, then the lime juice just until the mixture thickens (do not overbeat as the custard may separate). Pour the filling into the unbaked crust. Bake the pie for 10 minutes, then transfer to a wire rack.

3 In a large bowl with an electric mixer on HIGH, beat the egg whites with the cream of tartar until fluffy. Gradually beat in the sugar until the meringue stands in glossy soft peaks. To "attach" the meringue, lightly score the filling with the prongs of a fork. Swirl the meringue in high peaks over the filling, mounding it in the center and sealing it well at the edges. Bake the pie for 10 minutes or just until golden. Let the pie cool for 3 hours or to room temperature before serving. Store in the refrigerator, then return to room temperature to serve.

1/9 pie = 651 calories, 21 g fat (12 g saturated), 174 mg cholesterol, 105 g carbohydrates, 14 g protein, 291 mg sodium, 1 g fiber

BANANA PRALINE PIE

Bananas were first imported from Cuba in 1804 and in 1876 were introduced as an exotic fruit for a "dime a banana" at the Philadelphia Centennial Exposition. By the 1900s, bananas were fast becoming one of our most popular fruits. Here, my mother's favorite recipe for banana pie. I've substituted brown sugar, for some of the white sugar, to give the pie a delicious praline flavor.

MAKES ONE 9-INCH DEEP DISH PIE
PREP TIME 45 MIN ✦ BAKE TIME 15 MIN
COOL / CHILL TIME 3¼ HR

½ recipe **BUTTERY CRUST** (page 15)

BANANA PRALINE CREAM FILLING
¾ **cup packed light brown sugar**
¼ **cup granulated sugar**
3 **tablespoons cornstarch**
2 **tablespoons all-purpose flour**
¼ **teaspoon salt**
1 **cup light cream**
1 **cup milk**
3 **large egg yolks**
1 **tablespoon unsalted butter (not margarine), at room temperature**
2 **teaspoons vanilla extract**
1 **teaspoon banana extract**
2 **cups slices ripe bananas (2 large)**

1 recipe **Decorator's Whipped Cream** (page 20)

1 Preheat the oven to 425°F and butter a 9-inch deep-dish pie plate. Roll, shape, and flute the pie shell. Prick the shell all over with a fork. Completely prebake the shell for 15 minutes or until golden (see Blind-Baking, page 12). Transfer the shell to a rack to cool. Reduce the oven temperature to 350°F.

2 In a medium-size saucepan, mix the sugars, cornstarch, flour, and salt. Slowly whisk in the cream and milk until smooth. Whisk constantly over medium heat for 8 minutes or until mixture boils and thickens. Remove from the heat.

3 Meanwhile, in a small bowl with an electric mixer on HIGH, beat the egg yolks until light yellow. Stir about 1 cup of the hot cream mixture into the yolks, then return this mixture to the saucepan. Stir over low heat for 2 minutes or until thickened (do not let boil). Remove from heat and stir in the butter and vanilla and banana extract. Cool for 15 minutes.

4 Spoon half of the filling into the baked shell. Cover with the banana slices, then the remaining filling. Lay a piece of plastic wrap directly on filling. Refrigerate the pie for at least 3 hours or until set. Pipe or spoon the Decorator's Whipped Cream around the edge and in the center of the pie. Refrigerate.

1/9 pie = 498 calories, 28 g fat (15 g saturated), 157 mg cholesterol, 56 g carbohydrates, 6 g protein, 172 mg sodium, 1 g fiber

BANANA CREAM PIE Increase the granulated sugar to 1 cup and omit the brown sugar.

> ✦ ISLAND LIMES ✦
>
> *In 1835, lime trees were planted in the Florida Keys which produced small yellowish limes with a highly aromatic, tart flavor, similar to very sour lemons. By the late 1850s, Key Lime Pies had made their debut. They coincided with the introduction of sweetened condensed milk, as fresh milk was scarce on the islands. Early pies were baked in a pastry crust, but now they're often made in a graham cracker crust. Originally pies were topped with a meringue. Today, they are often topped with whipped cream and even sometimes served frozen.*

◆ *Key Lime Pie*

COCONUT MERINGUE PIE

A rich creamy pie that bakes perfectly every time, thanks to the addition of a few tiny marshmallows to the filling.
It's a favorite selection with the "regulars" who dine frequently at Luby's Cafeterias.

MAKES ONE 9-INCH DEEP-DISH PIE
PREP TIME 15 MIN ✦ BAKE TIME 27 MIN
COOL / CHILL TIME 3 HOURS

½ **recipe BUTTERY CRUST
(page 15)**

COCONUT CREAM FILLING

2½ **cups half-and-half**
2 **tablespoons unsalted butter (not
margarine), at room temperature**
2 **large eggs**
½ **cup sugar**
2 **tablespoons cornstarch**
½ **teaspoon vanilla extract**
⅛ **teaspoon salt**
½ **cup miniature marshmallows
(about 1 ounce)**
1 **cup flaked coconut, divided**

MERINGUE

5 **large egg whites, at room
temperature**
½ **teaspoon cream of tartar**
⅔ **cup sugar**

1 Preheat the oven to 400°F and set out a 9-inch deep-dish pie plate. Roll, shape, and flute the pie shell. Prick it all over with a fork. Completely prebake the shell for 15 minutes or until golden (see Blind-Baking, page 12). Cool on a rack.

2 In a medium-size saucepan, stir the half-and-half and butter over medium heat just until the mixture comes to a boil. Remove from the heat. In a medium bowl, whisk together the eggs, the ½ cup sugar, cornstarch, vanilla, and salt until the cornstarch is completely dissolved. Stir about 1 cup of the hot half-and-half mixture into the eggs, then return this mixture to the saucepan. Cook and stir for 2 minutes or until thickened.

3 Stir the marshmallows and ¾ cup of the coconut into the hot custard. Cook, stirring occasionally, until the marshmallows melt and the mixture is blended. Remove from the heat. Gently spoon the filling into the baked shell. Lay a piece of plastic wrap directly on the warm filling. Refrigerate for at least 3 hours, or until set.

4 Preheat the oven to 350°F. In a medium-size bowl, with an electric mixer on HIGH, beat the egg whites with the cream of tartar until fluffy. Beat in the ⅔ cup sugar, 2 tablespoons at a time, and continue beating until the meringue stands in glossy soft peaks. Completely cover the filling with the meringue, sealing it well at the edges of the pie shell. Make high peaks with the back of a spoon as you go. Be sure no filling is peeking out. Sprinkle with the remaining ¼ cup of coconut. Bake for 12 to 15 minutes or until golden. Refrigerate.

1/9 pie = 440 calories, 23 g fat (13 g saturated), 105 mg cholesterol, 54 g carbohydrates, 8 g protein, 193 mg sodium, 1 g fiber

LEMON SOUR CREAM PIE

From Darlene Nolan comes this spectacular creation of the popular Florida Sour Cream Lemon Pie. She uses
less sugar in her pies than most recipes suggest, then replaces the traditional meringue with whipped cream and walnuts.

MAKES ONE 8-INCH PIE
PREP TIME 45 MIN ✦ BAKE TIME 15 MIN
COOL / CHILL TIME 2½ HOURS

½ **recipe BUTTERY CRUST
(page 15)**

LEMON SOUR CREAM FILLING

¾ **cup sugar**
¼ **cup cornstarch**
1 **teaspoon grated lemon zest**
¼ **teaspoon salt**
1⅓ **cups water**
½ **cup fresh lemon juice**
2 **large eggs**
1 **teaspoon unsalted butter (not
margarine), at room temperature**
½ **cup sour cream**

1 **recipe Decorator's Whipped Cream
(page 20)**

¼ **cup chopped walnuts
Candied Lemon Zest (page 21)**

1 Preheat the oven to 400°F and set out an 8-inch pie plate. Roll, shape, and flute the pie shell. Prick it all over with a fork. Completely prebake the pie shell for 15 minutes or until golden (see Blind-Baking, page 12). Cool on a rack.

2 In a medium-size saucepan, mix the sugar, cornstarch, lemon zest, and salt. Whisk in the water and lemon juice. Cook, whisking constantly, over medium heat for 5 minutes or just until the mixture comes to a full boil and thickens. (Whisk on the bottom to prevent filling from scorching.) Remove from the heat.

3 Meanwhile, in a small bowl, with an electric mixer on HIGH, beat the eggs until light yellow and thick. Stir about 1 cup of the hot sugar mixture into the eggs, then return this mixture to the saucepan. Cook and stir over low heat for 2 minutes or until thickened (do not let boil). Remove from the heat and stir in the butter. Cool for 30 minutes, then fold the sour cream into the filling. Spoon the filling into the baked crust and chill the pie for 1 hour.

4 Pipe or spoon the Decorator's Whipped Cream on top of the pie. Sprinkle with the walnuts and decorate with the Candied Lemon Zest. Refrigerate the pie at least 1 hour more or until set. Store in the refrigerator.

1/8 pie = 462 calories, 28 g fat (14 g saturated), 130 mg cholesterol, 47 g carbohydrates, 6 g protein, 183 mg sodium, 1 g fiber

◆ *Coconut Meringue Pie in a Buttery Crust*

JUNIOR'S STRAWBERRY CHEESE PIE

At Junior's restaurant in Brooklyn, New York, the Rosen family has been baking up their famous cheese pies since the 1930s. They begin each pie with a graham cracker crust, spoon on a rich cream cheese filling, and top with the prettiest strawberries.

MAKES ONE 9-INCH DEEP-DISH PIE
PREP TIME 30 MIN ✦ BAKE TIME 38 MIN
COOL / CHILL TIME 3 HR

1 recipe GRAHAM CRACKER
CRUMB CRUST (page 17)

CREAM CHEESE FILLING
¾ cup plus 2 tablespoons sugar
3 tablespoons cornstarch
30 ounces cream cheese, at room
temperature
1 jumbo egg
½ cup cold heavy (whipping) cream
¾ teaspoon vanilla extract

STRAWBERRY TOPPING
2 cups large, ripe fresh
strawberries, hulled
½ cup strawberry jelly, melted
½ cup chopped mixed nuts (almonds,
pecans, and/or walnuts)

1 Preheat the oven to 350°F and butter a 9-inch deep-dish pie plate. Press the graham cracker crumb mixture over the bottom and up the sides of the pie plate.

Bake for 8 to 10 minutes or just until set. Cool the pie crust on a wire rack. Increase the oven temperature to 375°F.

2 In a large bowl, combine the sugar and cornstarch. With an electric mixer on LOW, blend in the cream cheese. Beat in the egg, then beat in the cream, a little at a time. Beat in the vanilla. Mix the filling only until thoroughly blended, just like they do at Junior's. Do not overmix.

3 Spoon the filling into the baked crust. Bake the pie for 30 to 35 minutes or until puffed. The pie rises in the oven, then settles as it cools. Let the pie cool on a wire rack for 1 hour.

4 To make the Strawberry Topping, arrange the whole berries in circles on top of the pie, leaving a ½-inch border around the the edge. Spoon the warm jelly over the berries, covering the entire top of the pie. Sprinkle the nuts on the border of the pie. Refrigerate the pie for at least 2 hours or until serving time. If

there is any pie left over, cover with plastic wrap and store in refrigerator.

1/12 cheese pie = 573 calories, 39 g fat (22 g saturated), 129 mg cholesterol, 49 g carbohydrates, 9 g protein, 315 mg sodium, 2 g fiber

BLUEBERRY CHEESE PIE Substitute a 1-pound can of blueberry pie filling for the strawberries and strawberry jelly.

CHERRY CHEESE PIE Substitute a 1-pound can of cherry pie filling for the strawberries and strawberry jelly.

PINEAPPLE CHEESE PIE Make a pineapple topping to replace the strawberries and strawberry jelly: Drain the heavy syrup from a 1-pound can of crushed pineapple into a small saucepan. Mound the pineapple on top of the cooled baked cheese pie. Stir 2 tablespoons cornstarch and 1 tablespoon fresh lemon juice into the syrup. Bring to a boil over medium high and cook for 1 minute. Drizzle this sauce over the pineapple, covering the pie.

ANNIE B'S EVERYTHING CHEESE TART

Ann Bartholomay, a professional caterer and chef, bakes this cheese tart with a cookie crust for her clients who love chocolate. The chunky topping is her own creation: two kinds of chocolate, coconut, and walnuts.

MAKES ONE 12-INCH TART
PREP TIME 30 MIN ✦ BAKE TIME 50 MIN
COOL / CHILL TIME 2¼ HR

½ recipe ANNIE B'S TART SHELL
(page 15)

CREAM CHEESE FILLING
8 ounces cream cheese, at room
temperature
⅓ cup sugar
1 large egg
3 tablespoons cold heavy (whipping)
cream
¼ teaspoon vanilla extract
6 caramels (about 2 ounces)

CHUNKY CHOCOLATE TOPPING
1 cup shredded coconut
1 cup chopped walnuts

8 ounces semisweet chocolate,
chopped into chunks
8 ounces white chocolate, chopped
into chunks
1 cup sweetened condensed milk

1 Preheat the oven to 350°F and butter a 12-inch tart pan with a removable bottom. Roll, shape, and trim the crust. Prick the crust with a fork and refrigerate for 15 minutes. Partially prebake for 10 minutes or until set (see Blind-Baking, page 12). Cool the crust on a wire rack. Reduce the oven temperature to 225°F.

2 In a large bowl, with an electric mixer on HIGH, beat the cream cheese until smooth and light. Beat in the sugar, then

the egg, cream, and vanilla. Pour the filling into the partially baked shell. In a small saucepan, melt the caramels over low heat, then quickly swirl into filling. Bake the tart for 20 minutes or until set. Increase the oven temperature to 350°F.

3 In a medium-size bowl, toss together all of the ingredients for the Chunky Chocolate Topping except the milk. Spoon on the tart and drizzle with the milk. Bake for 20 minutes or until golden. Cool on a wire rack for 15 minutes. Refrigerate the tart for 2 hours or until serving time. Store in the refrigerator.

1/18 tart = 440 calories, 27 g fat (12 g saturated), 52 mg cholesterol, 46 g carbohydrates, 7 g protein, 134 mg sodium, 1 g fiber

◆ *Junior's famous cheese pies (top to bottom) — Strawberry, Pineapple, Cherry, and Blueberry*

JAMES BEARD'S LEMON SLICE PIE

From JAMES BEARD'S AMERICAN COOKERY *comes this Lemon Slice Pie, using paper-thin lemon slices.*
For a traditional variation, stir a cup of golden raisins into the cooked filling and serve with freshly whipped cream.

MAKES ONE 9-INCH PIE
PREP TIME 45 MIN • BAKE TIME 15 MIN
COOL / CHILL TIME 2½ HR

½ **recipe** BUTTERY CRUST
(page 15)

LEMON SLICE FILLING

- 1½ **cups thin slices unpeeled lemons,
  plus 12 thin slices for garnish
  (9 large lemons)**
- 1½ **cups water, divided**
- 2 **cups sugar, divided**
- 3 **large egg yolks**
- 7 **tablespoons all-purpose flour**
- ¼ **teaspoon salt**
- 2 **tablespoons unsalted butter (not
  margarine), softened**

1 Preheat the oven to 375°F and set
out a 9-inch pie plate. Roll, shape,
and flute the pie shell. Prick it all over
with a fork. Completely prebake the shell
for 15 minutes or until golden (see Blind-
Baking, page 12). Cool on a rack.

...A LEMON IS NOT JUST A LEMON...

*When buying lemons for pies, look for
bright ripe yellow ones with no tinges of
green. Fruit should be firm, not soft or
overripe. They should have smooth, even
skins, as wrinkled skins usually mean
the lemons are old. Most importantly,
select lemons that feel heavy in your
hand for their size, for this means they
are full of juice. Expect to get about
1 teaspoon grated zest from each large
lemon and about 3 tablespoons of juice.*

2 In a medium-size saucepan, place the
1½ cups lemon slices in 1¼ cups of
the water. Simmer about 10 minutes or
until the rind is very tender. Add 1 cup of
the sugar and let simmer 5 minutes more.

3 Meanwhile, in a small bowl, whisk the
egg yolks with the remaining 1 cup
of sugar and ¼ cup water, the flour, and
salt. Whisk in some of the hot lemon
mixture and return to the saucepan.
Cook and stir over low heat until clear
and thickened. Do not overcook or the
acid from the lemons may thin the filling.
Add the butter and cool for 30 minutes.
Pour into the baked shell. Garnish with
the 12 lemon slices. Chill for at least
2 hours. Store in the refrigerator.

*1/9 pie = 392 calories, 13 g fat (6 g saturated), 103 mg
cholesterol, 75 g carbohydrates, 5 g protein, 137 mg
sodium, 2 g fiber*

MILE-HIGH LEMON PIE

*Light, lemony, and luscious — this is one of my most favorite pies. The secret of a mile-high meringue is to beat it
until stiff peaks form and no grains of sugar remain. Then swirl it into peaks onto a warm, not hot, filling before browning.*

MAKES ONE 9-INCH PIE
PREP TIME 1 HR • BAKE TIME 27 MIN
COOL / CHILL TIME 3½ HR

½ **recipe** BUTTERY CRUST
(page 15)

LEMON CUSTARD FILLING

- 1⅓ **cups sugar**
- ½ **cup cornstarch**
- 2 **teaspoons grated lemon zest**
- 1⅔ **cups water**
- 4 **large egg yolks**
- ⅔ **cup fresh lemon juice**
- 2 **tablespoons unsalted butter (not
  margarine), at room temperature**

MERINGUE

- 5 **large egg whites**
- ½ **teaspoon cream of tartar**
- 1 **cup sugar**

1 Preheat the oven to 375°F and set out
a 9-inch pie plate. Roll, shape, and
flute the pie shell. Prick the shell all over
with a fork. Completely prebake the pie
shell for 15 minutes or until golden (see
Blind-Baking, page 12). Cool on a rack.
Reduce the oven temperature to 350°F.

2 In a medium-size saucepan, mix the
sugar, cornstarch, and lemon zest.
Whisk in the water. Whisk constantly
over medium heat for 5 minutes or just
until the mixture comes to a full boil and
thickens. Do not overcook, as this can
break the "gel" and result in a thin filling
that will not set. Remove from the heat.

3 Meanwhile, in a small bowl, with an
electric mixer on HIGH, beat the egg
yolks until light yellow and thick. Stir
about 1 cup of the hot sugar mixture into
the egg yolks, then return this mixture to
the saucepan. Cook and stir over low
heat for 2 minutes or until thickened (do
not let boil). Remove from the heat and
stir in the lemon juice and butter. Pour
the filling into the baked shell.

4 In a medium-size bowl, with an
electric mixer on HIGH, beat the egg
whites and cream of tartar until fluffy.
Gradually beat in the sugar, about
2 tablespoons at a time, and beat until
the meringue stands in glossy soft peaks.

5 To attach the meringue, likely score
the filling with the prongs of a fork.
Gently spoon the meringue on top of the
hot filling, starting at the edges of the pie
shell and working toward the center. Be
sure no filling is peeking out. Make peaks
with the back of a spoon as you go. Bake
12 to 15 minutes or until golden brown.
Cool for 3 hours at room temperature.
Store any leftover pie in the refrigerator.

*1/8 pie = 416 calories, 13 g fat (6 g saturated), 127 mg
cholesterol, 72 g carbohydrates, 5 g protein, 119 mg
sodium, .5 g fiber*

✦ *James Beard's Lemon Slice Pie in a Buttery Crust with a fancy rope edging*

GRASSHOPPER PIE

Darlene Nolan began making this recipe during her college days. She often makes two different versions to take to holiday parties — a green one flavored with crème de menthe and a red one flavored with blackberry brandy. Grasshopper pies began appearing at dinner parties in the 1950s and soon became the dessert-of-choice for special celebrations.

MAKES ONE 9-INCH DEEP-DISH PIE
PREP TIME 1 HR ✦ BAKE TIME 8 MIN
CHILL / FREEZE TIME 4⅓ HR

1 recipe CHOCOLATE COOKIE
   CRUMB CRUST (page 17)

GRASSHOPPER CREAM FILLING
¾ cup milk
50 large marshmallows (10 ounces)
¼ cup plus 2 tablespoons crème de
   menthe
¼ cup white crème de cacao
3 cups cold heavy (whipping) cream,
   divided
   Few drops green food coloring
   (optional)

   Sprigs of fresh mint
   Chocolate-covered square mints,
   cut diagonally (optional)

1 Preheat the oven to 375°F and butter a 9-inch deep-dish pie plate. Press the crumb mixture over the bottom and up the sides of the pie plate. Completely bake the crust for 8 to 10 minutes or just until set. Cool completely on a wire rack before filling.

2 In a large saucepan, bring the milk to a simmer over medium-high heat. Add the marshmallows and cook, stirring constantly, until the marshmallows have melted completely. Transfer this mixture to a large bowl and refrigerate for 20 minutes or until the mixture mounds when dropped from a spoon. Stir in the crème de menthe and crème de cacao.

3 In a medium-size bowl, with an electric mixer on HIGH, beat 2 cups of the heavy cream until soft peaks form. Fold the whipped cream into the marshmallow mixture. Add green food coloring, if you wish, drop by drop until you get the color you like. Pour this mixture into the baked crust.

4 Cover the pie with plastic wrap and freeze for at least 4 hours. For a decorative finish, whip the remaining 1 cup of whipping cream until stiff peaks form. Using a pastry bag fitted with a medium star tip (#17), pipe a border of overlapping whipped cream shells around the outside edge of the pie. Then, pipe a lattice design across the top with a small star tip (#14 or #15). Or apply the cream with a spoon or a cone made from parchment paper. Garnish with the sprigs of mint. Add the chocolate-covered mints if you wish. Store any leftover pie in the freezer.

1/10 pie = 493 calories, 38 g fat (21 g saturated), 120 mg cholesterol, 57 g carbohydrates, 5 g protein, 227 mg sodium, .3 g fiber

BLACKBERRY BRANDY ALEXANDER PIE Substitute ¼ cup blackberry brandy for the green crème de menthe. Omit the green food coloring and add red coloring if you wish.

MILLION-DOLLAR PIE

From Princess Cameron in the Lone Star state comes this pie that is so rich that it "tastes like a million." It reminds me of the fresh fruit ambrosia we served for the holidays, folded into a creamy whipped filling and spooned into a crumb crust. This recipe makes two pies — serve only one and freeze the other, if you wish.

MAKES TWO 9-INCH PIES
PREP TIME 30 MIN ✦ BAKE TIME 8 MIN
CHILL TIME 1 HR

2 recipes GRAHAM CRACKER
   CRUMB CRUST (page 17)

MILLION-DOLLAR FILLING
1 12-ounce carton frozen whipped
   topping, thawed for 15 minutes
1 14-ounce can sweetened condensed
   milk
¼ cup fresh lemon juice
2 cups fresh strawberries, hulled
   and sliced ¼ inch thick
1 8-ounce can crushed pineapple,
   drained

1 cup flaked coconut
½ cup finely chopped pecans

1 Preheat the oven to 375°F and butter two 9-inch pie plates. Press the graham cracker crumb mixture over the bottoms and up the sides of the two pie plates. Completely bake the crusts for 8 to 10 minutes or just until set. Cool both crusts thoroughly on wire racks.

2 In a large bowl, beat the whipped topping, condensed milk, and lemon juice with a wooden spoon. With a rubber scrapper, fold in the strawberries, pineapple, coconut, and pecans. Divide evenly between the two pie shells.

3 Cover the pies with plastic wrap and refrigerate for at least 1 hour before serving. If you wish, serve just one pie. Wrap the other pie well and freeze it for up to 1 month. (To serve the frozen pie, transfer it from the freezer to the refrigerator at least 1 hour before serving.) Slice the pie with a knife dipped in hot water. Store any leftover pie in the refrigerator.

1/9 pie = 398 calories, 20 g fat (12 g saturated), 31 mg cholesterol, 51 g carbohydrates, 5 g protein, 164 mg sodium, 2 g fiber

◆ *Grasshopper Pie, topped with a lattice of whipped cream and sprigs of fresh mint*

◆ *Orange Dream Pie, decorated with petite whipped cream flowerettes*

ORANGE DREAM PIE

Ice cream pies are among the easiest pies to make — and one of the simplest ways to impress guests.
The popular ice-cream-on-a-stick made with vanilla ice cream and coated with orange sherbet inspired this pie.

MAKES ONE 9-INCH DEEP-DISH PIE
PREP TIME 30 HR ✦ BAKE TIME 10 MIN
COOL / STAND TIME 45 MIN
FREEZE TIME 3 HR

1 recipe ALMOND CRUNCH CRUMB CRUST (page 17)

ORANGE DREAM FILLING
1 **quart vanilla ice cream, softened**
1 **quart orange sherbet, softened**
⅓ **cup orange marmalade, melted and cooled slightly**
1 **cup cold heavy (whipping) cream**

1 Preheat the oven to 375°F and butter a 9-inch deep-dish pie plate. Press the almond crumb mixture over the bottom and up the sides of the pie plate. Bake the pie crust for 10 minutes or until golden and set. Cool the crust completely on a wire rack before you make the filling.

2 Spoon half of the vanilla ice cream into the baked crust, then top with half of the orange sherbet. Repeat with a layer of the remaining vanilla ice cream and the remaining orange sherbet on top. Using the back of a spoon, make deep swirls in the filling. Don't let the filling melt. If the ice cream or sherbet should

> ✦ *BAKER'S TIP* ✦
>
> *To serve a frozen ice cream pie or whipped cream pie, let the pie stand in the refrigerator for 1 hour before serving, or at room temperature for 15 minutes. To cut the pie, use a slicing knife with a long thin straight blade, dipped in hot water.*

appear to be melting, return the pie to the freezer to firm up before proceeding.

3 Cover the pie with plastic wrap and freeze for 1 hour. Drizzle the top of the pie with the warm marmalade and swirl with a knife to marble the top. Cover and return to the freezer for 2 hours more or until firm.

4 About 15 minutes before serving, remove the pie from the freezer and let it stand at room temperature. In a small bowl, with an electric mixer on HIGH, beat the cream until stiff peaks form. Pipe or spoon small flowerettes or swirls in a ring on top of the pie. Store any leftover pie in the freezer.

1/10 pie = 530 calories, 32 g fat (17 g saturated), 97 mg cholesterol, 59 g carbohydrates, 6 g protein, 137 mg sodium, 1 g fiber

PHILLIP STEPHEN SCHULZ'S PEANUT BUTTER PIE

Cookbook Author Phillip Stephen Schulz shares one of his favorite pies. It's a refrigerator pie
made with a chocolate crumb crust and a rich filling whipped up from peanut butter and cream cheese.
Fluffy whipped cream and decorative chocolate curls top it off.

MAKES ONE 9-INCH PIE
PREP TIME 30 HR ✦ BAKE TIME 8 MIN
CHILL TIME 4 HR

1 recipe CHOCOLATE COOKIE CRUMB CRUST (page 17) or GRAHAM CRACKER CRUMB CRUST (page 17)
1 **teaspoon ground cinnamon**
1 **teaspoon instant coffee powder**

PEANUT CREAM FILLING
4 **ounces cream cheese, at room temperature**
1½ **cups chunky or smooth peanut butter**
1 **cup confectioners' sugar, sifted**
½ **cup milk**
2 **teaspoons vanilla extract**

2 **cups cold heavy (whipping) cream Chocolate Curls (page 20)**

1 Preheat the oven to 350°F and butter a 9-inch pie plate. Pick a crust recipe. Mix the crust, adding the cinnamon and instant coffee powder to the crumb mixture. Press the crumb mixture over the bottom and up the sides of the pie plate. Bake the crust for 8 to 10 minutes or just until set. Cool the baked crust thoroughly on a wire rack while you make the filling.

2 In a large bowl, with an electric mixer on HIGH, beat the cream cheese and peanut butter until creamy and well blended. Add the sugar and beat until fluffy, then beat in the milk and vanilla.

3 In a medium-size bowl, with an electric mixer on HIGH, beat the cream until stiff peaks form when the beaters are lifted. Set aside 1 cup of the

whipped cream in the refrigerator for decorating the pie. (You will have about 3 cups whipped cream remaining.)

4 Stir a third of the remaining 3 cups of whipped cream into the peanut butter mixture until it is well blended. Then gently fold in the remaining cream from the bowl (do not worry if some streaks of cream are still visible).

5 Spoon the filling into the baked crust. Spread the reserved 1 cup of whipped cream over the top of the pie, making peaks with the back of a spoon. Sprinkle generously with Chocolate Curls. Refrigerate the pie for at least 4 hours. Store in the refrigerator.

1/10 pie = 610 calories, 55 g fat (22 g saturated), 99 mg cholesterol, 51 g carbohydrates, 14 g protein, 425 mg sodium, 3 g fiber

MARION CUNNINGHAM'S PUMPKIN PIE

"It's doubtful that the Indians and Pilgrims shared pumpkin pie at that first Thanksgiving in Plymouth," says Marion Cunningham, editor of THE FANNIE FARMER COOKBOOK (13th edition). "They ate pumpkin, but likely baked in its own shell."

MAKES ONE 9-INCH PIE
PREP TIME 1 HR ✦ BAKE TIME 45 MIN
COOL TIME 2 HR

1 recipe MARION CUNNINGHAM'S PIE PASTRY (page 15)

PUMPKIN FILLING
1 1¾-pound pie pumpkin (such as sugar baby)
⅔ cup sugar
1 teaspoon ground cinnamon
½ teaspoon salt
¼ teaspoon ground ginger
   Pinch ground cloves
1½ cups evaporated milk
2 eggs, lightly beaten

   Pastry leaves (page 20) (optional)

1 Cut the pumpkin into large pieces, discarding the seeds and pith. Fit a large pot with a steaming rack, fill with about 2 quarts water, and bring to a boil over high heat. Carefully place the unpeeled pumpkin on the rack, cover the pot, and steam the pumpkin for about 30 minutes or until the pulp is soft. Cool the pumpkin, then scrape the pulp from the skin into a food processor. Purée until smooth. Transfer the pumpkin purée to a large bowl. Stir in the sugar, cinnamon, salt, ginger, cloves, milk, and eggs.

2 Preheat the oven to 400°F and butter a 9-inch pie plate. On a lightly floured surface, roll the chilled dough into a 15-inch round, then ease into the pie plate. Using a paring knife, trim the edges, allowing a 1-inch overhang, then fold and flute. Decorate the edge with pastry leaves if you wish. Pour the pumpkin mixture into the shell.

3 Bake the pie for 15 minutes, then reduce the oven temperature to 350°F. Bake the pie 30 to 40 minutes more or until the filling is set and a kitchen knife inserted in the center comes out clean. Cool on a wire rack for at least 2 hours before serving. Top with pastry leaves, if you wish. Refrigerate.

1/8 pie = 308 calories, 16 g fat (5 g saturated), 60 mg cholesterol, 36 g carbohydrates, 6 g protein, 237 mg   3 sodium, 1 g fiber

CANNED PUMPKIN PIE Substitute 1½ cups canned pumpkin for the fresh pumpkin (Step 1). Increase the spices to 1½ teaspoons cinnamon, ½ teaspoon ginger, and ¼ teaspoon ground cloves.

HOLIDAY EGGNOG PIE

The word nog comes from an Old English term for "ale." In England, eggnog is often made with red wine, but on this side of the Atlantic Ocean, we usually use brandy and rum. This pie turns popular eggnog into a light and airy chiffon dessert.

MAKES ONE 9-INCH DEEP-DISH PIE
PREP TIME 45 MIN ✦ BAKE TIME 15 MIN
STAND / CHILL TIME 3 HR

½ recipe PÂTE BRISÉE (page 15)

EGGNOG CHIFFON FILLING
¼ cup cold water
1 tablespoon plain unflavored gelatin
2½ cups milk
1 cup granulated sugar
¼ teaspoon salt
4 large egg yolks
2 tablespoons dark rum
   or 1 teaspoon rum extract
1 tablespoon brandy or vanilla extract
2 cups cold heavy (whipping) cream

   Fresh raspberries
   Sprigs of fresh mint

1 Preheat the oven to 400°F and butter a 9-inch deep-dish pie plate. Roll, shape, and flute the pie shell. Prick the shell all over with a fork. Completely prebake the shell for 15 minutes or until golden (see Blind-Baking, page 12). Cool on a wire rack.

2 Pour the water into a small saucepan and sprinkle the gelatin over the top. Stir, then let stand for 5 minutes to soften. Stir over low heat until the gelatin is completely dissolved. Set aside.

3 In a medium-size saucepan, whisk the milk, sugar, and salt and bring to a boil over medium-high heat. Remove from the heat.

4 Meanwhile, in a small bowl, with an electric mixer on HIGH, beat the egg yolks until light yellow and thick. Stir about 1 cup of the hot milk mixture into the yolks, then return this mixture to the saucepan. Cook over low heat, stirring constantly, for 2 minutes or until thickened (do not boil). Remove from the heat and whisk in the dissolved gelatin, the rum, and brandy. Pour into a heatproof bowl and lay a piece of plastic wrap directly on the filling. Chill for 1 hour or until the custard mounds when dropped from a spoon.

5 Meanwhile, in a small bowl, with an electric mixer on HIGH, beat the cream until soft peaks form. Fold 2 cups of the whipped cream into the eggnog custard, then spoon the filling into the baked shell. Chill the pie for 2 hours or until set. Cover and refrigerate the remaining whipped cream.

6 Decorate the pie by piping or spooning peaks of the reserved whipped cream into a wreath around the edge. Garnish with clusters of whole raspberries and mint leaves. Store any leftover pie in the refrigerator.

1/9 pie = 460 calories, 31 g fat (18 g saturated), 194 mg cholesterol, 38 g carbohydrates, 7 g protein, 187 mg sodium, 1 g fiber

◆ *Marion Cunningham's Pumpkin Pie, decorated with fancy cinnamon-dusted pastry leaves*

COUNTRY KITCHEN PIES

♥

Fresh, old-fashioned pies, just like grandma used to make. Nothing fancy ... just homespun pies that are great tasting and oh-so-good. Here are everybody's favorites — red cherry laced up under a lattice crust, apple orchard pie with a touch of cinnamon, and juicy blueberry under a crisp streusel. Some country kitchen pies turn into pudding pies as they bake. Others buckle and slump under their buttery crusts. Still others bake into spoon cobblers or flip into upside-down pies. They're all best served proudly, with a smile, and straight from the dish they're baked in, naturally.

♦ *Fruit Orchard Pies (top to bottom, clockwise) —*
Country Apple Pie (see recipe, page 128),
Laced-Up Cherry Pie (page 126), and
Blueberry Streusel Pie (page 126)

LACED-UP CHERRY PIE

Fresh cherry pie is one of the treats of summer. May, June and July are the best months to bake a cherry pie. From early May through July, look for the sweet golden cherries with red blushing color known as Royal Ann or Queen Anne. In late June and July, try the tart red Montmorency cherries. Both kinds of cherries make great pies ... just adjust the sugar.

MAKES ONE 9-INCH DEEP-DISH PIE
PREP TIME 45 MIN ✦ BAKE TIME 50 MIN
COOL TIME 2 HR

- 1 recipe PÂTE SUCRÉE (page 15)
- 3 tablespoons heavy cream, divided

SOUR CHERRY PIE FILLING

- 1¼ to 1½ cups sugar, plus
  2 tablespoons for sprinkling
- 3 tablespoons cornstarch
- 2 tablespoons quick-cooking tapioca
- ¼ teaspoon salt
- 2¼ pounds fresh sour red pie cherries,
  pitted, or 6 cups drained, canned
  tart red pitted cherries in juice
- 1 tablespoon fresh lemon juice
- ¾ teaspoon almond extract
  Few drops of red food coloring
  (optional)
- 2 tablespoons unsalted butter (not
  margarine), cut into pieces

1 Preheat the oven to 375°F and butter a 9-inch deep-dish pie plate. Line a baking sheet with waxed paper. Divide and shape the pastry into 2 equal disks. On a lightly floured surface, roll out each disk into a large circle, ⅛ inch thick. Trim one round to a 16-inch circle and the second to a 13-inch circle. Fit the larger round into the pie plate, leaving a 1½-inch overhang. Brush the shell with 1 tablespoon of the cream and refrigerate. Transfer the remaining pastry round to the baking sheet and refrigerate.

2 In a large bowl, mix the 1¼ to 1½ cups of sugar (depending on sweetness of cherries), the cornstarch, tapioca, and salt. Toss with the cherries, lemon juice, and almond extract, plus a few drops of food coloring, if you wish. Spoon into the shell. Dot with the butter.

3 To make the lattice crust, with a fluted pastry wheel, cut the remaining pastry round into 12 strips, 1 inch wide.

Weave a lattice top over the cherries and flute the edge (see Lattice Crust, page 14). Brush the lattice with the remaining 2 tablespoons of cream and sprinkle with the remaining 2 tablespoons of sugar. Bake the pie for 50 minutes or until the crust is golden and the filling is bubbling. Cool on a wire rack for at least 2 hours. Serve at room temperature and store in the refrigerator.

1/9 pie = 457 calories, 16 g fat (10 saturated), 76 mg cholesterol, 76 g carbohydrates, 5 g protein, 206 mg sodium, 1 g fiber

SWEET CHERRY PIE Substitute 2¼ pounds fresh sweet Queen Anne cherries for the sour cherries. Reduce the sugar in the filling to 1 cup.

BLACKBERRY LATTICE PIE Substitute 6 cups ripe fresh blackberries for the cherries and 1 tablespoon of crème de cassis for the almond extract.

BLUEBERRY STREUSEL PIE

Choose the biggest, juiciest blueberries you can find and discard any that look shriveled. If you're not using the berries right away, refrigerate them, without washing, in a moistureproof container. Wash the berries immediately before using. This recipe tops the pie with a traditional crumbly streusel, from the German word for "sprinkle" or "strew."

MAKES ONE 9-INCH DEEP-DISH PIE
PREP TIME 30 MIN ✦ BAKE TIME 45 MIN
COOL TIME 2 HR

- ½ recipe PÂTE BRISÉE (page 15)
- 2 tablespoons light cream

FRESH BLUEBERRY FILLING

- ⅔ cup packed light brown sugar
- ½ cup granulated sugar
- ⅓ cup quick-cooking tapioca
- ¼ teaspoon salt
- 6 cups fresh blueberries
- 1 tablespoon fresh lemon juice
- 2 teaspoons grated lemon zest
- 2 tablespoons unsalted butter (not
  margarine), cut into pieces

STREUSEL TOPPING

- ⅔ cup all-purpose flour
- ½ cup granulated sugar
- ½ teaspoon ground cinnamon
- 5 tablespoons cold unsalted butter
  (not margarine), cut into pieces

1 Preheat the oven to 375°F and set out a deep-dish 9-inch pie plate. Roll, shape, and flute the pie shell. Brush the shell with the cream and refrigerate while you make the filling.

2 In a large bowl, combine both sugars, the tapioca, and salt. Toss with the blueberries, lemon juice and lemon zest. Spoon into the pie shell, mounding the berries in the center. Dot with the butter.

3 To make the topping, in a small bowl, mix the flour, sugar, and cinnamon. Cut in the butter until crumbs form. Sprinkle over the filling, covering it completely. Bake the pie for 20 minutes or until the top begins to brown. Reduce the oven heat to 350°F and bake 25 minutes more or until the topping is light brown and the filling is bubbling. Cool the pie on a wire rack for at least 2 hours. Store in the refrigerator.

1/9 pie = 444 calories, 17 g fat (10 saturated), 45 mg cholesterol, 78 g carbohydrates, 3 g protein, 119 mg sodium, 3 g fiber

RASPBERRY CRUMB PIE Substitute 6 cups fresh red raspberries for the blueberries. Use only ¼ cup tapioca (Step 2).

◆ *Cherry Pie, all laced up with a Lattice Crust*

COUNTRY APPLE PIE

This old-fashioned apple pie tastes as if it just came out of the oven in a country farm kitchen.
Pick firm, ripe apples with no soft spots — some sweet, tart, and red; others crisp and green or yellow.

MAKES ONE 9-INCH DEEP-DISH PIE
PREP TIME 45 MIN ✦ BAKE TIME 1 HR
COOL TIME 2 HR

1 **recipe PÂTE SUCRÉE (page 15)**

TART & SWEET APPLE FILLING
  2 **pounds sweet-tart red apples, such as McIntosh or Jonathan**
1½ **pounds sweet-tart green or yellow apples, such as Granny Smith or Golden Delicious**
  1 **teaspoon grated lemon zest**
  3 **tablespoons fresh lemon juice**
  ¾ **cup packed light brown sugar**
  ⅔ **cup granulated sugar, plus 2 tablespoons for sprinkling**
  ⅓ **cup all-purpose flour**
  1 **tablespoon ground cinnamon**
  ½ **teaspoon ground nutmeg**
  ½ **teaspoon salt**
  ⅓ **cup apple cider**
  2 **tablespoons heavy cream**

1 Butter a 9-inch deep-dish pie plate. On a lightly floured surface, roll out half of the chilled pastry to a large round,

⅛ inch thick. Trim it to a 15-inch circle and fit into the pie plate, leaving a 1½-inch overhang (do not prick). Chill the shell while you make the filling.

2 Meanwhile, peel and core the apples. Finely chop 3 of the red apples into a ¼-inch dice and place in a large bowl. Slice the remaining red and all of the green apples ¼ inch thick and add to the bowl. Add the lemon zest, lemon juice, brown sugar, the ⅔ cup granulated sugar, the flour, cinnamon, nutmeg, and salt to the apples and toss to coat.

3 Preheat the oven to 425°F. Mound the apples in the chilled shell. Drizzle the cider over the apples.

4 Roll out the remaining pastry into another large round, ⅛ inch thick, and trim to a 13-inch circle. Using a small apple cutter (about 1 inch in size), cut out 3 or 4 apples from the crust, reserving the cutouts. Cover the pie with

the top crust, seal the edges with a little water, and flute with a pinch-push flute. "Glue" the apple cutouts to the top crust with a little water (or an egg white beaten with a little water, see page 63). Brush the top crust with the cream and sprinkle the pie with the remaining 2 tablespoons of granulated sugar.

5 Bake the pie for 20 minutes. Lower the temperature to 375°F and bake 40 minutes more or until the apples are tender when tested with a fork. If the crust browns before the pie is done, loosely cover the pie with a foil tent. Let the pie cool on a rack for at least 2 hours before serving. Refrigerate any leftover pie. This pie is at its best when served slightly warm or at room temperature.

1/9 pie = 500 calories, 14 g fat (8 saturated), 80 mg cholesterol, 94 g carbohydrates, 5 g protein, 266 mg sodium, 5 g fiber

RAY'S APPLE CRUMB PIE

Chef Ray Norton likes his fresh fruit pies very lightly seasoned — with just enough sugar and spice to complement the natural fruit flavors. He uses crisp Granny Smith apples and golden raisins, then tops off the pie with buttery brown sugar crumbs.

MAKES ONE 9-INCH DEEP-DISH PIE
PREP TIME 30 MIN ✦ BAKE TIME 45 MIN
COOL TIME 1 HR

½ **recipe PÂTE BRISÉE (page 15)**

APPLE & RAISIN FILLING
3½ **pounds Granny Smith apples (about 7 large)**
  ½ **cup golden raisins**
  ⅓ **cup packed light brown sugar**
  ¼ **teaspoon ground cinnamon**

CRUMB TOPPING
  ½ **cup cold unsalted butter (not margarine), cut into small pieces**
  ⅔ **cup packed light brown sugar**
  1 **cup all-purpose flour**

1 Preheat the oven to 425°F and butter a 9-inch deep-dish pie plate. Roll, shape, and flute the pie shell (do not prick). Freeze the shell while you make the filling.

2 Peel and core the apples and slice them ¼ inch thick. Place the apples in a large bowl them with the raisins, brown sugar, and cinnamon. Toss the apples and raisins until they are well coated with the sugar-cinnamon mixture. Spoon this filling into the pie shell, mounding it high in the center.

3 In a medium-size bowl, place all of the ingredients for the topping. Using an electric mixer on MEDIUM,

beat the mixture just until crumbs form (do not overmix). Sprinkle this topping mixture over the apple filling, covering it completely.

4 Bake the pie for 45 minutes or until the apples are tender and the topping and crust are golden brown. If the crust browns before the apples are tender, loosely cover the pie with a foil tent. Let the pie cool on a rack for at least 1 hour before serving. Store any leftover pie in the refrigerator.

1/9 pie = 483 calories, 18 g fat (11 saturated), 45 mg cholesterol, 83 g carbohydrates, 4 g protein, 80 mg sodium, 5 g fiber

Country Apple Pie in a Pâte Sucrée Crust, decorated with apple cutouts and finished with a pinch-push flute (page 13)

DEBORAH'S TARTE TATIN

This classic upside-down French apple tarte was created by the two unmarried Tatin sisters in their restaurant at Lamotte-Beuvron on the Loire River. The authentic recipe is completely oven-baked and requires great skill to turn it out upside down without it collapsing. In this recipe, created by Food Editor Deborah Mintcheff, caramelized apples are tightly packed into a pan, then baked under a buttery blanket of pastry. The finished tarte turns out easily, without sticking.

MAKES ONE 9-INCH DEEP-DISH TARTE
PREP TIME 1 HR ◆ BAKE TIME 20 MIN
COOL TIME 30 MIN

½ **recipe PÂTE BRISÉE (page 15)**

TARTE TATIN

1 **cup (2 sticks) unsalted butter (not margarine)**
2 **cups plus 2 tablespoons sugar**
3 **pounds Golden Delicious apples, peeled, cored, and quartered**
2 **tablespoons fresh lemon juice**

1 **recipe Crème Fraîche (page 20) (optional)**

1 Prepare the pastry and chill. Line a 9-inch deep-dish pie plate with foil and butter generously. Set aside.

2 In a large skillet, preferably cast iron, melt the butter over low heat. Stir in the sugar until mixed, but not dissolved. Place all of the apples, rounded-sides down, in the skillet (they will shrink as they cook). Sprinkle with the lemon juice. Increase the heat to medium-high.

3 Cook the apples for 20 to 25 minutes or until they are richly glazed and the syrup has begun to thicken. Stir occasionally, shifting and moving the apples in the center to the side of the pan. Increase the heat to high and cook the apples 10 minutes longer or until they turn a deep brown. As the apples turn brown, transfer them to the foil-lined pan: Working from the outside to the center of the pan, arrange the apples in tight concentric circles, rounded-sides down, overlapping them to fit. Set the apples aside to cool to room temperature.

4 Preheat the oven to 425°F. On a lightly floured surface, roll out the pastry to a large round, ⅛ inch thick.

Trim to a 10-inch circle. Place the pastry over the apples, tucking the edges of the dough down between the apples and the sides of the pan. Prick the dough all over with a fork.

5 Bake the tarte for 20 minutes or until the pastry is golden and the juices are bubbling. Remove the tarte from the oven and immediately invert it onto a heatproof serving plate. Remove the pie plate, then peel away the foil. Serve warm, with Crème Fraîche, if you wish.

1/9 tarte = 551 calories, 28 g fat (17 saturated), 73 mg cholesterol, 81 g carbohydrates, 2 g protein, 73 mg sodium, 4 g fiber

BLUSHING PEAR TARTE TATIN
Substitute 3 pounds ripe pears (Anjou or Bartletts), peeled, cored, and quartered, for the apples. Sprinkle 1 cup of fresh raspberries over the caramelized pears (at the end of Step 3).

MARIAN BURROS'S PLUM TORTE

At the request of her readers, New York Times *Food Editor Marian Burros has included this recipe in her newspaper column every year since the 1980s. Technically it's not a pie, although it looks a little like one. Actually, it's a plum torte held together with a cakelike batter and it's baked in a springform pan, not a pie plate.*

MAKES ONE 9- OR 10-INCH TORTE
PREP TIME 30 MIN ◆ BAKE TIME 40-50 MIN
COOL TIME 15 MIN

1 **cup all-purpose flour, sifted**
1 **teaspoon baking powder**
   Pinch salt
¾ **cup sugar, plus extra for sprinkling**
½ **cup (1 stick) unsalted butter (not margarine), at room temperature**
2 **large eggs**
12 **large ripe fresh plums, halved and pitted**
1 **teaspoon ground cinnamon, or to taste**

1 Preheat the oven to 350°F and butter a 9- or 10-inch springform pan. In a small bowl, mix the flour, baking powder, and salt.

2 In a large bowl with an electric mixer on HIGH, cream the ¾ cup of sugar and butter until light yellow. Reduce the speed to LOW, add the flour mixture and eggs, and beat for 2 minutes or until well blended. Spoon the batter into the pan.

3 Place the plum halves, skin-side down, on top of the batter. Mix the cinnamon with 1 or 2 tablespoons sugar, depending upon the sweetness of the fruit. Sprinkle this mixture on the plums.

4 Bake the torte for 40 to 50 minutes or until a pick inserted in the center comes out clean. Cool for 15 minutes before serving. Store any leftovers in the refrigerator or freezer. To freeze the torte, double-wrap it in foil, place in a plastic bag, and seal. To serve, unwrap the torte, then defrost and reheat it in a 300°F oven about 10 to 15 minutes or until warm.

1/9 torte = 263 calories, 12 g fat (7 saturated), 75 mg cholesterol, 38 g carbohydrates, 4 g protein, 52 mg sodium, 2 g fiber

GRANDMA PHYLLIS'S FRESH RASPBERRY PIE

Aimee Rinehart loves watching Grandma Phyllis DeKoninck make pies. Grandma knows exactly when she has cut the shortening into the flour just enough, and when the dough is right for rolling. Best of all, Grandma's pies come out looking and tasting great every time. She's known for many different kinds — her sugar pies, chocolate, rhubarb, butterscotch, pecan, and black raspberry. We could only find the smaller red raspberries — and discovered homemade heaven.

MAKES ONE 9-INCH DEEP-DISH PIE
PREP TIME 30 MIN ✦ BAKE TIME 40 MIN
COOL TIME 1 HR

1 recipe GRANDMA'S
   SHORTENING CRUST (page 15)

   RASPBERRY FILLING
6 **cups fresh red raspberries**
½ **cup water**
¾ **cup sugar, plus 1 tablespoon for
   sprinkling**
5 **tablespoons quick-cooking tapioca**
2 **tablespoons unsalted butter (not
   margarine), cut into pieces**

1 Preheat the oven to 400°F and butter
a 9-inch deep-dish pie plate. Line a
baking sheet with waxed paper. On a

lightly floured surface, roll out half of the pastry ⅛ inch thick, and trim to a 16-inch circle. Fit into the pie plate, leaving a 1½-inch overhang. Refrigerate the shell and the remaining pastry.

2 In a large bowl, toss the raspberries with the water. In a small bowl, mix the sugar and tapioca, then toss with the berries until well coated. Spoon into the pie shell. Dot with the butter.

3 Roll out the rest of the pastry ⅛ inch thick, trim to a 13-inch circle, and transfer to the top of the pie. Seal the edges with a little water and flute. Using a knife, cut 7 or 8 slits (about 1 inch long)

in the top crust for steam vents. Sprinkle with the remaining tablespoon of sugar.

4 Bake the pie for 20 minutes, then reduce the oven temperature to 375°F and bake 20 to 25 minutes more or until the filling is bubbling through the slits onto the top crust. Cool on a wire rack for at least 1 hour. Serve the pie warm or at room temperature. Store any leftover pie in the refrigerator.

1/9 pie = 495 calories, 28 g fat (8 saturated), 31 mg cholesterol, 58 g carbohydrates, 5 g protein, 246 mg sodium, 5 g fiber

FRESH BLACK RASPBERRY PIE
Substitute 5 cups fresh black raspberries for the red raspberries.

ORANGE CUSTARD CREAM PIE

Oranges are one of my favorite fruits, but not just for their juice. In this recipe, they're cooked into a silky, creamy custard with just a hint of orange zest, then spooned into a baked, sweet pie shell. It's a great pie to serve for a party, because you can make it the day before, chill it overnight, and then quickly garnish it with orange wedges right before serving.

MAKES ONE 9-INCH DEEP-DISH PIE

PREP TIME 15 MIN ✦ BAKE TIME 15 MIN
COOL / CHILL TIME 2¾ HR OR OVERNIGHT

½ **recipe PÂTE SUCRÉE (page 15)**

   ORANGE CREAM FILLING
1 **cup sugar**
6 **tablespoons cornstarch**
¼ **teaspoon salt**
1 **tablespoon grated orange zest**
1½ **cups fresh orange juice**
4 **large eggs**
1 **cup cold heavy (whipping) cream**

1 **large orange, for garnish**

1 Preheat the oven to 400°F and set out
a 9-inch deep-dish pie plate. Roll,
shape, and flute the pie shell. Prick it all
over with a fork. Completely prebake the

shell for 15 minutes or until golden (see Blind-Baking, page 12). Cool the shell on a wire rack while you make the filling.

2 In a medium-size saucepan, mix the sugar, cornstarch, and salt. Stir in the orange zest and orange juice. Cook over medium heat, whisking constantly, for 8 minutes or just until the mixture comes to a full boil and thickens. Remove the custard mixture from the heat.

3 In a small bowl with an electric mixer on HIGH, beat the eggs until light yellow and thick. Stir about 1 cup of the hot orange mixture into the eggs, then return this mixture to the saucepan. Cook and stir over low heat for 2 minutes or until thickened (do not let boil). Remove from the heat.

4 Pour the filling into a medium-size bowl and let stand at room temperature for 15 minutes. Chill in the refrigerator for 30 minutes or just until the mixture is cool to the touch.

5 In a large bowl, with the mixer on HIGH, whip the cream to stiff peaks. Fold in the chilled orange mixture. Spoon the filling into the baked shell. Chill the pie for at least 2 hours or overnight. To garnish, halve the orange lengthwise, then cut each half lengthwise into wedges, ½ inch thick. Arrange the orange slices in a pinwheel design on top of the pie. Store any leftover pie in the refrigerator.

1/9 pie = 366 calories, 18 g fat (10 saturated), 168 mg cholesterol, 40 g carbohydrates, 6 g protein, 168 mg sodium, 1 g fiber

SNICKERDOODLE FRUIT PIE

Baking cookies at Christmastime for my friends is one of my family's traditions — cinnamony Snickerdoodles are always on the list. I've created a pie crust from this traditional cookie that's perfect for filling with fresh fruits and berries.

MAKES ONE 9-INCH DEEP-DISH PIE
PREP TIME 45 MIN ✦ BAKE TIME 45 MIN
COOL TIME 1 HR

1 recipe BETH'S SNICKERDOODLE COOKIE CRUST (page 19)
3 tablespoons sugar
1 teaspoon ground cinnamon

CINNAMON-FRUIT FILLING

¾ cup sugar
2 tablespoons all-purpose flour
2 tablespoons quick-cooking tapioca
⅛ teaspoon salt
2 pounds ripe nectarines or peaches, peeled, pitted, and sliced ¼ inch thick (4 cups)
2 cups fresh blackberries or raspberries
1 teaspoon ground cinnamon
½ teaspoon grated orange zest
2 tablespoons fresh orange juice
2 tablespoons unsalted butter (not margarine), cut into small pieces

1 Preheat the oven to 400°F and set out a deep-dish 9-inch pie plate. On a lightly floured surface, roll out half of the chilled pastry into a large round, ⅛ inch thick. Trim it to a 15-inch circle and fit it into the pie plate, leaving a 1½-inch overhang (do not prick). Toss the sugar with the cinnamon, then sprinkle half of this mixture over the pie shell. Chill the pie shell while you make the fruit filling. Set the rest of the sugar mixture aside.

2 In a small bowl, combine the sugar, flour, tapioca, and salt. In a large bowl, toss the nectarines or peaches with the berries, cinnamon, orange zest, and orange juice; let stand for 10 minutes. Spoon the fruit mixture into the pie shell, mounding the fruit in the center. Scrape the bowl well to get all of the juices. Dot the fruit with the butter.

3 On a lightly floured surface, roll out the remaining pastry to another large round, ⅛ inch thick, and trim to a 13-inch circle. Place over the top of the pie and finish with a zigzag flute. Cut a few steam vents in the top crust. Cut out leaves from the remaining scraps of dough, if you wish, and "glue" on the top of the pie with a little water.

4 Sprinkle the pie with the reserved sugar-cinnamon mixture. Bake the pie for 25 minutes or until the top begins to brown. Reduce the heat to 350°F and bake 20 minutes more or until the crust and topping are golden brown and the filling is bubbling. Cool on a wire rack for at least 1 hour before serving. Store any leftover pie in the refrigerator.

1/9 pie = 459 calories, 17 g fat (9 saturated), 82 mg cholesterol, 75 g carbohydrates, 6 g protein, 177 mg sodium, 5 g fiber

OLIVE DAVIS'S SCHNITZ PEACH PIE

Elizabeth Baird, Food Director of Canadian Living *magazine, shares this rich and wonderful recipe from her mother, Olive Davis. Elizabeth calls her mother the Pie Queen "because," she says, "I think she makes the best pies to be found in Canada." Elizabeth believes that this one, like all peach pies, is at its best while still just warm, when the crust is flaky and crisp and the filling gorgeously runny.*

MAKES ONE 9-INCH DEEP-DISH PIE
PREP TIME 30 MIN ✦ BAKE TIME 40 MIN

½ recipe CRISP FLAKY CRUST (page 15)

FRESH PEACH FILLING

⅔ cup firmly packed light brown sugar
3 tablespoons all-purpose flour
   Pinch of salt
2 tablespoons cold unsalted butter (not margarine), cut into small pieces
6 large ripe peaches, peeled, halved, and pitted
2 teaspoons fresh lemon juice
¼ cup heavy (whipping) cream

1 large egg yolk
½ teaspoon ground cinnamon

1 Preheat the oven to 425°F and butter a 9-inch deep-dish pie plate. Roll, shape, and flute the pie shell (do not bake or prick). Refrigerate the shell while you make the filling.

2 In a small bowl, mix the sugar, flour, and salt. Add the butter and mix with a fork or your fingers until crumbly. Spoon about one third of this mixture into the pie shell.

3 Cut each peach half into 3 slices and arrange the peach slices attractively over the crumbs. Sprinkle with the lemon juice. In a cup, whisk the cream with the egg yolk and pour over the peaches. Sprinkle on the rest of the crumbs. Dust with the cinnamon.

4 Bake the pie for 10 minutes. Reduce the oven temperature to 375°F and bake 30 to 35 minutes more or until the peaches are tender and the crust is crisp and golden. Store any leftover pie in the refrigerator.

1/8 pie = 331 calories, 17 g fat (8 saturated), 60 mg cholesterol, 44 g carbohydrates, 3 g protein, 128 mg sodium, 2 g fiber

◆ *Snickerdoodle Fruit Pie, finished with a zigzag flute (page 13), decorated with pastry leaves, and showered with cinnamon sugar*

CROSS-MY-HEART COBBLER

Traditional cobblers are made with biscuit dough. In this recipe, it's cut into hearts and lattice strips, which top a juicy fresh-fruit filling. This is the recipe for those summer fruits — nectarines, plenty of berries, and plump cherries. Purchase the red sour cherries if you can find them, or use the sweet red cherries and ⅓ cup less sugar.

MAKES ONE 13 × 9-INCH COBBLER
PREP TIME 45 MIN ◆ BAKE TIME 50 MIN

1 recipe MOM ALLEN'S
   SHORTCAKE DOUGH (page 19)

FRESH FRUIT FILLING
1½ pounds ripe fresh nectarines,
   peeled, pitted, and sliced ¼ inch
   thick (4½ cups)
 2 cups pitted, halved sweet Bing or
   red sour cherries
 2 cups fresh blueberries
 2 cups fresh raspberries
 2 cups fresh strawberries, hulled and
   sliced ¼ inch thick
 1 to 1⅓ cups sugar (based on
   sweetness of cherries), plus
   2 tablespoons for sprinkling
2½ tablespoons quick-cooking tapioca
 2 tablespoons cornstarch

 1 teaspoon grated lemon zest
 2 tablespoons fresh lemon juice
 2 to 3 tablespoons cherry brandy
 2 tablespoons unsalted butter (not
   margarine), melted

 1 recipe Crème Fraîche (page 20)
   (optional)

1 Generously butter a 13 × 9 × 3-inch
   baking dish. Mix the shortcake
dough, shape into a 8-inch disk, and
chill for 30 minutes.

2 Meanwhile, in a large bowl, toss the
   nectarines, cherries, all of the berries,
the 1 to 1⅓ cups sugar, the tapioca,
cornstarch, the lemon zest and juice, and
the brandy to taste. Evenly spread the
fruit and any juices in the baking dish.

3 Preheat the oven to 425°F. On a
   lightly floured surface, roll out the
shortcake dough into a large rectangle,
⅛ inch thick. Make a crisscross Lattice
Crust (page 14) from about half of the
dough. Using a 2-inch heart cutter, cut
out hearts from the remaining dough
(you will need about 24 hearts). Attach
hearts around the edge and on the lattice
strips, fastening them with ice water.
Brush with the butter and sprinkle with
the remaining 2 tablespoons of sugar.
Bake for 20 minutes, then reduce the
heat to 350°F and bake 30 minutes more
or until the juices are bubbling. Serve
with Crème Fraîche, if you wish.

*1/12 cobbler = 410 calories, 16 g fat (9 saturated),
63 mg cholesterol, 65 g carbohydrates, 5 g protein,
231 mg sodium, 4 g fiber*

TWICE-BAKED FRESH PEACH COBBLER

For generations, cooks have been using pie pastry to make deep-dish fruit cobblers. This recipe uses the old-fashioned method of baking half of the filling under half of the crust, just long enough so the crust is no longer doughy, but has not browned. Then it's topped with the remaining filling and crust and baked a second time, until the top pastry is crisp and the filling is bubbly.

MAKES ONE 13 × 9-INCH COBBLER
PREP TIME 45 MIN ◆ BAKE TIME 65 MIN

 1 recipe PÂTE SUCRÉE (page 15)

FRESH PEACH FILLING
1½ cups sugar, plus 2 tablespoons for
   sprinkling
 3 tablespoons all-purpose flour
½ teaspoon ground cinnamon
3½ pounds ripe fresh peaches, peeled,
   pitted, and sliced ¼ inch thick
   (10 cups)
 1 teaspoon grated lemon zest
 2 tablespoons fresh lemon juice
 1 cup cold water, divided
 6 tablespoons (¾ stick) unsalted
   butter (not margarine), divided

1 Preheat the oven to 375°F and
   generously butter a shallow 13 × 9 ×
3-inch baking dish. Mix the pastry, shape
into two equal 6-inch disks, and chill. In

a small bowl, toss the 1½ cups of sugar
with the flour and cinnamon. Set aside.

2 In a large bowl, toss the peaches with
   the lemon zest and lemon juice, then
spread half of the fruit over the bottom
of the baking dish. Drizzle with ½ cup of
the water and half of the sugar mixture.
Dot with 2 tablespoons of the butter.

3 On a lightly floured surface, roll out
   one pastry disk into a 13 × 9-inch
rectangle, ⅛ inch thick. Lay the pastry
over the peaches and make 6 steam
slits. Bake the cobbler, uncovered, for
20 minutes or just until the crust begins
to set. Transfer the cobbler to a wire rack.

4 Meanwhile, roll out the remaining
   pastry disk into a 14 × 10-inch
rectangle, ⅛ inch thick. Top the cobbler
with the remaining peaches and ½ cup of

water, the rest of the sugar mixture, and
2 tablespoons of the butter. Cover with
the remaining pastry rectangle and slit as
before. Melt the remaining 2 tablespoons
of butter and brush on top of the cobbler.
Sprinkle the cobbler with the remaining
2 tablespoons of sugar. Bake 45 minutes
more or until the crust is crisp.

*1/12 cobbler = 387 calories, 15 g fat (9 saturated),
72 mg cholesterol, 64 g carbohydrates, 4 g protein,
107 mg sodium, 3 g fiber*

FALL FRUIT COBBLER For the
peaches, substitute 1 pound red tart
apples (Jonathans or McIntosh) and
1 pound Granny Smith apples, peeled,
cored, and sliced ¼ inch thick — plus
6 ounces dried blueberries, 6 ounces
dried cranberries and 1 cup golden
raisins, cooked in boiling water until
plump, then drained.

◆ *Cross-My-Heart Cobbler*

CHOCOLATE PUDDING PIE

Here's a fancier version of Mom's chocolate pudding. It bakes into a pie with a puffy cake-like layer on top and a hot fudge sauce on the bottom. Start with premium-quality chocolate, preferably an imported one, that's high in cocoa butter, rich in flavor, and smooth in texture. Serve this rich pudding pie hot, straight from the oven, with Rum Crème Anglaise.

MAKES ONE 11-INCH PUDDING PIE
PREP TIME 30 MIN ✦ BAKE TIME 9 MIN

- **14 ounces bittersweet or semisweet chocolate, chopped**
- **¼ cup (½ stick) unsalted butter (not margarine), cut into pieces**
- **⅛ teaspoon salt**
- **8 large egg yolks**
- **⅓ cup plus 2 tablespoons granulated sugar, divided**
- **4 large egg whites**
- **1 teaspoon fresh lemon juice**
- **3 tablespoons sifted confectioners' sugar**

- **1 recipe Rum Crème Anglaise (page 20) (optional)**
- **1 cup fresh raspberries**

1 Preheat the oven to 475°F and generously butter an 11-inch flan or quiche dish, about 1 inch deep, preferably a fluted one. Melt the chocolate and butter with the salt (see page 21). Set aside to cool to room temperature.

2 Meanwhile, in a large bowl, with an electric mixer on HIGH, beat the egg yolks with the ⅓ cup of granulated sugar until light yellow and thick ribbons form.

3 In a medium-size bowl, with the mixer on HIGH, beat the egg whites and lemon juice with clean beaters until frothy. Add the remaining 2 tablespoons of granulated sugar and beat until soft peaks form (do not overbeat, or the pudding may get grainy and it will be more difficult to fold in the whites).

4 Fold about one third of the egg whites into the batter, then gently fold in the remaining whites just until incorporated. Specks of the whites will still remain, but that's just fine. Do not overfold, as this will prevent the pie from rising up high and puffy in the oven.

5 Carefully spoon the batter into the tart pan (it will almost reach the top). Bake for 9 to 10 minutes or until the top and sides of the pudding are set but the center still jiggles. Do not overbake as you want the center to be warm and saucy. While pudding bakes, spoon the Crème Anglaise onto dessert plates. Top with spoonfuls of the pudding, making sure you get some of the fudgy chocolate sauce. Scatter some raspberries around each serving. Store any leftovers in the refrigerator. Warm up before serving.

1/9 pudding pie = 361 calories, 19 g fat (5 saturated), 203 mg cholesterol, 45 g carbohydrates, 6 g protein, 97 mg sodium, 1 g fiber

LEMON DAINTY PUDDING PIE

Here's an old Southern recipe, handed down through generations of my family. It has always been called Lemon Dainty, though I've never been able to discover why (except it's light, dainty, and delicate). It begins as a soufflé-like batter with plenty of fresh lemon flavor. As the pudding pie bakes, a cake-like layer rises to the top, hiding a creamy pudding underneath.

MAKES ONE 12-INCH PUDDING PIE
PREP TIME 30 MIN ✦ BAKE TIME 20 MIN

- **1¼ cups plus 1 tablespoon granulated sugar, divided**
- **5 large eggs, separated**
- **2 tablespoons grated lemon zest**
- **⅓ cup fresh lemon juice**
- **⅓ cup all-purpose flour**
- **⅛ teaspoon salt**
- **6 tablespoons (¾ stick) unsalted butter (not margarine), melted**
- **1½ cups milk**

Sifted confectioners' sugar

1 Preheat the oven to 400°F and generously butter a 12-inch flan or quiche dish, about 1 inch deep, preferably a fluted one. Sprinkle the 1 tablespoon of granulated sugar over the bottom of the dish.

2 In a large bowl, with an electric mixer on HIGH, beat the egg yolks with 1 cup of the remaining granulated sugar until light yellow and thick ribbons form. Reduce the speed to LOW and beat in the lemon zest, lemon juice, flour, salt, and butter just until blended. Beat in the milk just until blended through the batter.

3 In a medium-size bowl with the mixer on HIGH, beat the egg whites with clean beaters until frothy. Add the remaining ¼ cup of granulated sugar and beat until soft peaks form (do not overbeat).

4 Fold about one third of the egg whites into the batter, then gently fold in the remaining whites just until incorporated. Specks of the whites will still remain, but that's just fine. Do not overfold, as this will prevent the pie from rising up high and puffy in the oven.

5 Carefully spoon the batter into the dish (it will almost reach the top). Bake for 20 to 25 minutes or until the top and sides are set but the center still jiggles. Do not overbake, as you want the center to be warm and saucy. Sprinkle with confectioners' sugar and serve immediately. Store in the refrigerator.

1/9 pudding pie = 259 calories, 12 g fat (7 saturated), 145 mg cholesterol, 35 g carbohydrates, 5 g protein, 92 mg sodium, .5 g fiber

BANANA SPOON PIE

Spoon pies are exactly what their name says — a pie that's scooped out, then eaten with a spoon. This one's adapted from the banana-wafer pudding, popular in the mid-20th century. Wafers make the shell and tiny puffs of meringue top it off.

MAKES ONE 10-INCH SPOON PIE
PREP TIME 30 MIN ✦ BAKE TIME 12 MIN
COOL / CHILL TIME 1¼ HR

- 1 **12-ounce package vanilla wafers (5 cups)**
- 1½ **cups sugar, divided**
- 3 **tablespoons cornstarch**
- 2 **tablespoons all-purpose flour**
- ¼ **teaspoon salt**
- 3 **cups milk**
- 4 **large eggs, separated**
- 2 **tablespoons unsalted butter (not margarine), cut into small pieces**
- 1 **tablespoon vanilla extract**
- 1 **teaspoon banana extract**
- 4 **cups ripe banana slices, ¼ inch thick (4 large)**
- ¼ **teaspoon cream of tartar**

1 Butter a 10-inch round baking dish with 2-inch sides. Set aside 20 wafers to make the side "crust." Crumble the remaining wafers, sprinkling ¼ cup over the bottom of dish. Save rest of crumbs.

2 In a medium-size saucepan, mix ¾ cup of the sugar with the cornstarch, flour, and salt. Whisk in the milk until smooth. Cook over medium heat, whisking constantly, for 8 minutes or just until the mixture comes to a full boil and thickens. Remove from the heat.

3 In a small bowl with an electric mixer on HIGH, beat the egg yolks until light yellow and thick. Stir 1 cup of the hot cream mixture into the eggs, then return this mixture to the saucepan. Cook and stir over low heat for 2 minutes or until thickened (do not let boil). Remove from the heat and stir in the butter, vanilla and the banana extract. Cool for 15 minutes.

4 Preheat the oven to 350°F. Over the crumbs in the dish, layer half of the banana slices, half of the pudding, and half of the reserved wafer crumbs, then repeat. Slip the reserved 20 wafers around the edge, rounded-side out.

5 To make the meringue, in a medium-size bowl, with an electric mixer on HIGH, beat the egg whites and cream of tartar until soft peaks form. Gradually add the remaining ¾ cup of sugar and beat until stiff peaks form. Pipe or spoon into small puffs over the top of the pie. Bake for 12 to 15 minutes or until the meringue is lightly browned. Chill for at least 1 hour before serving. Refrigerate.

1/9 spoon pie = 470 calories, 13 g fat (5 saturated), 136 mg cholesterol, 81 g carbohydrates, 8 g protein, 220 mg sodium, 1 g fiber

Pipe tiny meringue puffs, covering pie completely

TAPIOCA PUDDING PIE

Here's the forever-favorite of tapioca pudding, made extra-creamy, then spooned into a crumb crust. It's topped with a garland of whipped cream and a cluster of fresh raspberries, then chilled until it's firm enough to slice.

MAKES ONE 9-INCH PUDDING PIE
PREP TIME 30 MIN ✦ BAKE TIME 8 MIN
COOL / CHILL TIME 3¼ HR

- 1 **recipe GRAHAM CRACKER CRUST (page 17)**

TAPIOCA PUDDING FILLING
- 3 **large eggs, separated**
- ⅔ **cup plus 2 tablespoons sugar**
- 2⅓ **cups milk**
- ⅔ **cup quick-cooking tapioca**
- 1 **tablespoon vanilla extract**

- 1 **cup cold heavy (whipping) cream**
- 1 **cup fresh raspberries**

1 Preheat the oven to 350°F and set out a 9-inch deep-dish pie plate. Mix the crust mixture and press the crumbs over the bottom and up the sides of the pie plate. Bake for 8 minutes or until set. Place the crust on a wire rack to cool.

2 In a large bowl, with the mixer on HIGH, beat the egg yolks and the ⅔ cup of sugar until light yellow and thick. Transfer to a large saucepan and whisk in the milk and tapioca. Let stand for 5 minutes. Cook the pudding over medium-high heat, whisking frequently, for 7 minutes, or until it reaches a full rolling boil. Remove from the heat.

3 Meanwhile, in a large bowl, with the mixer on HIGH, beat the egg whites with clean beaters until frothy. Sprinkle in the remaining 2 tablespoons of sugar and beat until stiff glossy peaks form.

4 Reduce the mixer speed to LOW. Gradually pour in the hot egg mixture and then the vanilla, beating just until blended. Cool for 15 minutes, then refrigerate the pudding for 1 hour or until cooled but not set.

5 In a small bowl, with the mixer on HIGH, whip the cream until stiff peaks form. Fold ½ cup of the whipped cream into the cooled pudding, then spoon the pudding into the pie plate. Using a pastry bag fitted with a fluted tip (#3 or #4) or with a spoon, make a garland around the edge of the pie with the remaining whipped cream. Arrange the raspberries in the center of the pie. Chill 2 hours more or until serving time. Store any leftover pie in the refrigerator.

1/9 pudding pie = 462 calories, 23 g fat (13 saturated), 137 mg cholesterol, 58 g carbohydrates, 7 g protein, 182 mg sodium, 2 g fiber

FRESH BLUEBERRY SLUMP

Spoon pies begin with fabulous fruits, but no bottom crust — only a top crust of soft dumplings, a rich pastry, or a crunchy topping. As the name implies, they are not cut into wedges, but served and eaten with a spoon. This is one of my most favorite spoon pies, scrumptious and pretty enough to serve for company. Fresh blueberries are covered with a cream cheese and sour cream layer, then sweet slump-dumplings are spooned on top. The dumplings rise and then slump into the filling during baking.

MAKES ONE 13 × 9-INCH PIE
PREP TIME 30 MIN ◆ BAKE TIME 25 MIN

BLUEBERRY FILLING
- 3 tablespoons cornstarch
- ⅔ cup water
- 1⅔ cups granulated sugar, divided
- 8 cups fresh blueberries (2 quarts)
- 1 teaspoon grated lemon zest
- 1 8-ounce package cream cheese, at room temperature
- 1 cup sour cream
- 2 tablespoons fresh lemon juice
- 2 teaspoons vanilla extract

SLUMP-DUMPLINGS
- 1½ cups all-purpose flour
- ⅓ cup packed light brown sugar
- 1 tablespoon baking powder
- ½ teaspoon salt
- ¾ cup milk
- 1 large egg
- ¼ cup (½ stick) unsalted butter (not margarine), melted

1 Preheat the oven to 400°F and generously butter a 13 × 9 × 3-inch baking dish.

2 In a large saucepan, stir the cornstarch into the water until completely dissolved, then stir in 1 cup of the granulated sugar. Bring the mixture to a boil over medium-high heat and boil for 2 minutes. Remove from the heat and gently stir in the blueberries and lemon zest. Spread the berries evenly in the baking dish.

3 In a medium-size bowl with an electric mixer on HIGH, beat the cream cheese, sour cream, the remaining ⅔ cup of granulated sugar, the lemon juice, and vanilla until smooth and creamy. Gently and evenly spread the cheese mixture on top of the berry filling.

4 Make the dumplings by mixing the flour, brown sugar, baking powder, and salt in a medium-size bowl. In a small bowl, whisk the milk, egg, and butter. Make a well in the center of the flour mixture, pour in the milk mixture, and stir until well mixed (do not overbeat as this may cause the dumplings to become tough). Drop the batter by spoonfuls on top of the filling.

5 Bake the slump for 25 minutes or until the filling is bubbly and the dumplings are golden and puffy.

1/10 slump = 482 calories, 19 g fat (12 g saturated), 72 mg cholesterol, 75 g carbohydrates, 7 g protein, 312 mg sodium, 3 g fiber

INDIVIDUAL PEACH-RASPBERRY CRISPS

These luscious little crustless pies are quick to mix and need only twenty-three minutes to cook. Their name comes from the buttery brown sugar and oat topping that bakes and then broils up crisp and crunchy before serving.

MAKES 6 FIVE-INCH INDIVIDUAL CRISPS
PREP TIME 15 MIN
BAKE / BROIL TIME 23 MIN

PEACH-RASPBERRY FILLING
- 3 pounds peaches, peeled, pitted, and sliced ¼ inch thick (6 cups)
- 2 cups fresh raspberries
- ⅓ cup granulated sugar
- 2 teaspoons grated lemon zest

CRISP TOPPING
- ½ cup (1 stick) unsalted butter (not margarine)
- 1¼ cups packed light brown sugar
- ½ cup old-fashioned oats (not instant)
- ½ cup all-purpose flour
- ¾ cup chopped walnuts
- 1 teaspoon ground cinnamon
- ¼ teaspoon ground mace
- ¼ teaspoon salt

1 Preheat the oven to 375°F and butter 6 five-inch individual shallow gratin (broiler-proof) dishes, about 1½-cup capacity each. In a large bowl, toss the peaches, raspberries, granulated sugar, and lemon zest together and set aside.

2 In a medium-size saucepan, melt the butter over medium heat. Remove from the heat and stir in the remaining topping ingredients.

3 Divide the fruit mixture and any juices that have collected evenly among the dishes. Sprinkle each pie with about ⅓ cup of the topping.

4 Bake the crisps for 20 minutes or until the peaches are tender when tested with a knife. Turn on the broiler. Place the crisps 6 inches from the heat and broil for 3 to 4 minutes or until the topping is crisp and bubbly (watch carefully as the topping can brown fast).

1 crisp = 626 calories, 26 g fat (11 g saturated), 42 mg cholesterol, 98 g carbohydrates, 7 g protein, 107 mg sodium, 8 g fiber

APPLE-BLACKBERRY CRISPS
Substitute 3 pounds sweet-tart red apples (such as McIntosh or Jonathan) for the peaches. Peel, core, and slice them ¼ inch thick. Substitute 2 cups fresh blackberries for the raspberries. Substitute ¼ teaspoon ground ginger for the mace.

APPLE-CRANBERRY PANDOWDY

This homey dessert is typically made with fresh apples, sweetened with sugar or molasses, and then baked under a biscuit batter until the top becomes crisp. The name's origin is not clear, though many think it comes from the fact that the dessert looks quite dowdy as it bakes. I like to top it with a buttery pie dough, making it look a little less dowdy.

MAKES ONE 13 × 9-INCH PANDOWDY
PREP TIME 45 MIN ✦ BAKE TIME 1¼ HR

**1 recipe CRISP FLAKY CRUST
(page 15)**

APPLE-BERRY FILLING

2½ pounds tart-sweet red apples, such as McIntosh, peeled, cored, and sliced ¼ inch thick (7½ cups)
2 cups dried cranberries
½ cup sugar, plus 2 tablespoons for sprinkling
1 teaspoon ground cinnamon
½ teaspoon ground nutmeg
½ teaspoon salt
½ cup maple syrup
⅓ cup water
¼ cup (½ stick) unsalted butter (not margarine)
2 tablespoons heavy cream

1 Butter a 13 × 9 × 2-inch baking dish. Mix the dough, shape into a 6-inch disk, and chill for 30 minutes.

2 Meanwhile, in a medium-size bowl, mix the apples, cranberries, the ½ cup of sugar, the cinnamon, nutmeg, and salt. Spread the mixture evenly in the baking dish. In a small saucepan, heat the syrup, water, and butter until the mixture comes to a full boil and the butter melts. Pour the boiling syrup over the fruit.

3 Preheat the oven to 400°F. On a lightly floured surface, roll out the dough into a large rectangle, ⅛ inch thick. Trim the pastry to a 16 × 12-inch rectangle and place on top of the fruit, leaving a 1½-inch overhang. Flute the edges. Brush the pastry with the cream and the remaining 2 tablespoons of sugar. Bake for 15 minutes. Remove the pandowdy from the oven and reduce the oven temperature to 325°F.

4 With a sharp knife, "dowdy" the dessert by cutting across the crust diagonally about 6 times, then 6 more times in the opposite direction. Push the crust down slightly with a spoon, allowing the crust to absorb the juices. Bake the pandowdy 1 hour more or until the apples are tender when tested with a knife and the top is crisp and golden.

1/10 pandowdy = 547 calories, 22 g fat (11 g saturated), 42 mg cholesterol, 88 g carbohydrates, 4 g protein, 250 mg sodium, 5 g fiber

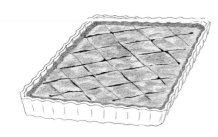

To "dowdy" the top crust, diagonally cut across it 6 times in each direction with the tip of a sharp knife, allowing the juices to bubble over the crust

BLACKBERRY-NECTARINE COBBLER WITH SWEET SHORTCAKE DUMPLINGS

Here's a cobbler that takes little pastry know-how, bakes up perfectly every time, and tastes as if a master baker created it.

MAKES ONE 13 × 9-INCH COBBLER
PREP TIME 30 MIN ✦ BAKE TIME 25 MIN

1 recipe MOM ALLEN'S SHORTCAKE DOUGH (page 19), made with 1 cup heavy (whipping) cream, plus 2 tablespoons cream for brushing

BLACKBERRY-NECTARINE FILLING
3 pounds ripe nectarines, peeled, pitted, and sliced ¼ inch thick (6 cups)
3 cups fresh blackberries
1 cup granulated sugar, plus 2 tablespoons for sprinkling
3 tablespoons quick-cooking tapioca
1 teaspoon grated lemon zest

2 to 3 tablespoons blackberry liqueur (crème de cassis)
½ teaspoon ground cinnamon

SOUR CREAM TOPPING
2 cups sour cream
1 tablespoon milk

1 Butter a 13 × 9 × 3-inch baking dish. Make the shortcake dough, using 1 cup of cream, plus a tablespoon more if needed, to give a sticky, wet dough.

2 Preheat the oven to 400°F. In a large bowl, toss the nectarines, blackberries, the 1 cup of sugar, the tapioca, and lemon zest. Flavor to taste with the liqueur. Spread the fruit mixture in the baking dish.

3 Make the shortcake dumplings by dropping the dough by large spoonfuls on top of the fruit mixture. Brush with the remaining 2 tablespoons of cream. Toss the remaining 2 tablespoons of sugar with the cinnamon and sprinkle on the cobbler.

4 Bake the cobbler for 25 to 35 minutes or until the nectarines are tender when tested with a knife and the top is golden brown. While the cobbler bakes, mix the sour cream and milk. Spoon the cobbler into dishes and top each with a heaping spoonful of sour cream.

1/12 cobbler = 469 calories, 22 g fat (13 g saturated), 75 mg cholesterol, 66 g carbohydrates, 6 g protein, 249 mg sodium, 5 g fiber

CAROL'S BUMBLEBERRY PIE

Bumbleberry has joined the list of the most popular Canadian pies. But there's not just one Bumbleberry Pie. According to Carol Ferguson, Food & Nutrition Director of Homemaker's Magazine *in Toronto,"Bumbleberry fillings use various combinations of available berries, usually with apples, and sometimes include rhubarb or other fruits." If you can't find blackberries, use extra blueberries. The filling is delectably soft and juicy — perfect for serving warm or at room temperature.*

MAKES ONE 9-INCH DEEP-DISH PIE
PREP TIME 30 MIN ◆ BAKE TIME 50 MIN
COOL TIME 1 HR

1 recipe BUTTERY CRUST (page 15)

FRUIT FILLING

2 **cups peeled apple slices (¼ inch thick)**
1 **cup fresh blackberries**
1 **cup fresh blueberries**
1 **cup fresh raspberries**
1 **cup sliced fresh strawberries**
2 **teaspoons fresh lemon juice**
¾ **cup granulated sugar, plus 2 tablespoons for sprinkling**
6 **tablespoons all-purpose flour**
¼ **teaspoon ground cinnamon**
1 **large egg yolk**
2 **teaspoons water**

1 Preheat the oven to 425°F and set out a deep-dish 9-inch pie plate. Using half of the chilled pastry, roll out and shape the bottom shell, leaving a 1½-inch overhang (do not prick). Chill the pie shell while you make the filling.

2 In a large bowl, toss the apples with all of the berries. Sprinkle with the lemon juice. In a small bowl, mix together the ¾ cup of sugar, the flour, and cinnamon. Add to the fruit mixture and toss gently to coat. Spoon the fruit mixture into the pie shell, mounding it high in the center.

3 On a lightly floured surface, roll out the remaining pastry into a large round, ⅛ inch thick; trim it to a 13-inch circle. Place on top of the filling, then seal the edges with a little water. Finish with a braided edge. Cut steam vents in the top crust. In a small bowl, beat together the egg yolk and water, then brush over the top crust. Sprinkle with the remaining 2 tablespoons of sugar.

4 Bake the pie for 15 minutes. Reduce the oven temperature to 350°F and bake 35 to 40 minutes more or until the crust is golden brown. Cool the pie on a wire rack for at least 1 hour before cutting. Refrigerate any leftovers.

⅛ pie = 522 calories, 20 g fat (9 g saturated), 84 mg cholesterol, 82 g carbohydrates, 7 g protein, 160 mg sodium, 5 g fiber

MINCEMEAT PIE

Eliza Smith (The Compleat Housewife, *London, 1729) describes how to make mince "pyes" from four pounds of boiled leg of veal, shredded with nine pounds of beef suet, eight pippins [apples], and four pounds of raisins. She says to season the mixture well with "one ounce of nutmegs grated, half an ounce of cloves, as much mace, a large spoonful of salt, above a pound of sugar, the peel of a lemon shred exceeding fine ... and just as the pies go into the oven, put into every one a spoonful of sack [dry white wine] and claret." Today, most pies leave out the meat and they are often flavored with brandy instead of claret.*

MAKES TWO 9-INCH PIES
PREP TIME 1 HR ◆ BAKE TIME 45 MIN
COOL TIME 1¼ HR

2 recipes CRISP FLAKY CRUST (page 15)

MINCEMEAT FILLING

1 **large lemon**
1 **small orange**
1¼ **cups sugar, plus 2 tablespoons for sprinkling**
½ **cup water**
3 **tablespoons molasses**
1 **teaspoon ground cinnamon**
½ **teaspoon ground cloves**
½ **teaspoon ground nutmeg**
½ **teaspoon salt**
4½ **pounds sweet-tart apples, such as Granny Smith or Pippin, peeled, cored, and coarsely chopped**
1 **cup dark raisins**
1 **cup golden raisins**
½ **cup candied citron, finely chopped**
¾ **cup brandy or apple cider**
2 **tablespoons heavy cream**

1 Butter two 9-inch pie plates. Using half of the chilled pastry, roll and shape the 2 bottom pie shells, leaving a 1½-inch overhang (do not prick); chill. Shape the rest of the pastry into two equal 6-inch disks and chill.

2 Halve the lemon and orange, remove the seeds, and place in a food processor. Add the 1¼ cups of sugar, the water, molasses, cinnamon, cloves, nutmeg, and salt; process just until well blended but not smooth. Transfer to a large saucepan and stir in the apples, raisins, and citron. Cook over low heat for 30 minutes, stirring often to prevent sticking. Stir in the brandy, remove from the heat, and cool 15 minutes.

3 Preheat the oven to 425°F. Divide the mincemeat between the 2 pie shells. On a lightly floured surface, roll out each pastry disk ⅛ inch thick and trim to a 13-inch circle. Top each pie with a pastry circle, seal, and flute. Cut steam vents in the top. Decorate with apple cutouts made from the pastry scraps. Brush the pies with the cream and sprinkle with the remaining 2 tablespoons of sugar. Bake for 15 minutes; lower the oven temperature to 350°F and bake 30 to 40 minutes more or until golden. Cool for 1 hour. Refrigerate any leftover pie.

⅛ pie = 545 calories, 22 g fat (10 g saturated), 34 mg cholesterol, 84 g carbohydrates, 5 g protein, 227 mg sodium, 4 g fiber

◆ *Bumbleberry Pie with a braided edging (page 13)*

Bold italic numbers refer to photos of pies. *Light italic* numbers refer to suggested crusts.

METRIC EQUIVALENTS

LIQUID – VOLUME

American Standard	Metric	
1 teaspoon	5	milliliters
1 tablespoon	15	milliliters
⅛ cup (2 tablespoons/1 ounce)	30	milliliters
¼ cup (4 tablespoons/2 ounces)	60	milliliters
⅓ cup (5⅓ tablespoons)	80	milliliters
½ cup (8 tablespoons/4 ounces)	120	milliliters
1 cup (16 tablespoons/8 ounces)	240	milliliters
1 pint (2 cups/16 ounces)	480	milliliters
1 quart (4 cups/32 ounces)	960	milliliters
	(.96	liter)
1 gallon (4 quarts/128 ounces)	3.785	liters

WEIGHT

	Metric	
1 ounce	28.35	grams
½ pound (8 ounces)	227	grams
1 pound (16 ounces)	454	grams
2.2 pounds	1,000 grams (1 kilogram)	

TEMPERATURE

Fahrenheit	Celsius
32° F (water freezes)	0°C
212° F (water boils)	100°C

Oven Temperatures

Fahrenheit	Celsius	
250° to 300°F	120° to 150°C	Warm – very slow cook
300° to 325°F	150° to 160°C	Warm – slow cook
325° to 350°F	160° to 180°C	Medium – slow cook
350° to 375°F	180° to 190°C	Medium
375° to 400°F	190° to 200°C	Medium hot
400° to 425°F	200° to 220°C	Hot – fast cook
450° to 475°F	230° to 250°C	Hot – very fast cook
500° to 525°F	260° to 275°C	Hot – extremely fast cook

BAKEWARE – VOLUME*

American Standard		Metric	
Regular pie plate			
8 × 1½ inches	4 cups	1	liter
9 × 1½ inches	5 cups	1.25	liters
10 × 1½ inches	6 cups	1.5	liters
Deep-dish pie plate			
9 × 2 inches	6 cups	1.5	liters
10 × 2 inches	7 cups	1.75	liters
Quiche dish			
10 × 1½ inches	6 cups	1.5	liters
12 × 1½ inches	8 cups	2	liters
Tart pan			
10 × 1 inches	5 cups	1.25	liters
11 × 1 inches	6 cups	1.5	liters
12 × 1 inches	7 cups	1.75	liters
Individual tart pan			
4 × ¾ inches	⅔ cup	160	milliliters
5 × ¾ inches	¾ cup	180	milliliters
Barquette & tartlet molds			
3½ × ½ inches – boat	1 tablespoon	15	milliliters
4½ × ½ inches – boat	2 tablespoons	30	milliliters
2½ × ½ inches – heart	2 tablespoons	30	milliliters
3 × ½ inches – round	2 tablespoons	30	milliliters
Ramekin			
4 × 2 inches – round	1½ cups	360	milliliters
Baking pan/dish			
8 × 8 × 1½ inches	6 cups	1.5	liters
9 × 9 × 2 inches	8 cups	2	liters
13 × 9 × 3 inches	16 cups	4	liters
Springform pan			
10 × 2½ inches	12 cups	3	liters
Deep-dish pizza pan			
14 × 1½ inches	12 cups	3	liters
Deep skillet			
10 × 2 inches	8 cups	2	liters
12 × 2 inches	12 cups	3	liters

* Bakeware volumes are approximate.

CREDITS

RECIPES

Page 42: *Tourtière de Fleur-Ange recipe from* A TASTE OF QUEBEC *by Julian Armstrong. Copyright © 1990. Reprinted by permission of Macmillan Canada.*

Page 70: *Julia Child's Free-Form Fresh Apple Tart recipe from* THE WAY TO COOK *by Julia Child. Copyright © 1989 by Julia Child. Reprinted by permission of Alfred A. Knopf, Inc.*

Page 92: *Maida Heatter's Salted Almond Chocolate Pie recipe from* GREAT AMERICAN DESSERTS *by Maida Heatter. Copyright © 1985 by Maida Heatter. Reprinted by permission of Maida Heatter.*

Page 94: *Joe's Chocolate Fudge Pie recipe from* MAIDA HEATTER'S BEST DESSERT BOOK EVER *by Maida Heatter. Copyright © 1990 by Maida Heatter. Reprinted by permission of Random House, Inc.*

Page 97: *Larry Forgione's Pennsylvania Dutch Chocolate Nut Pie recipe from* AN AMERICAN PLACE *by Larry Forgione. Copyright © 1996 by Larry Forgione. Reprinted by permission of William Morrow & Company, Inc.*

Page 108: *Mrs. Grace Coolidge's Custard Pie recipe from* THE FIRST LADIES COOKBOOK *by Margaret Brown Klapthor. Copyright © 1966 by Parents' Magazine Press. Reprinted with permission of Gruner + Jahr USA Publishing ("G & J").*

Page 109: *Marlborough Tart recipe from* THE AMERICAN HERITAGE COOKBOOK. *Copyright © 1964 by American Heritage Publishing Co., Inc. Reprinted by permission of* AMERICAN HERITAGE *Magazine, a division of Forbes, Inc. © Forbes, Inc.*

Page 112: *Coconut Meringue Pie recipe from* LUBY'S CAFETERIA 50TH ANNIVERSARY RECIPE

COLLECTION. *Copyright © 1996 by Luby's Cafeterias, Inc. Reprinted by permission of Luby's Cafeterias.*

Page 116: *James Beard's Lemon Slice Pie recipe from* AMERICAN COOKERY *by James Beard. Copyright © 1972 by James A. Beard; Illustrations Copyright © 1972 by Little, Brown and Company (Inc.). Reprinted by permission of Little, Brown and Company.*

Page 122: *Marion Cunningham's Pumpkin Pie recipe from* THE FANNIE FARMER COOKBOOK *by Marion Cunningham. Copyright © 1996 by Marion Cunningham. Reprinted by permission of Alfred A. Knopf, Inc.*

Page 130: *Marian Burros's Plum Torte recipe. Reprinted with the permission of Simon & Schuster from* THE NEW ELEGANT BUT EASY COOKBOOK *by Marian Burros and Lois Levine. Copyright © 1998 by Foxcraft Ltd. and Lois Levine.*

Page 132: *Olive Davis's Schnitz Peach Pie recipe from* GREAT CANADIAN RECIPES: APPLES, PEACHES, & PEARS *by Elizabeth Baird. Copyright © 1977 by Elizabeth Baird. Reprinted by permission of Lorimer & Company, Publishers.*

Page 140: *Bumbleberry Pie recipe by Carol Ferguson, from* HOMEMAKER'S *Magazine. Copyright © June/July, 1997. Reprinted by permission of Tele Media.*

ACCESSORIES

Page 1: *Pie plate — Annyx, Sag Harbor, 150 Main Street, Sag Harbor, NY 11963 / (516) 725-9064.*

Pages 8-9: *Pie Bird — From the Collection of Lillian Cole, 14 Harmony School Road, Flemington, NJ 08822 / (908) 782-3198.*

Pages 22-23: *Table — Bittersweet Interiors, 110 Greene Street, New York, NY 10012 / (212) 343-2322.*

Page 25: *Fork — Fortunoff, 681 Fifth Avenue at 54th Street, New York, NY 10022 / (800) FORTUNOF.*

Page 27: *Table — Barton-Sharpe, Ltd., 66 Crosby Street, New York, NY 10012 / (212) 925-9562. Quiche dish — Royal Worcester's "Evesham Vail" Porcelain from The Royal China & Porcelain Co.,*

Inc. / (800) 257-7189. Silver liner — Fortunoff, 681 Fifth Avenue at 54th Street, New York, NY 10022 / (800) FORTUNOF. Area rug — Fiezy / (800) 779-0877.

Page 29: *Plates and salt shaker — Ceramica, 59 Thompson Street, New York, NY 10012 / (800) 228-0858.*

Page 45: *Table — ercole, inc., 116 Franklin Street, New York, NY 10013 / (212) 941-6098.*

Page 47: *Table and chair — Rooms & Gardens, 290 Lafayette Street, New York, NY 10012 / (212) 431-1297.*

Pages 48, 49 and 51: *Napkins — Archipelago / (212) 334-9460.*

Page 59: *Tray — Christofle USA / (800) 799-6886. Napkins — Archipelago / (212) 334-9460.*

Page 75: *Pie plate — Annyx, Sag Harbor, 150 Main Street, Sag Harbor, NY 11963 / (516) 725-9064.*

Pages 86-87: *Pie plate — Annyx, Sag Harbor, 150 Main Street, Sag Harbor, NY 11963 / (516) 725-9064.*

Page 107: *Tea cart — Barton-Sharpe, Ltd., 66 Crosby Street, New York, NY 10012 / (212) 925-9562. China — Royal Worcester's "Purple Vine" Fine Bone China from The Royal China & Porcelain Co., Inc. / (800) 257-7189. Silverware — Christofle USA / (800) 799-6886.*

Page 120: *Pie plate — Annyx, Sag Harbor, 150 Main Street, Sag Harbor, NY 11963 / (516) 725-9064.*

Page 123: *Buffet, glass compote, and sugar bowl — Barton-Sharpe, Ltd., 66 Crosby Street, New York, NY 10012 / (212) 925-9562. China — Royal Worcester's "Lavinia" Fine Bone China from The Royal China & Porcelain Co., Inc. / (800) 257-7189. Flatware — Fortunoff, 681 Fifth Avenue at 54th Street, New York, NY 10022 / (800) FORTUNOF. Plate stand and teapot — Michael Feinberg, 225 Fifth Avenue, New York, NY 10011 / (212) 532-0311. Silverleaf tray — Vietri / (800) 277-5933.*

Pages 126-127 and 129: *Blue Spatterware pie plate — Annyx, Sag Harbor, 150 Main Street, Sag Harbor, NY 11963 / (516) 725-9064.*

Bold italic *numbers refer to photos of pies.* Light italic *numbers refer to suggested crusts.*